Anders Lustgarten

Plays: 1

A Day At the Racists,
If You Don't Let Us Dream, We Won't Let You Sleep,
Black Jesus, Shrapnel: 34 Fragments of a Massacre,
Kingmakers, The Insurgents

A Day At the Racists: 'The real wow of the week is *A Day at the Racists* by Anders Lustgarten, a political actvist turned breathtakingly competent playwright.' *The Independent on Sunday*

If You Don't Let Us Dream, We Won't Let You Sleep: 'Lustgarten demonstrates an ear for what's happening in parts of Britain, and how the relentlessness of economic crisis – even if it is no longer sharp or deep – eats away at people's hope, patience and decency.' Paul Mason, BBC

Black Jesus: 'In this new 75-minute piece, [Lustgarten] tackles Zimbabwe; the result . . . is intriguing and eye-opening . . . Lustgarten opens up new dramatic territory . . . [and] also raises important questions about post-conflict societies: he suggests that the past has to be faced, but that guilt and innocence are never absolute and that community service is better than retributive punishment.' *Guardian*

Shrapnel: 34 Fragments of a Massacre: 'The Roboski massacre is a further wake-up call to the inefficiency and brutality of the use of drones in the "war on terror". Anders Lustgarten's [play] personalises this terrible tragedy. He humanises the army's soulless, technological tactics by putting names to the numbers. It's a journalistic undertaking. All aspects of the fallout are explored, from the victims and their families through to the extreme views spawned by the pervasively peddled nightmare of the "enemy within".' *Stage*

Kingmakers: 'Lustgarten's jokey *Kingmakers* [is] set in 1225, ten years after the Runnymede signing, with Monty Python barons closing ranks with King John's son and heir in iambic pentameters . . . The rich, says Sprocket, . . . the mediating wheeler-dealer in *Kingmakers,* hold us in contempt: they laugh at us from yachts.' *Whatsonstage*

By the same author

Black Jesus
The Damned United (*stage adaptation*)
A Day at the Racists
If You Don't Let Us Dream, We Won't Let You Sleep
Lampedusa
Shrapnel: 34 Fragments of a Massacre
The Sugar-Coated Bullets of the Bourgeoisie

ANDERS LUSTGARTEN

Plays: 1

A Day at the Racists
If You Don't Let Us Dream, We Won't Let You Sleep
Black Jesus
Shrapnel: 34 Fragments of a Massacre
Kingmakers
The Insurgents

with an introduction by the author

Bloomsbury Methuen Drama
An imprint of Bloomsbury Publishing Plc

B L O O M S B U R Y
LONDON · OXFORD · NEW YORK · NEW DELHI · SYDNEY

Bloomsbury Methuen Drama

An imprint of Bloomsbury Publishing Plc

50 Bedford Square
London
WC1B 3DP
UK

1385 Broadway
New York
NY 10018
USA

www.bloomsbury.com

**Bloomsbury, Methuen Drama and the Diana logo
are registered trade marks of Bloomsbury Publishing Plc**

This collection first published 2016

A Day At the Racists first published in 2010 by Methuen Drama
© Anders Lustgarten, 2010, 2016

If You Don't Let Us Dream, We Won't Let You Sleep first published in 2013
by Methuen Drama © Anders Lustgarten 2013, 2016

Black Jesus first published in 2013 by Methuen Drama
© Anders Lustgarten 2013, 2016

Shrapnel: 34 Fragments of a Massacre first published in 2015
by Methuen Drama © Anders Lustgarten 2015, 2016

Kingmakers first published in this volume in 2016 by Methuen Drama
© Anders Lustgarten 2016

The Insurgents first published in this volume in 2016 by Methuen Drama
© Anders Lustgarten 2016

This collection copyright © Anders Lustgarten 2016
Introduction copyright © Anders Lustgarten 2016

British Library Cataloguing-in-Publication Data
A catalogue record for this book is available from the British Library.

ISBN: HB: 978-1-3500-0594-5
PB: 978-1-3500-0593-8
ePDF: 978-1-3500-0595-2
ePub: 978-1-3500-0596-9

Library of Congress Cataloging-in-Publication Data
A catalog record for this book is available from the Library of Congress.

Cover design: Adriana Brioso. Cover image: Charles Maraia/Getty Images.

Typeset by Country Setting, Kingsdown, Kent CT14 8ES

Contents

Anders Lustgarten
Chronology

2007   *The Insurgents* (Finborough Theatre, London)

       The Punishment Stories (Soho Theatre, London); finalist for Verity Bargate Award

       The Police, an adaptation of the Polish play by Slawomir Mrozek (Battersea Arts Centre, London)

2008   *Enduring Freedom* (Finborough Theatre)

2009   *Death and the Kit Kat* (*A Torture Comedy*) (Finborough Theatre)

2010   *A Day at the Racists* (Finborough Theatre)

2011   *The Fat Man* (Theatre Uncut)

       Recipient of the inaugural Harold Pinter Playwright's Award (Royal Court Theatre, London)

2012   *Socialism is Great* (National Theatre Connections Festival)

       Blair's Children (Cockpit Theatre)

2013   *If You Don't Let Us Dream, We Won't Let You Sleep* (Royal Court, London)

       Black Jesus (Finborough Theatre)

       The Breakout (Theatre Uncut)

2014   *The Finger of God* (Theatre Uncut)

2015   *Shrapnel: 34 Fragments of a Massacre* (Arcola Theatre, London)

       Lampedusa (HighTide; Soho Theatre)

       Kingmakers (One of the Magna Carta Plays, Salisbury Playhouse)

Introduction

I didn't plan to do this.

I have a British passport, German surname, American parents
and Scandinavian first name (though zero connection to
Scandinavia). I have a BA, MA and most of a PhD in Chinese
language and politics. I was an international athlete (Scottish
400m champion, though zero connection to Scotland). I taught
on Death Row in San Quentin, California, for two years, then
full-time for three years in the British prison system. I worked
for a Kurdish human rights organisation for a year, then ran
a campaign against a particularly noxious BP oil pipeline for
two years, then spent nearly a decade fighting the modern-
day imperialism of development banks. I was involved in the
Occupy movement and the Egyptian revolution.

So I don't write for the usual reasons. I write because
mainstream politics is dead: bought and paid for by an insatiable
capitalism and motivated by a hateful, vicious brutality. Hatred
of ordinary people, even more than greed, is the defining
characteristic of global elites in the twenty-first century. How
else can you describe a Tory government that systematically
starves the poor and persecutes the disabled? A European
Union whose ten-point communiqué on 'alleviating the
problems of migration' had seven points involving bombing
migrant boats and/or military intervention? A European
banking system which crushed and immiserated the people of
Greece when they dared to vote for a humane alternative to
austerity? All across the globe, we're seeing the rise of a new
capitalist totalitarianism which has nothing but contempt for us.

Now there's a range of ways you can respond to hate-fuelled
totalitarian bullying. You can try to placate it, to mitigate the
worst of it. We'll call that the Tony Blair approach, the
essence of New Labour – capitalism is unavoidable so let's
give it its head and reap the side 'benefits'. That approach
ends with the death of the orthodox left, a million people
dead, the Middle East in turmoil, and you with a splinter of

cold terror lodged in your blackened heart at the prospect of prosecution at The Hague for war crimes. That's a no.

You can submit to bullying, embrace its values. Try to create a world where you only listen to an echo chamber of your own opinions. That way lies Jeremy Hunt on one side and No Platforms and trigger warnings on the other. I'll give that a miss. Or you can stand up for yourself, tell a different tale to the one that's in the media and most of the places of fiction, one you think is important and interesting, and see who comes to listen and what happens next. That's me.

Theatre got to me because of its capacity for empathy, for compassion, for entertainment, and for hope: the four great absences of modern politics. There are things we can achieve in theatre it seems to me we can't readily achieve in almost any other arena in modern life. Things to do with empathy and solidarity and connection with other human beings. I think that's why it enrages me so much when other people don't make proper use of that opportunity, to expand the bounds of human connection.

The greatest thing my plays have to offer, I think, is hope. The possibility of agency, of emotional connection with other people in an economic system predicated on fragmented isolation and comfort shopping. And it's that hope, perversely, that really offends certain people.

There's a pitifully predictable review I get when people don't want to think about the ideas in my plays, one that bangs on about my activism as if somehow it were incompatible with craftsmanship or poignancy or humour. The fact is there are a lot of people who are profoundly threatened by hope: the right, of course, but also the affluent liberal left, comfortable in their anomie and their gesture politics, self-absolved of their moral responsibilities and left free to consume by their prevailing delusion that neo-liberal capitalism can't be changed, that we're stuck with it forever. That, as my plays tend to illustrate, is bullshit.

There's a strong tendency in British theatre now (heavily influenced by a German dramaturgy which itself is played out and changing) to grandiose empty spectacle, to gesture politics on stage. That's the stuff you do if you want to win awards. Luckily for me, I don't want to win awards. I want to cause trouble. Hope is the best way to do that.

But after I put my stuff out there, it's all up to you. I trust you to get the best out of it, and if you violently disagree with me: cool. That's the whole point of art – the artist doesn't get to control or contain what happens next. That's the anarchic spirit of the relationship between artist and audience that I really love. I'm not even sure I want you to like my plays. 'Like' is a little neutral, a little milquetoast, no? I think I'd prefer you to love or to hate them, to be enraged or inspired by them, to go away thinking about the ideas within them. Maybe that's more arrogant and presumptuous than wanting you to like them. I don't know. I don't get to decide these things. I just get to say what I think, which is a massive privilege in this world. And you get to decide what to do with that.

There are a few elements I like to employ in my plays. The first is humour (you may not agree). The second is to come at you from an angle you weren't expecting.

The first play in the collection, *A Day at the Racists*, is about New Labour's abandonment of the working class, especially the white working class, and the consequent rise of the BNP. But what's provocative about an anti-BNP play? Far more interesting to follow the logic of a pro-BNP argument to its conclusion in an irreversibly multi-cultural society, and see what happens.

Another technique is hypothesis. Often my plays are set just on the far shoulder of reality, a little in the future. *If You Don't Let Us Dream, We Won't Let You Sleep* is about the financialisation of society – the way in which finance has inveigled itself into every crevice of modern power, the everyday impacts of capitalist totalitarianism. The second half is a blunt Brechtian alternative to austerity at a time when there just wasn't one anywhere. A lot of people said it did them good to hear that argument from the Royal Court main stage, in front of an audience of financiers. And I loved the debate, the rage, it provoked. That's what you should be after if you want to be a writer of integrity, not awards and praise.

Black Jesus is also hypothetical: set in Zimbabwe in the aftermath of Mugabe's death, a Truth and Reconciliation Commission investigates the worst of the atrocities carried out by the Green Bombers. Nobody is innocent and nobody is guilty, which is the way the real world always is. I spent a fair bit of time in Zimbabwe, a brilliantly erudite and argumentative country which I have a ton of time for, and took an early version to the Harare International Festival. It owes its presence here to David Mercatali, who made me fish it out and rewrite it.

Shrapnel is an attempt to look at the wider causes of things. A basic challenge of political playwriting is that plays tend to be focused on individuals, but events tend to be the products of complex processes, macro-systems. So a drone massacre in Turkey can be put down to an error, a single order, if you want to keep it simple. But what about the nationalist politicians, the media who stir up hatred, the economic repression that forces villagers to smuggle diesel in the mountains, the international arms traders, the techno-nerds for whom designing a missile is nothing more than a well-paid puzzle to solve. When do they take their share of responsibility?

Kingmakers takes the piss. Out of our preoccupation with the monarchy, the endless flood of cultural propaganda that turns the hapless plastic twats of our ruling class into grandiose Shakespearean heroes, out of the fact that having taken our money, the elite now want our sympathy into the bargain. All in iambic pentameter. We did it in Salisbury, the epicentre of true blue royalism. It went better than expected, overall.

The last play here, *The Insurgents*, is the very first play I wrote and looks it in places. But it's funny and prescient and I enjoyed it at the time, so here you go.

If you're a young writer, here are some things I've discovered, which might be helpful to you. Always challenge your audience. With content, not only with form, which is largely the politically evacuated cop-out choice of those who don't have any content. Find something to say. Get after it. Be unexpected. Don't hold back. Listen when people hate your work, sometimes they're right. And sometimes they're dead wrong and they prove to you exactly why your work is needed.

Enjoy yourself. You're very lucky to get to do this.

ANDERS LUSTGARTEN
March 2016

Acknowledgements

Apologies to those I've forgotten, it's not personal!

Beeper Beeper, Featured Creature
Laurence Lustgarten
Donna Dickenson
Chris Britton
Lloyd Trott
Neil McPherson
Esther Baker
Simon Stephens
Ryan McBryde
Stephanie Street
Dominic Cooke
Chris Campbell
David Mercatali
Mehmet Ergun
Gareth Machin
Scrapper

A Day at the Racists

You start from the presumption that only you
are intelligent and sensitive enough to see
how bad capitalist society is.

Trevor Griffiths, *The Party*

Racism is like a Cadillac.
There's a new model every year.

Malcolm X

For Zena Birch
for all the help and advice

Acknowledgements

Thanks to Lisa and Nina at Soho; Ben and Lily at Curtis Brown; the Debnath and Rochlitz hospitality, enjoyed across the world; Laurence Lustgarten; Donna Dickenson and Chris Britton; Stephanie Street; Sarah Grochala and Anna Kerth for the Polish; everyone who helped with interviews, sources, readings and comments.

This play is written in testament to the (forgotten) history of British working-class activism.

A Day at the Racists was first performed at the Finborough Theatre, London, on 2 March 2010 with the following cast and creative team:

Peter Case	Julian Littman
Driver	Gwilym Lloyd
Polish Lady	Vanessa Havell
Burka Woman 1	Thusitha Jayasundera
Burka Woman 2	Zaraah Abrahams
African Guy	Trevor A. Toussaint
Labour MP	Vanessa Havell
Mark Case	Sam Swainsbury
Clinton Jones	Trevor A. Toussaint
Gina White	Thusitha Jayasundera
Zenobia	Zaraah Abrahams
Tony McDonald	Gwilym Lloyd
Rick Coleman	Nick Holder
Housewife	Vanessa Havell
Journalist	Vanessa Havell

Black Man *and* **Asian Woman** *played by members of the cast.*

Director   Ryan McBryde
Designer   Mila Sanders
Sound Designer   George Dennis
Lighting Designer   Dan Hill

Characters

Peter Case
Driver
Polish Lady
Burka Woman 1
Burka Woman 2
African Guy
Labour MP
Mark Case
Clinton Jones
Gina White
Zenobia
Tony McDonald
Rick Coleman
Housewife
Journalist
Black Man
Asian Woman

Act One

Lights up on a bus stuck in traffic. **Pete Case**, *a white man in his fifties, is late for work. He is trying to read a book on local history, but his frustration distracts him. A jaunty tune starts up.*

'We came to England through the tunnel last night
(That's right, that's right)
We claim asylum now they're treating us right
(So right, so right)
Oh something tells me, Ahmed, this is the place to be
Cos here we're getting everything and we're getting it for free.

Oh I've got a brand new leather jacket and a brand new mobile phone
Brits they live in cardboard boxes while we get furnished homes
Legal aid, driving lessons, central heating and free bills
Oh we get all the benefits and you get all the bills.'

Pete *looks at his watch. A fat woman in a bright pink jumpsuit in front of him is on her mobile phone, yelling in Polish. We follow what she says on surtitles.*

Woman in Pink Jumpsuit *(into mobile)* Nie! Tak ci powiedział? A ty co mu powiedziałaś?
(No! He said that? What did you say to him?)

Pete *sighs and checks his watch again. The bus jumps forward, then grinds to a sudden halt again. The driver opens the door.* **Pete** *tries to control his anger. Tune:*

'They drove a lorry from Ikea straight away
(You pay, you pay)
TVs and furniture, it was mostly OK
(You pay, you pay)
But flat it wasn't suitable, the council's run by fools,
After crossing fifteen countries we need heated swimming pools.

Oh I've got a brand new leather jacket and a brand new mobile phone

Brits they live in cardboard boxes while we get furnished homes
Legal aid, driving lessons, central heating and free bills
Oh we get all the benefits and you get all the bills.'

Pete's *phone rings.*

Pete   Yeah, hello?

Two women in burkas plump themselves down on top of him, shoving him along the seat, as they carry on a loud conversation in Arabic.

Burka Woman 1   ه ىلإ تلق تنأ اذامو ؟هو قال أنّ !إضفـر
(No! He said that? What did you say to him?)

Burka Woman 2   هو قالني كان هاتف جوّاله مكسور
(He told me his mobile was broken.)

Pete   On the bus.

The woman in the pink jumpsuit pulls some smelly-looking foodstuff out of her bag, takes a huge mouthful and shouts into her phone, spraying bits of food everywhere.

Woman in Pink Jumpsuit (*into mobile*)   Co powiedział?
Że mu się popsuła komórka? Dupek! Zasługujesz na kogoś lepszego!
(Is that what he said? That his mobile was broken? Arsehole! You can do better than him, you know.)

Burka Woman   1   يستطيع أتمّت كثيرا حسنت من يعرف ه ![لوسرـرأ]
نأ ,أنت
(Arsehole! You can do so much better than him, you know.)

Pete   I'm trying to, mate, believe me I'm trying.

*An **African Guy** sneezes violently, wipes his hands on the bus seat, then pulls a thick stack of money from his pocket as he sings along to his iPod far too loud.*

African Guy   'Who the fuck cares
      I'm stanky rich
      I'ma die tryna spend this shit
      Southside's up in this bitch'

*The **Bus Driver** shouts something out of the window. Horns start to blare.*

Pete   Because I went to see our useless fucking MP is why. (*Beat.*) Have a guess.

The woman in the pink jumpsuit turns around and removes her top to reveal a sensible suit and blouse. She is now his local Labour MP.

Pete   So there's nothing you can do for me?

MP   I'm sorry, Mr Case. This is not something over which I have any control.

Pete   Even though we've been here however many years . . .

MP   The current method of housing allocation –

Pete   Paid our taxes? Done our bit?

MP   . . . is based on objective need, rather than length of residency. The policy has been that way for some time.

Pete   And he has an objective need!

MP   It's a policy that's intended to favour the needs of families rather than –

Pete   He's got the little one.

MP   *Large* families, families that would otherwise have / nowhere else –

Pete   He's in my front room. He's kipping on the couch in my front room.

MP   That is unfortunate, and I'm sure difficult for you, but the policy is geared towards the most vulnerable, those with large families, whom I know you wouldn't –

Pete   Large families of who? (*Beat.*) Come on, large families of who? Cos I thought the birth rate in Britain was right down.

Beat.

MP   Mr Case.

Pete   Speaking.

MP   That's not a particularly constructive attitude, if I may say so.

Pete   Oh?

MP   To bring immigration into the discussion is frankly −

Pete   *Me* bring it into the discussion?

MP   This borough operates a policy of absolute equality.

Pete   You're rigging the system in favour of people from outside the area −

MP   Absolute non-discrimination and / equality.

Pete   Instead of the people round here who've put the work in!

MP   It's something I personally feel very strongly about.

Pete   Do you now?

MP   I do. As a matter of fact. Yes.

Pete   That's nice. Absolute equality. So how come you've got five houses and my son don't have one?

MP   I'm not going to dignify that with a −

Pete   I forget; did you put in for the moat or the massage chair?

MP   I have other constituents who are equally deserving of my time.

Pause.

Pete   Know what's funny? (*She shrugs awkwardly.*) I've voted for you lot every time.

Beat.

MP   Good. (*Brief smile.*) Thank you.

Pete   I've voted Labour in every election since 1974. I dragged my carcass round the factory floor every lunchtime and tea break for a month before every election, getting bums off seats and down the polling station for ya. Even after Kinnock slung me out the bloody *party*, I've kept voting for you.

MP   And I hope we can persuade you to continue to do so.

Pete   You must think I'm a proper mug. Don't you? Go on. At least give me that much. You must think I'm a proper mug.

Beat. The woman digs into her bag, takes a huge bite of the dodgy food and spits it all over **Pete** *as, pulling her pink top back on, she morphs back into the Polish woman.*

Woman in Pink Jumpsuit (*into mobile*)   Myślę, że powinnaś uciąć mu tego jego bezużytecznego fiuta i sprzedać na "Ibeju"! (I think you should chop off his worthless dick and sell it on EBay!)

She turns back away from him. The song continues

'We go to garage to buy nice motor car
(Price is no bar)
Flash BMW cos we've come so far
(Price is no bar)
It costs many thousands, but man oh what the heck
We come back tomorrow and we pay with welfare cheque.'

Pete (*into phone*)   Mark with ya?

'Oh I've got a brand new leather jacket and a brand new mobile phone
Brits they live in cardboard boxes while we get furnished homes
Legal aid, driving lessons, central heating and free bills
Oh we get all the benefits and you get all the bills.'

Burka Woman 1   تقدّم إنكلترا يكون يذهب أن يتمّ هذا المساء, ناك امهم
كيف أنت
(Anyway, how do you reckon England are gonna do tonight?)

Pete (*simmering*)   You're gonna have to speak up, Clint. It's a little noisy here.

Burka Woman 2   اثنان وحاولت أن يهاجم نزولا إلى .حقاّ,دمتعي
ةحنجألا أنا أفكرّ هم سوفت ذهبت أربعة أربعة
(Depends, really. I think they should go 3-5-2 and try to attack down the wings.)

African guy   'Yeah, I talk the talk, and I walk the walk
          Like a Teflon Don, but I run New York'

Pete   You told him yet?

Woman in Pink Jumpsuit (*into mobile*)   To nie jest Polska, Waleska, nie musisz tkwić w tym gównie!
(This is not Poland any more, Valeska: you don't have to take this shit!)

Drilling. The driver leans on his horn and yells out the window. Horns blare in reply.

Burka Woman 1   مه [ووش ,] تشدحيس اذام فـرعت تـنأ
وسيذهب هو كلّ حلمة فوق ثانية [درـبمل] فـلخلا ىلإ نورضحيس
(You know what'll happen they'll bring back Lampard and it'll all go tits up again.)

Burka Woman 2   [يإ] [فوكيـنغ] حالة كره فرنكـتك [درـبمل]
(I fucking hate Frank Lampard.)

Pete   I tried to, mate. Last night.

Pete's son **Mark**, *a good-looking lad in his early twenties, comes on dribbling a football dextrously.* **Pete** *smiles. Suddenly* **Mark** *boots the ball violently off stage and looks away into a mirror, sorting his hair out.*

Pete   What is it tonight? D'n'B, R'n'B?

Mark   That's very good, Dad. B'n'B's more your line. (*Fiddles with hair.*) Dubstep.

Pete   Dubstep? They just make it up these days, don't they? That's not even a word.

Mark   Can you let me get ready, please? I'm well late.

Pete   Dubstep . . . Who's going down with ya?

Mark   Why? You don't care who I'm kotchin down some club with, do ya? (*Beat.*) Trev and Kamal, and Bolota's gonna meet us down there.

Pete   Bolota's the Ethiopian kid?

Mark   Eritrean. His mum is.

Pete   Close enough.

Mark   Cos they both begin with 'E'?

Pete   No, smartarse, cos they used to be the same place, didn't they.

Mark   You tell me.

Pete   I am telling you. They was one country 'til one split from the other. About twenty year back.

Mark   I don't think Bolota's been east of Dagenham in his life. Right, I'ma bounce. Don't wait up, you get me?!

Pete   What time you getting back?

Mark   Here we go.

Pete   I'm just saying, be on time tomorrow.

Mark   I told ya, I'll go to work from the club.

Pete   You know what Clint's like.

The **African Guy** *rises. He becomes* **Clinton Jones**, *a no-nonsense Cockney mate of* **Pete**'s *in painter's overalls who owns the small firm that employs* **Pete** *and* **Mark**.

Clint   Where the hell you been? Them walls s'posed to paint 'emselves?

Clint *makes his way over to a housing association flat being renovated. Plaster on the walls; painting and decorating tools lie around.*

Mark   When was I last late?

Clint   Thursday!

Mark   Six months without a sickie, trying to show both of ya I ain't no charity case –

Pete   Fair enough. (*He holds up a £20 note.*) Buy 'em a drink on me. Your mates.

Mark   I don't need your money.

Pete   I know. If you *needed* it, I'd make you earn it. But you've been grafting like a good 'un, I'll buy you and your mates a drink. (*Beat.*) We're strange like that, fathers.

Mark   Takes all sorts. (*Beat. He takes the money.*) Ta.

Pete   My pleasure.

Mark   And thank you for looking after Ella for tonight.

Pete   You know I love having her around.

Mark   Enjoy it while it lasts, Dad, yeah? Have me deposit soon.

Pete   Listen, Mark –

Mark   Make sure she gets her juice in the morning.

Pete   I will.

Mark   And her vitamins.

Pete   I have done this before, you know. With you, for a start.

Mark   And see how that turned out.

Pete   Mark.

Mark   Yeah?

Beat.

Pete   It's been good having you around, these last few months. It's been good getting to know you again. Don't rush off, whatever happens. (*Pause.*) Look after yourself.

Mark   I do, Dad. All day, every day.

He goes over to join **Clint** *at the flat.*

Pete   I couldn't, mate. It's your decision, you do it . . . (*The bus hasn't moved an inch.* **Pete** *checks his watch.*) Look, hang on, I'll be right there. (*He rises and tries to force his way past the women.*) Excuse me. Excuse me. Excuse me. Get out the bloody –

He shoves past them and approaches the driver. The women glare at him.

Burka Woman 1   تـنأ ,يتلقّى هذا رجال إنجليزيّة ما من إحترام لنساء فـرـعت؟

(These English men have no respect for women, you know?)

Woman in Pink Jumpsuit   Ej, zasrańcu, może nieco
grzeczniej, co?
(Hey, shithead, try to be polite maybe?)

Pete   What's going on, mate?

Driver   Station Barking.

Pete   Do what?

Driver   The bus go station Barking.

Pete   Yeah, but it's not though, is it?

Driver   Excuse me please?

Pete   The bus ain't going to Barking, is it? On account of
we're just sat here, do you know what I mean?

Beat.

Driver   Excuse me please?

Pete *slaps his hands together and inhales deeply.*

Pete   Do you know where you are going?

Driver   The bus go station Barking.

Woman in Pink Jumpsuit (*into mobile*)   Nie wiem, jakiś
palant przeszkadza kierowcy. Hej kolo!!
(I don't know, some wanker is distracting the driver. Hey
buddy!)

Pete   And do you know where station Barking is, old son?

Burka Woman 1   هو فقط يحاول أن يتمّ شغله, دارفـنـاب هتـاكرت
(Leave him alone, he is only trying to do his job!)

Driver (*smiling apologetically, palms up*)   No.

*Someone bangs on the side of the bus and unleashes a torrent of abuse.
The sound of a jackhammer.* **Pete** *rips the doors of the bus open and
storms away. The song:*

'Our friends in Parliament are all on our side
(Cock-eyed, cock-eyed)

Sometimes they talk tough but you know it's a lie
(Cock-eyed, cock-eyed)
Immigration is a good thing, on that they all agree
The only ones who'll stop it are the wicked BNP.

Oh I've got a brand new leather jacket and a brand new
mobile phone
Brits they live in cardboard boxes while we get furnished homes
Legal aid, driving lessons, central heating and free bills
Oh we get all the benefits and you get all the bills.'

The cast turns to the audience and collectively shouts:

'TO STOP ALL THIS NONSENSE, VOTE BNP!'

Pete *heads to the flat, where* **Clint** *and* **Mark** *are wrestling with an oversized cistern.*

Clint   Bit more your end.

Mark   I've got my end.

Clint   No you ain't. (**Mark** *hefts his end up a little more.*) Float valve.

Mark   Eh?

Clint   How loud was the music in that gaff?

Mark   Thass Benga for you! Nasty, *dutty* bass, blood!

He holds out a fist for **Clint** *to bump.* **Clint** *glares at him.*

Clint   That was a . . . one a them questions you ask yourself, Mark. Pass us the fucking float valve.

Mark (*passing him the float valve*)   You've got the right hump this morning, dontcha Clint? Big night last night, was it?

Clint   No. It wasn't.

Mark   Not as big as mine anyway! This one gyal, yeah . . . (*Points to his arm.*) See that? What are those, mate?

Clint (*not looking*)   Stab wounds, hopefully.

Mark   Scorch marks! Thass how hot this chick was, you know! Oh my days! (**Pete** *enters.*) Alright Dad? Hear what, you're lucky your little couch ain't got space for two cos it woulda got *bruk* up last night! I woulda rode dat ting like the Grand National! I'm talking about up and over, up and over, you know what I mean?!

Pete *looks at* **Clint** *with a 'You told him yet?' expression.* **Clint** *shakes his head.* **Mark** *starts singing some dancehall tune about hotness.*

Clint   You turn off the stopcock on the rising main?

Mark   Course.

Clint   Course? Says the twat who set off indoor Niagara Falls on his first day. We had geezers turning up in barrels and everything.

Mark   Clinton, I've come in and saved *your* arse.

Clint   You may have improved but you ain't what you think you are, Mark.

Mark   It was Titanic in here this morning.

Clint   I've got stuff on my mind.

Mark   I had to pull Kate Winslet out the shower curtain. You were miles away.

Clint   Get on with your work!

Mark *looks hurt. Pause.*

Pete   We lost the Mandela House contract.

Mark   What? (**Clint** *busies himself with the cistern.*) Who to?

Beat.

Clint   Them Polish fellas that're doing Harrison's.

Mark   But they shouldn't even . . . They haven't got their City and Guilds. Do they have City and Guilds in Poland? You can't get the contracts now unless . . .

He looks around as if appealing to an invisible referee. **Clint** *bangs his spanner hard against the cistern by way of reply.*

Pete   Cheaper bid.

Mark   Course cheaper bid, they're not fucking qualified! How can the council give 'em the contract? (*Pause. Neither of them will meet* **Mark***'s eye. He clocks what this means. To* **Pete**.) *I've* got my City and Guilds. Eight months I spent getting 'em, cos you told me there'd be work at the end of it.

Pete   There is / work.

Mark   But not here. Come on then, spit it out. I might be thick but I ain't stupid. Mandela House, that's half the order book. (*Beat.*) At least be straight with me, Clint.

Pause.

Clint   As it stands, I don't have enough work for three.

Mark   Well that's that then.

Pete   Hold on –

Clint   As it stands.

Pete   There's ways / around it –

Clint   If things pick up –

Mark   Nah nah nah, bollocks. *Bollocks.* The way it is out there right now? Don't take the piss out of me *and* take my job.

Pete   He hasn't taken your job. It's not his –

Mark   No. But you have. I'm better than you, Dad, don't pretend I'm not. Alright, I was shit when I started, but I've done my courses and I've knuckled down and now I'm better than you. I'm faster and I've got a better eye. It's true, ain't it Clint?

Beat. **Clint** *looks away.*

Pete   I need my job an all, Mark.

Clint   It was him got you the place here.

Mark   I made the most of this, you know? I fucking *hated* being here when I started, I'd've hated anything that wasn't football, but the white spirit in yer eyes and the boredom of it . . . When you've had thousands of people shouting for ya and then it's just you in a room with a roller and some spackling, it's quite hard to take.

Pete   You're making a meal of this.

Mark   I knuckled down and I got *good* at it, Dad.

Pete   There's other jobs. That Tesco's just opened up.

Mark (*glaring*)   Raise my daughter on five pound an hour?

Pete   You've almost got yer deposit.

Mark   Yeah, what about *rent*?

Pete   You can stay with me a bit more, I like having you there.

Mark   That's nice.

Pete   I can carry you –

Mark   I don't want to be fucking *carried*, Dad! (*Beat.*) Fuck it. It don't matter anyway.

Pete   There's gotta be a way we can get you into one of these places.

Mark   Aw, come on now –

Pete   You should have this place. We should be doing up this place for *you*.

Mark   It's a *waste of time*.

Pete   You been down for it since the year dot, they can't just take it away from ya –

Mark   They've changed the rules.

Pete   Then they can change 'em back again!

Clint   He's right, Pete. They don't care about local people, do they?

Mark   I'm gonna leave the country. I've been thinking about it and I'm gonna leave the country.

Pause.

Pete   No.

Mark   That's what I'm gonna do though.

Pete   And go where?

Mark   Somewhere hot with a beach, birds in bikinis and drinks with fruit in 'em. Somewhere away from this shithole. (*Beat.*) Gary's in Malaga working on sites and that, he reckons he can sort me out with some labouring work.

Pete   In Spain? Do you not read the papers? They're in worse shit than we are!

Mark   I'll find something.

Pete   Sat in some bar watching Sky Sports, dreaming of home?

Mark   I won't be dreaming of home.

Pete   What about your football? The fella from the Orient said get your knee sorted –

Mark   I'm twenty-three. Nobody gets picked up at twenty-three. There's nothing here for me no more.

Pete   What about Ella? What about . . . me and Ella?

Beat.

Mark   I'll take her with me. When I get settled.

Pause.

Pete   You know what your problem is, Mark? You've got no bottle. Never have done. When the going gets tough, Mark Case bottles it. Even when you was little.

Mark   Is that right?

Clint   Mark, I need you to go get me –

Pete   Oh yeah, no problem when you was head and shoulders above everybody else on the pitch, you pissed it then, thought you was the best thing since sliced, but when the standard got a little bit tougher, games got a little bit harder –

Mark (*bitter*)   I got hurt.

Pete   You couldn't hack it. You did a runner, just like you're doing now.

Mark   Runs in the family then.

Clint   Right, that's it, both of you back to –

Mark   The big man, the rebel. What the fuck have you done for the last ten years? A jobbing painter and decorator, takes the bus to work. Embarrassing.

Pete   The rest of the world is busting a gut to get over here, climbing in back of lorries and under trains, risking life and limb, and you, you lot can't wait to get away. If it ain't all on a plate, you'd rather do a few Es, get off your heads.

Mark   And all that effort, all them strikes done you so much good, ain't they?

Pete   You're lazy, Mark. Lazy and weak. (*Beat.*) Where's it gone, the energy, the confidence, the belief we used to have in this country? The only people who's got it now are the immigrants. Where's it gone, Mark? Where's yours gone?

Beat. **Mark** *leaves. Pause.* **Pete** *circles the room.*

Clint   Go after him.

Pete   D'you know what they told me down the social? You know what they told me?

Clint   Go after him, Pete.

Pete   I sat there two and a half hours, waiting. Like the United Nations it was. Every language under the sun except English, all at two hundred decibels. I dunno why these backpacking cunts go all the way to India when they could just spend a couple of hours down the DSS. And then the woman calls me in, not being funny but she barely speaks English herself –

Clint   Course.

Pete   And she gives me the line about criteria and need and points, and in the end she tells me, 'The only way you can get your son on the housing list is to make him homeless.' That's my government telling me that. My own government is telling me I should kick my boy out on the street and then *maybe* they'll think about helping him.

Clint   Peter. He's disappointed enough in himself. You can't be an all.

Pete   Who says I'm disappointed in him?

Clint   Come on, son.

Pete   He's got no spark, no *courage* to him now. He's gotta pick himself up, get –

Clint   Did you see the way he looked at ya? Like a kicked puppy.

Pete   How can he leave?

Beat.

Clint   Go on. I can cover it here.

Beat.

Pete   What'm I supposed to do, Clint? If he goes, that's the last of Ell I'm gonna see.

Clint   Go after him.

Pete   I'm gonna lose my son and my granddaughter, both of 'em, just like that.

A young, well-dressed, Asian-looking woman appears alongside him, clutching a stack of electoral materials. She calls herself **Gina White**.

What am I supposed to do?

Gina   Hello again.

Pete *turns. They are in his doorway. In his hand he holds the history book he was reading on the bus.*

It's Pete, isn't it?

Pete   It is, yeah.

Gina   I'm Gina.

Pete   Yeah, I remember.

She holds her hand out, business-like. He shakes it, somewhat uncomfortable. Pause.

Gina   So, have you had the chance to read the stuff I left you?

Pete   I haven't, no. Work, you know how it is.

Gina   What do you do?

Pete   Painter and decorator.

Gina   Right.

Pete   It was a, what do they call it now? A 'career rebrand', you could say.

Gina   Meaning you got fired.

Pete   Yeah.

Gina   What'd you do before?

Pete   Union organiser. (*Nods his head down the road.*) Car factories.

Gina   Oh yeah? Interesting.

Pete   That's one word for it. 'Outdated' would be another. What's that other thing they want now? 'Transferable skills'? I've got the opposite of that.

Gina   What's the book?

Pete   Local history stuff. A geek, my son calls me. I've got piles of stuff in here.

Beat.

Pete   I'd better get back to . . .

Gina   I could pop back in an hour or two? Give you a chance to look at what I left?

Pete   Yeah. No. No. Yeah.

Gina (*smiling*)   So yes *and* no?

Pete   You're all right.

Gina   All right you want me to come back or all right you want me to stay?

Beat. **Pete** *pulls a handful of crumpled leaflets from his back pocket.*

Pete   Do you really mean this?

Gina   We do.

Pete   You really *mean* it?

Gina   I do, yes.

Pete   Cos this is like going back in time for me. 'Nationalise public services.' 'End the privatisation of schools and hospitals.'

Gina   They care about big business, we care about ordinary people.

Pete   'No more bank bailouts.'

Gina   They 'can't interfere with the market' when it sends our jobs to China, but they'll bend over backwards for the bankers?

Pete   'Local residence the key for council house allocation.' Nobody's saying this sort of thing!

Gina   We are, Pete.

Pete   My son, right, born and raised in this area, and I went down the social and they've got *nothing* for him, nothing, it's all gone to these immigrants on the basis of greater need. And maybe they have got needs, those people, and good luck to 'em, but *so do we.* And we was here first. Nothing against them but we was here first and more than that, we put our shift in. I've paid my taxes and I put a shift in and I want what's coming. Not to me, because I'm a worn out old bugger, Gina –

Gina I wouldn't say that.

Pete But to the people who's important to me. And you look at who's in charge nowadays, the *contempt* they have for working-class people, taking away pensions and healthcare that people've been paying for for decades and then bang, just like that, privatised, gone . . . And you can take it from scum like the Tories cos they've always been that way, but from the Labour Party . . .

He hesitates for a moment.

Gina Carry on.

Pete Cos we made the Labour Party, do you know what I mean? Froze our bollocks off on picket lines, went on strike and lived off fresh air and fuck all for six months at a time. And now we've turned to dust in their eyes, ain't we? We're the fucking *problem* now: chav scum, ASBO meat. A source of *laughter*. Prime time TV entertainment. I hate them for it. I bloody hate them for it. (*Pause.*) Sorry. Sorry.

Gina It's fine.

Pete (*hand on chest*) Phwoah. Bloody hell. Sorry.

Gina It's good to hear.

Pete Dunno where that came from.

Gina I agree. I agree with everything you've said.

Beat.

Pete Ah, this is a joke! I used to have proper tear-ups with you lot in the Seventies!

Gina Those were not my lot.

Pete (*Pointing to his cheek.*) See there? That's where one of yours stuck his blade in.

Gina Those were not mine, Pete.

Pete You ask your bosses, they'll remember me. Pete Case, Head Case they used to call me. We was on the national news once, when they blackballed us from the factory. I've been called a 'socialist agitator' by Moira Stewart on national TV, that's my claim to fame. Got the tape somewhere, but it's Betamax, useless.

Gina   Join the British National Party, Pete.

Pete   I'm not gonna join the bloody BNP when I've spent half me life fighting 'em.

Gina   Do you think we should be building council houses for people like your son, instead of 'luxury accommodation' for parasitic tosspots?

Pete   I'm not a *fascist*, Gina, I'm not a racist!

Gina   Do you think we should cut back on the number of immigrants in this country, who undercut British workers and put them out of jobs?

Pete   I don't have a problem with people trying to feed their –

Gina   Do you think we should cut back on the number of immigrants –

Pete   Yes, I do, I do, alright.

Gina   Do you think we should restore our sense of dignity, of community, of pride?

Pete   I'm older than you, Gina. I know what these people are about.

Gina   Do you think anybody, and I mean anybody, in power gives two rancid shits about people like you and me, Pete Case, Head Case? (*Pause. Pete can't look at her.*) Then tell me what are you waiting for?

The sound of children playing. Parents' evening, **Ella**'s *school.* **Mark** *and* **Pete** *being shown round by her teacher,* **Zenobia,** *a young, middle-class black woman.*

Mark   Who's this?

Zenobia   That's Mary Seacole, the first black nurse in Britain. She went with the British to the Crimea.

Mark   I went with the British to Ayia Napa meself. Coulda used some medical attention there, no word of a lie. Which one's Ella's?

Zenobia   This one.

Mark   Rah, that is good, you know!

Zenobia   She's talented, your daughter.

Mark   She thinks the world of you.

Zenobia   And a lovely little girl too.

Mark   Always singing your praises.

Zenobia   Well, they do at that age, don't they?

Mark   I can see why.

Zenobia   They grow out of it eventually. I'm not that special.

Mark   I'd have to disagree.

Zenobia   That's sweet of you. Now if you'll excuse me, there are other parents –

Pete   So is this the same thing she was doing a few weeks ago?

Beat.

Zenobia   No, that was Diwali, Mr Case.

Pete   Right. It's just they seem quite similar, you know. To an ignoramus.

Zenobia   Not especially.

Pete   Easy to muddle up, maybe.

Zenobia   That was an Asian festival. This is Black History Month.

Pete   OK. Fair enough. (*He looks around.*) Lot of . . . lot of ethnic stuff she's getting at the minute.

Mark   It's Black History Month, Dad.

Zenobia   It's the time of year. Come back at Christmas or Easter, it'll be different.

Pete   Other made-up stuff, you mean?

Zenobia   Pardon?

Pete   When does she study the rest of it?

Zenobia   The rest of what?

Pete   Her heritage. British history.

Zenobia   This is part of British history.

Pete   Part of, yes. And I can understand that, why you want to give her all this lot, it's something your generation probably never got.

Zenobia   It's not my choice, Mr Case. I don't set the curriculum.

Pete   Don't get me wrong, I think it's fair enough. I just think you can go too far the other way, you know?

Zenobia   I only teach what they ask me to teach.

Mark   What's she missing then?

Pete   I told ya, British history.

Mark   The empire and all that? You always taught me 'Queen and Country' was bollocks. (*To* **Zenobia**.) He took my school textbook away one time cos it said Wellington won the battle of Waterloo. (*Parody of* **Pete**.) 'Wot, on his fackin own?'

Zenobia *tries to hide a smile.*

Pete   I'm talking about her roots.

Mark   When he wants cheering up a bit, this geezer pops in the Diana crash tape.

Pete   Mark, shut up for a minute. (*To* **Zenobia**.) Her society. What's made her.

Zenobia Isn't this part of what's made her?

Pete Of course it is, I'm not denying that. I'm talking about the bits you've forgotten.

Zenobia I haven't *forgotten* –

Pete See, it upsets me a little bit how people (*to* **Mark**), *uneducated* people, go on like British history is nothing but theft and murder. Because of some chinless wonders a couple of hundred years ago, an aristocracy I've got *nothing* in common with –

Zenobia If you'd come to the previous –

Pete The working-class movement, right, started right down this road! The first independent trade union was here gasworkers, 1867. First Labour MP, West Ham –

Mark Dad, she's five.

Pete And she should know the history of where she's from! In 1919, the London dockers refused to load arms for the White armies fighting the Russian revolution.

Zenobia And in 1940 they helped load refugee Jews back onto the boats that returned them to Germany. I did history at uni.

Pete Demonstrations against Mosley in the East End.

Zenobia Demonstrations *for* Mosley in the East End!

Pete Why do you have to contradict me?

Zenobia Because things were not, are not, and never will be, all one way.

Pete So she shouldn't get only the black stuff!

Mark (*incredulous*) The 'black stuff'?!

Zenobia With respect, have you *seen* Ella lately?

Pete Why's it matter so much what she looks like?

Mark Dad, lock it off, *now*.

Pete   You're shoving her into a box and telling her who she can and can't be, cos of what she looks like! You know what she said to me last week? 'Where am I from? Cos Razana's from Pakistan and Angelika's from Poland and Khalifa's from Somalia, but I'm not from anywhere special.'

Mark   Where's all this come from?

Pete   I want what's best for my granddaughter.

Mark   And she's trying her best to give it to her. Like she was trying to say but you wouldn't let her, if you'd come to the one at Easter –

Pete   I was / working.

Mark   If you'd come to the one at Easter, you'da seen all chicks and fluffy bunnies and you wouldn'ta gone off on this mad BNP turnout. (*Beat.*) I'm surprised at ya.

Pause.

Pete   I've got to go. Thank you for teaching my granddaughter.

Zenobia   It's fine. It's my job.

He leaves. Beat.

Mark   I've never met that geezer before in my entire life.

Beat. They both laugh a little.

Zenobia   It's just, no offence, but I get the same routine from the white parents *every single day* . . .

Mark   I know.

Zenobia   'Why do the kids have to do this black stuff? Why can't they study 'our' culture?'

Mark   He's not like that, I swear.

Zenobia   'How long has it been a crime to be white?'

Mark   He ain't got no Staff. He ain't coming in with a spider's web tattooed on his face, know what I mean?

Zenobia   No, I know, but –

Mark   He's a decent man, I promise.

Beat. She smiles.

Zenobia   I had one bloke in last week, he'd lost one of his fingers, probably in some bizarre prison ritual or something, so across his knuckles it said LOVE and HAT. (*They break up laughing.*) The worst bit was, he kept ranting on about how bad his kid's spelling was! Inside I was *pissing* myself! Sorry, I probably shouldn't say that . . .

Mark   Nah, nah, it's funny . . . (*Beat.*) Listen, Ms Williams . . . I don't know if this is, like . . . and you can shoot me down proper if you don't . . . cos I know it probably ain't professional and I don't wanna say you ain't professional, like . . . cos professional's one of the nicest things about ya . . . not that it's the only nice thing about ya, I mean –

Zenobia   Mr Case.

Mark   Mark. Sorry. Probably not the best time to lyrics ya –

Zenobia   I'm sorry, Mr Case, but this isn't acceptable. I'm afraid I have to hold you responsible for what happened today.

Mark   What?

Zenobia   You're going to have to write out some lines for me.

Mark   *What?*

Zenobia   Got a pen and paper?

Mark (*scrabbling in his jacket for a scrap of paper to write on, he can only find a Rizla packet, which he holds up apologetically*)   Yeah, I mean sort of . . .

Zenobia   That'll do. Ready? Oh seven nine four seven, six eight seven three four one. You get that?

Mark   Oh yeah. I'm a very good student. When the teaching's right.

Zenobia   I'm glad to hear it.

Mark   When do I have to hand this in?

Zenobia   How about Friday night?

Mark   That should work. That should definitely work.

Pete *on the doorstep with* **Gina**.

Gina   Why does she have to be one or the other, you mean?

Pete   Exactly! I thought you'd understand . . . (*Beat.*) Cos the thing is, right, if you say anything, you sound –

Gina   Sound racist.

Pete   And there's no comeback to that, is there? What can you say, 'My best friend is a black geezer'? You sound like a prick. You say anything, you get some social worker who's missed five Baby Ps before lunch round your gaff lecturing you on 'tolerance', like you eat off the floor, you're some kind of animal. (*He stops himself. Pause.*) I'm a nice man, really, Gina. Promise. I'm not normally like this.

Gina   Can I come in, Pete?

Beat.

Pete   Ella's just gone to bed. I don't wanna wake her, you know.

Gina   How old is she? Ella?

Pete   She's five.

Gina (*smiling*)   Nice age.

Pete   That's her there, look.

He hands over a picture from his wallet. The photo appears as a poster above their heads: a mixed-race (black and white) photogenic little girl with a happy smile.

Gina   Lovely little thing, isn't she?

She hands the photo back. Pause.

Pete   Who are you, Gina?

Gina   I'm your BNP election candidate.

Pete   Not what are you, who are you?

Gina   How'd you mean?

Pete   Where are you from, who's your family?

Gina   I'm not that comfortable talking about my personal life.

Pete   Well you might wanna get used to it, love. I think a few people might have questions, d'you know what I mean?

Pause.

Gina   My mum's English, Irish if you go back far enough, my dad's Pakistani.

Pete   Big families on both sides then.

Gina   Except neither side wanted the marriage and they cut them off. I have six aunts, seven uncles and thirty-seven cousins, and I've met a total of three of them. I think the isolation was what did for my parents, turned them in on each other.

Pete   It's hard when you get isolated.

Gina   Is that what happened to you and Mrs Pete? There must have been a –

Pete   Carry on with yer story.

Beat.

Gina   When I was a kid, we moved around a lot. I don't know if it was for my dad's work or to distract them from hating each other. All I know is I was never at home.

Pete   OK.

Gina   Right away, wherever we'd land up, they'd have me in one box or another, like you say about Ella, even if it was just the 'reject/don't fit in' box. I won't be put in a box, Pete. You know what lives in boxes? Toys.

Pete   Different nowadays, though, innit? I see Mark with his mates, all colours under the sun, they don't even care.

Gina   Oh, it's still there, under the surface, trust me. All these little groups, hiving themselves off, marking out their territory so they can get council grants. It's skin deep, this liberal tolerance.

Pete   Call me a liberal and I guarantee we'll fall out.

Gina   When were you last part of something? When's the last time you lost yourself in something bigger?

Pete   Work.

Gina   Painting and decorating?

Beat.

Pete   Factory days.

Gina   When else? The times I've been happiest, Pete, when I've made the most sense, are times of *patriotism*. Diana's death. Last Night of the Proms. The World Cup.

Pete   The World Cup is when you've been happiest?

Gina   Lost in the group, the heart pumping, something to be proud of. What is anyone *proud* of now, Pete? The answer should be all around us: England. Its pride, its passion, its greatness. The rivers and the hills and the beauty around you.

Pete   It's flat as a roadkill sarnie round here.

Gina   A thousand years of history and nobody knows who we are any more? But you know that history. You know you're part of something.

Pete   I read your new constitution. (*Pulls it out.*) 'The British National Party stands for the preservation of the national and ethnic character of the British people –'

Gina   That's me.

Pete   '– and is wholly opposed to any form of racial integration between British and non-European peoples. It is committed to reversing the tide of non-white immigration and to restoring the overwhelmingly white make up of the British population.'

Gina   They have to say that, don't they?

Pete   Do they?!

Gina   *For now*, so they don't lose the base. But in the long run, they'll adapt or die. People aren't out and out racist any more, not like they used to be. But they are still patriotic. And sick and fucking tired of spongers, whether it's wanker bankers with their hands out who fuck off to Dubai the moment anyone mentions tax, or bearded freaks with seven wives all claiming housing benefit. We, the British people, the way we are *now*, we've had enough. Whatever we look like, whoever we sleep with, whoever we pray to, the British people have had enough. Kick out the parasites, pull up the drawbridge and let's get on with it. (*Pause.*) Come to the next meeting. (*Beat.*) Please.

McDonald   No fucking way.

Pete *melts away.* **Gina** *with the BNP's local organiser, an unreconstructed but not unintelligent racist named* **Tony McDonald**. *Suddenly she is all steel again.*

Gina   I don't think it's up to you. Orders from above.

McDonald   From Rick the Prick, the one-eyed wanker? He can go fuck himself. I'm the regional organiser here.

Gina   Which is why I need your help to put the campaign together.

McDonald   I already told you.

Gina (*smiling*)   Give me a go.

McDonald   No fucking way.

Gina   What's wrong with me?

McDonald   Look at you. You think I can get my members to campaign for that? You think I can get my members out on the streets for a –

Gina   Where are you from, Tony?

Beat.

McDonald   Where am *I* from?

Gina   Yeah. Where's your family from?

McDonald   Becontree.

Gina   No, *originally*. Scottish name, McDonald, correct?

Beat.

McDonald   Celtic warriors. Conquerors.

Gina   Immigrants.

McDonald   Not as recently as your lot.

Gina   We're all outsiders, originally. But we're here now, aren't we? And we both want what's best for Britain.

Pause.

McDonald   Fucking European elections. Coleman wins two seats in the Europeans, *two seats* out of seventy odd, and all of a sudden it's 'time for the party to enter the political mainstream'.

Gina   You don't see winning seats as an important aim for a political party?

McDonald   Not as much as marking your territory, no. Standing up and saying who we are.

Gina   I think that attitude may be the reason Rick sent me here, Tone.

McDonald   Winning is secondary to staking out who we are, not letting people forget White Britain exists. Always has been. But two seats in the Euros and Coleman, the opportunist cunt, who in my opinion has never been a true member of this party, shits himself, rubs out the fucking Party constitution like it's a pub throwing order, and parachutes in some cocky little half-breed to stick her nose in like she owns the place. Classic Coleman. No local knowledge whatsoever.

Anyone knows the first thing about this area knows there is zero fucking chance –

Gina   Call me a Paki. (*Beat.*) Come on. Call me a Paki. Get it over with.

Beat. **Pete** *materialises in a doorway, unseen by either of them.*

McDonald   Look me up on Stormfront, darling, you'll see who you're dealing with.

Gina   Call me a Paki.

Beat.

McDonald   Paki.

Gina   Can't hear you. Louder.

McDonald   Paki.

Gina   Again.

McDonald   PAKI.

Gina   BOOOOORRRRRIIING! Is that the best you can do? How old are you, Tony? Fifty, fifty-five? And that's the sum total of wisdom those years have granted you? You should be embarrassed, mate. You want to win this election?

McDonald   Of course I do.

Gina   I will do that.

McDonald   But not at any price.

Gina   See, you might think you're radical, Tony, 'not like all the rest', but really you think like the lefties. All either of you see is my face. They see my face and they tell me about their yoga classes and their challenging Indian gap year. You see my face and you want to stick a pint glass in it. But it's the same thing. I'm here for a reason.

McDonald   Because this is your only chance of becoming a celebrity.

Gina   Because this is the only party that believes what I believe, in the greatness of Britain and of British identity.

McDonald   British identity doesn't include you.

Gina   I could have signed up as 'ethnic outreach officer' for the Tories or Labour. They're gagging for people like me. That would have been the easy way.

McDonald   Wouldn't have *stood out* quite so much though, would ya?

Gina   I could've got onto the lists of 'faces to watch' and had all the Westminster village idiots queuing up.

McDonald   Wouldn't be quite so 'controversial'. Don't think, because I'm true to myself, that I don't know what's going on.

Pete (*entering*)   Always been a step behind the times, aintcha Tony?

Gina   Pete!

Pete (*kissing **Gina**'s cheek, winking at **McDonald***)   Alright son?

Gina   You two know each other?

Pete   Oh yeah. We go way back.

McDonald   I've seen it all now. The Yanks have a nig-nog president, the BNP have a Paki candidate and Red Case strolls into my office.

Pete (*pointing to his face*)   I told you how I got this? That was Tony's handiwork.

McDonald   You want a matching pair? Then get the fuck out of my sight.

Pete   Can't. Gina invited me.

McDonald   This is your idea?

Gina   It is, yeah. Pete's exactly the kind of person I'm trying to draw into the party.

McDonald   Do you have a fucking clue what you're doing?

Gina   I think so.

McDonald   This Red trash, this Marxist scum, you want him in the *party*? The whole *point* of the party is to have cunts like this in the gutter, flush them out and punish them, let the red blood flow so people can see how weak they are, how weak and feeble are the Yids and the Reds and all the other mongrels and mixers.

Pete   I remember you pissing your pants in the New Cross Road.

McDonald   Scum like this are the reason for the party's existence.

Pete   The Battle of Lewisham, August of '77. Literally pissed his pants.

McDonald   He does not join the party.

Pete   Bricks and smoke bombs raining down and all I remember is this big stain spreading across Tony McDonald's denims.

McDonald (*springs to his feet and into* **Pete***'s face*)   What is your fucking game? What is your fucking game? What is your fucking game? (**Pete** *bristles. They are chin to chin. Pause.* **McDonald** *steps back.*) Who are you trying to kid? A fucking Red and a Paki working for the BNP? You're not even funny.

Gina   No, I'm not.

McDonald   You're mad if you think this is the last of this.

He storms out. **Gina** *calls after him.*

Gina   Give Rick my love! (*She turns to* **Pete**.) That was *amazing*! The look on his face! The way you put him in his place, that was *exactly* what I need –

Pete   I'm gonna go home now, Gina.

Gina (*face suddenly falling*)   What?! Why?

Pete   Feel a bit sick actually.

Gina   You need to sit down?

Pete   It was alright when I was winding him up but I think I might puke now. (*He bends over to catch his breath. Pause.*) Look at me. Fucking look at me. I'm actually in the BNP offices. I was actually thinking of joining the BNP.

Gina   You *are* –

Pete   I may have come down in the world but I ain't sunk that low. See ya, Gina.

He makes to leave. She bars his way.

Gina   No. No. Bollocks. Alright, you've run into an old adversary, it's jarred you a bit. You'll get over it.

Pete   Gina –

Gina   Has anything in the real world changed? Any of the things that brought you here tonight, have they changed?

Beat.

Pete   Look, it might have made sense, when we was *talking*, when I was reading your stuff in my flat –

Gina   And it still does.

Pete   But you talk about the real world the real world is people like him.

Gina   People like him are a dying breed. I'm the future. *I* am.

Pete   Yeah, but . . .

Gina   Look at me, is that what you're gonna say? Who's the racist now, Pete? 'You're a Paki, you stay with the other Pakis.'

Pete   You know I don't –

Gina   I thought this country was about freedom, where's the freedom in that? Fuck any system that says my dad can come over here and keep his disgusting Paki ways –

Pete   Gina –

Gina   That is what they are, Pete! What kind of freedom says my Dad can marry me off to some obese stinking fifty-year-old peasant from his village who signs his name with his thumbprint and tries to stick his cock up my arse on the wedding night? And then my white mother and all her kind tell me it's 'my culture' and I should be *grateful* to have it, because she's too fucking scared and lost and weak to know what's hers and so in her mind she's *brave* for sucking my Dad's dick and getting his passport because she didn't have to, she could've married that ginger IT engineer from Huddersfield and never had the neighbours whispering. Fuck all that.

Pete   I'm gonna go home.

Gina   Don't go. What made you come in? Once you saw Mr Knuckle-dragger there, you could have slipped back out the way you came. What made you stay?

Pete   Wanted to wind him up, didn't I?

Gina   Was that all? (*Beat.*) There is a great mass of humanity out there, lost and lonely and afraid, that we can reach. Help me find what the people need and want and dream of. Give them a little of what's been stolen from them and they will be ours forever.

Mark *enters the finished flat. He stares around.*

I can make a real difference in people's lives.

Mark   Fucking hell.

Gina   But I need an organiser.

Pete   No.

Mark (*walks around in some disbelief*)   Bloody fucking hell.

Gina   A man with experience.

Pete   Not me. No. No way.

Gina   A man with passion and intelligence, whose passion and intelligence are being criminally wasted as of now.

Mark (*jingles a set of keys*)   Bloody fucking fucking bloody hell.

Gina   A man who wants to make a difference in other people's lives, and his own.

Mark *does a little dance of ecstasy as he takes in the room.* **Pete** *enters the flat.* **Gina** *watches him.* **Pete** *and* **Mark** *stare at one another. Pause.*

Mark   I can't believe we was working on this place and now . . .

Pete   I know.

Beat.

Mark   Here's your bit, look.

Pete   How'd you know that was my bit?

Mark   Look at the finish on this.

Pete   Looks alright to me.

Mark   That is a crap finish. You never could finish. If I'd known I was on the list for the gaff, I'd have done it meself.

Pete   You weren't on the list.

Pause. They look at one another.

Mark   What about the rent?

Pete   You'll have to earn it, won't you.

Mark   That's my point.

Pete   I reckon Clint'll take you back on.

Mark   Where's he got new work from?

Pete   You'd be doing my stuff.

Mark   What are you gonna do?

Gina   I want you to run my campaign, Pete.

Pause.

Pete (*to* **Mark**)   I'm thinking of taking this job.

Mark   Doing what?

Gina   Will you do it?

Pete   With the council. I haven't decided yet. (*He looks at* **Gina**. *Beat.*) I don't want to do anything public.

Gina   It's nothing to be ashamed of.

Pete   Not until you've proved yourself. Alright?

Gina   There's no reason to hide –

Pete   *Alright?*

Gina   As you like. Whatever you like, Pete.

Mark   Dad?

Pete   Yeah?

Beat.

Mark   Thank you.

Pete   It's my pleasure.

Beat.

Mark   I didn't think you had it in you.

Pete   Well I do.

Mark   You didn't have to do no-one, did ya? I'm not gonna find some poor Somali bird and her three kids under the floorboards?

Pete   Connections. The way it works, always has done. (*Beat. To* **Gina**.) You did it.

Gina   I told you I would.

Pete   I've been trying to get him one of those places for five years.

Gina   When I say I'll do something, Pete, I do it.

Mark   I thought you give up all that politics stuff from time?

Pete   I never gave up politics, Mark. Politics gave me up.

Gina   What do you say, Pete?

Beat. **Mark** *looks around the room again.*

Mark   Dad?

Pete   Yes, mate?

Mark   You reckon Clint can sort me out some pink matt cheap?

Pete   Why?

Gina   Will you do it?

Mark   For Ella's room. Don't suppose you fancy giving me a hand?

Pete   With my finish?

Mark   If you can be arsed.

Gina   I want you, Pete.

Beat.

Pete (*to both*)   Yes. I'd love to. I would love that.

Lights gradually down.

Act Two

Pete, *smartly dressed, energised, buzzing around with papers in hand.*
Gina *enters.*

Pete   Right, here's the plan.

Gina   The plan is coffee.

Pete   You know them three tower blocks by the motorway?

Gina   Did you drink it all?

Pete   No party's been up there for going on twenty years.
Too scary, lifts are fucked, no-one fancies the smell of piss in
their clothes afterwards.

Gina   Look at you! You did drink it all!

Pete   You're going up there this morning. What are you
talking about?

Gina   Coffee.

Pete   I ain't made any coffee. Why are you talking about coffee?

Gina   Because it's eight o'clock in the morning.

Pete   There's hundreds and hundreds of people lives up
there, Gina! How d'you reckon them people are gonna react
when they see someone gives a shit about them?

Gina (*smiling, moves across and takes the papers from him*)   If
they're anything like me, they're going to be charmed, and just
a little scared, by your enthusiasm.

Pete   I'm not the one going.

Gina   Thank you for the suggestion, I think it's an excellent
idea. I will get up there as soon as I can.

Pete   You need to get up there now.

Gina   They're tower blocks, Pete, they're not going anywhere.

Pete   It sends a message. It shows no-one's gonna be left
behind, that we're here for the people no-one else cares about –

Gina (*smiling, passing him back the papers*)   I've got to go somewhere first. Stay here. Keep having good ideas. And try not to explode.

She takes a seat at a table with **McDonald**, *clutching a pint, and the party leader,* **Rick Coleman**, *whose polished veneer cracks at times to let through something very dark.* **Pete** *looks at the papers, hesitates, then strides purposefully out of the door.*

Coleman   That was an excellent speech, Gina.

Gina   Thank you, Rick.

Coleman   Exactly on message. Well done. One or two cracking jokes as well.

McDonald   You like a joke, don't you, Gina?

Gina   I try to entertain as well as inform.

McDonald   Which of us do you reckon is funnier?

Gina   I don't –

McDonald   Why are blacks like bicycles? Cos they only work with chains on. (*No reaction.*) Here's a good one: bloke goes into a bar with a crocodile. He says to the barman, 'Do you serve niggers in here?' Guv'nor says, 'Course we do, we're not racist.' 'Right then, I'll have a pint of lager and a nigger for the crocodile.' (*Beat.*) Laugh, Rick.

Coleman   I tend not to laugh at things I don't find funny, Tony.

McDonald   You used to love all that.

Coleman   I don't think so.

McDonald   Oh, you did. I remember you standing on the bar after NF meetings, roaring out the Yid jokes. 'Why do Jews make the best magicians? Because they –'

Gina   Most men are in favour of the burka. It gives you somewhere to wipe your cock after a blow job. (*Beat.*) You've probably heard that one.

McDonald   I have, yeah. Different when you tell it though, innit. (*Pause.*) Thirty years fighting for blood and honour, fighting to purge White Britain of the taint –

Gina   And failing. Because there's more of us here than ever, aren't there? So on your own terms, you're a complete failure.

McDonald   Failure would be to surrender. Which I will never do.

Gina   Here's one for you: 'What's the difference between the BNP and the royal family? One's a group of neo-Nazi bigots who hate democracy, the other's the BNP.'

Coleman   That's very funny, Gina.

McDonald   She's walking down my streets holding my flag like I'm the one doesn't belong here. You any idea how much that hurts?

Coleman   You don't altogether understand politics, do you?

McDonald   Don't underestimate me, cunt.

Coleman   The point of the Party is not to serve as a vehicle for your pathetic little 'blood on the leather' rentboy paramilitary fantasies, Tony. The point of the Party is to operate as a modern political force.

McDonald   You're a parasite, Coleman.

Coleman   You see, most people don't share your embarrassingly crude reaction to the lies of multiculturalism.

McDonald   A worm in the guts.

Coleman   Whether that's because of the sheer volume of Third World sewage they wade through on the streets or the Marxist conspiracy in the media, I couldn't say. It really doesn't matter.

McDonald (*to* **Gina**)   You trust him, do ya?

Coleman   The point is, the British people are too indoctrinated to try to turn the clock back. It won't work. They have ethnics in their workplaces, ethnics in their families. A touch of the tar and all that.

McDonald   Do you trust him?

Gina   I've no reason not to.

McDonald *laughs a short bitter laugh.*

Coleman   But that doesn't mean they aren't angry. What people have done, you see, is they've *codified* their anger. People speak in code now. 'Knife crime' means, 'I'm afraid of black men', 'terrorism' means 'Brown people frighten me'. And they vent their rage over the breakfast table, with their orange juice and the *Daily Mail*, because nobody in politics will take the code to its logical conclusion. Except for us. Six million *Mail* readers and no political party to represent them. That is a very salient fact, Tony, one no nationalist should ignore. Now do you understand why she's here?

McDonald   Winning elections is not as important as staying pure.

Coleman   If you want to stop mass immigration, you have to achieve power within the mainstream political system. There is no other way.

McDonald   Two seats in the Euros and maybe, *maybe*, one in Parliament?

Gina   Once I win, people will look at us in a different way.

Coleman   Credibility, Tone. The people who want to vote BNP but think it's a waste? The people who vote Tory hoping they'll stop hugging and start hurting? All ours.

McDonald   People don't vote *for* anyone. They vote in *protest*.

Coleman   We will give them that outlet also. The decision has been taken.

McDonald   You'd fuck thirty years of my work, thirty years of my life, for a joke?

Coleman   You will give Gina the full extent of your co-operation –

McDonald   You don't tell me –

Coleman   Or you will be replaced –

With unnerving quickness **Tony** *picks up his pint and pours the last of it deliberately over* **Gina***'s head. He holds the empty glass close to her face. Pause.*

McDonald   The future isn't here quite yet.

The sound of heavy rain. **Mark** *and* **Zenobia** *in a restaurant. It's not going well.* **Zenobia** *fiddles with her fork. Beat.*

Mark   It's caning it down out there. It's like Katrina with white people.

Zenobia   Mmmm.

Beat.

Mark   I wouldn't say it's been raining a lot, but I was at B&Q today and this old bearded geezer was buying up all the wood. Said he was in a hurry to get to the zoo?

Zenobia   What were you doing at B&Q?

Mark   I wasn't . . . It was, like, a set-up? For the joke?

Zenobia   Right. Have you got a lot more rain jokes?

Mark   Nah –

Zenobia   Or a lot of other jokes that need a handout in advance?

Mark   Did I do something wrong?

Zenobia   Well, yes, Mark. When you offered to take me out for dinner, I was expecting a little more than Nando's.

Mark   What's wrong with Nando's? Ella loves Nando's.

Zenobia   Ella is five. If I was five, I'm sure I'd love Nando's too. The next time you want to impress a *woman*, you might wanna consider something a bit more upmarket. (*Beat.*) I'm sorry. I'm being a bitch.

Mark   You're not being a bitch.

Zenobia   I *am* being a bitch.

Mark   Maybe just a little bit.

Zenobia (*slaps him on the arm*)   Oi! You're not meant to agree with me!

Mark   What's the matter, you don't like fried chicken? You'll get kicked out the black person's union if you don't like fried chicken.

Zenobia   You do like to walk a fine line, don't you?!

Mark (*Johnny Cash*)   'Because you're mine, I walk the line.'

Zenobia   Ouch. I see how they got all those confessions at Guantanamo now.

Mark   See, you've given me an idea there. I'm gonna keep singing until you smile.

Zenobia   No.

Mark   'Just one Cornetto!'

Zenobia   Shut up!

Mark   'Give it to me!'

She shoves her hand over his mouth. He takes it and keeps hold of it.

Zenobia (*laughing*)   Stop it!

Mark   There's loads more where that came from. What about that Susan Boyle song?

Zenobia   Don't you *dare*!

Mark   Nah, I don't need to now, I've had my wicked way with ya. Got you to smile.

Beat. She gradually withdraws her hand from his and sits back in her chair.

So go on then. What's the drama?

Zenobia   What do you mean?

Mark   It ain't just the peri-peri giving you the hump, is it?

Beat.

Zenobia   They want to turn the school into an Academy.

Beat.

Mark   I don't actually know what that –

Zenobia   They're going to close the school down and reopen it on the waste land between the dump and the sewage works.

Mark   What?

Zenobia   Flog off the old site for 'executive housing', and rehire the teachers on half the pay, and everything based on test scores, and no time to give the immigrant kids basic English or show the British kids from the shitty estates how to brush their teeth or clean themselves properly.

Mark   They can't do that.

Zenobia   Read the papers.

Mark   Are you gonna stay?

Zenobia   Not on that money, with some box-ticker peering over my shoulder all day.

Mark   No.

Zenobia   It's not worth it, Mark!

Mark   They can't just do that!

Zenobia   Yes they can.

Mark   Who's doing it?

Zenobia   The council.

Mark   Then stop them. Batter them.

Zenobia   'Batter them', how are you gonna –

Mark   I don't know, Zenobia! They're elected, ain't they? Then do what my dad used to do get your lot together, pressure them, get new people in, get it out there what the bastards are up to. If that don't work, go round their houses and set them on fire.

Zenobia   Mark –

Mark   This is the first time Ella's been happy at school. She loves your class. Why should someone be able to take that away from her? Why should they? (*Beat.*) I'm not educated like you, Zenobia. I don't know how things work or why they work. Who needs education when you're gonna be the next David Beckham? But I'm not, am I? (*Beat.*) I don't want my girl to miss out, that's all. I'm sorry if –

Zenobia   Shut up. (*Beat.*) I'm gonna go home now, Mark.

Mark   Aw, look, I'm really sorry –

Zenobia   I'm going to go home and think about what you said. And maybe make a few phone calls. (*Beat.*) And next time, assuming you're up for a next time?

Mark (*grinning*)   I think I can fit you in.

Zenobia   Take me somewhere decent?

Coleman *and* **Gina**. *He watches her as she wipes the beer from her hair.*

Coleman   Are you alright?

Gina   I'm fine.

Coleman   You're soaked. Let me help you.

He pulls out a handkerchief and daubs at her brow. Something in his fastidiousness, the care he takes not to touch her skin with his bare hand, says more about the way he sees her than any amount of rhetoric. She realises this and disgusted and chilled, pulls strongly away. They study each other. He puts away the handkerchief.

Coleman   I'm sorry about that. I do hope it hasn't put you off.

Gina   Nothing I haven't dealt with before.

Coleman   Tony, I mean. If you want, I can have him disciplined, brought up before the committee –

Gina   I really don't need your protection, Rick.

Coleman   I know you don't, Gina. Or I wouldn't have chosen you.

Gina   Is that how it worked? I had the impression it was the other way round.

Coleman   I'm sure your memory is better than mine. (*Beat.*) One thing on your next speech.

Gina   Yes?

Coleman   Play up the Islamification of Britain a little more. Shariah law, immigration via the womb. You know, how quickly they breed –

Gina   Saw the update on the website, yep.

Coleman   I think that'll play very well down here.

Gina   I'll consider it, yes.

Beat.

Coleman   Well. Duty calls. Is there anything more I can do to help you, Gina?

Gina   There is, actually. Cutting out the references to 'Third World sewage' would probably be useful.

Coleman   In private conversation, between friends –

Gina   You used it in your speech last week. Three times.

Beat.

Coleman   What you have to do, you see Gina, you have to titillate them. It's like an erotic film. Do you watch erotic films, Gina? (*Beat.*) I don't, but I understand the principle. You know what they want, they want the naughty stuff. But you don't give them what they want, not up front. You hint at it, you suggest it, but you don't give it to them until they're gagging for it, then . . . bang.

Gina   You told me we would campaign on a positive line.

Coleman   It's like fishing. You ever go fishing, Gina?

Gina   A positive line about England. What England can be.

Coleman   Bait in the water, flick of the wrist. Get it to glimmer. Flick of the wrist.

Gina   Bait in the water.

Coleman   This *is* a positive line. *You* are our positive line.

Gina   Before I signed up to this, you agreed British nationalism's deeper meaning, it's not what you look like, it's where you're from, putting British people first –

Coleman   Whatever their colour. And I stand by those ideas one hundred percent, every one of them. The ideas of the future.

Gina   Then why are you –?

Coleman   They're not a very sophisticated electorate, the great British public. They don't adjust to change very well.

Gina   You're not giving them the chance.

Coleman   It's quite a complicated argument. Confused people tend not to vote.

Gina   Then make it clear what –

Coleman   Having you as our candidate makes it clear, surely?

Gina   Not if you keep undermining me, no.

Coleman   Once you're in position, we can roll out the more sophisticated stuff.

Gina   You told me –

Coleman (*losing patience*)   I also told you there were certain things you might have to swallow. If you wanted the high profile the Party can offer.

Pause.

Gina   Fine.

Coleman   Anything else you want to raise? Might as well get it on the table now.

Gina   Nothing.

Coleman   Sure?

Gina   Sure.

Beat.

Coleman   Good. Then I'll see you before the election, Gina.

Pete *leading a community clean-up day, collecting rubbish from a local estate. He puts a couple of things into a black plastic sack. A middle-aged housewife comes out of her door and watches him suspiciously.*

Housewife   What do you think you're doing?

Pete   Evening, madam.

Housewife   Never mind madam, what d'you think you're doing?

Pete   Community clean up. Helping make the area look like it used to.

Housewife   Who are you, council?

Pete   Not council, no.

Housewife   I bloody thought not, they're effing useless, council.

Pete   Tell me about it.

Housewife   Waste of bloody taxpayer money. Ain't seen council round here for donkey's.

Pete   That's Labour for you.

Housewife   I hope you're not expecting us to pay for that.

Pete   Course not, Madam. Community service.

Housewife   Oh yeah. What'd you do then?

Pete   Not that kind of –

Housewife   My old man's out on one a them now. A hundred and twenty hours for a knock-off DVD player, don't seem worth it really.

Pete   We provide a community service, I mean.

Housewife   Who's we?

Pete (*pulling out leaflets and handing her one*)   Compliments of the British National Party.

Housewife   Get off! You're never BNP!

Pete   We are.

Housewife   BNP's never done sod all round here apart from stand on the High Street gobbing at Pakis, excuse my French.

Pete   That's in the past.

Housewife (*examining leaflet*)   Who the bloody hell's that on there?

Pete   Gina is our candidate in the election.

Housewife   But she's a –!!

Pete   You get any more problems, graffiti, ASBO kids, you give us a bell on that number and we'll see what we can do for you.

Housewife   You're never BNP.

Pete   And I hope in return we can count on your vote on May 6th.

Housewife   You keep this up you might. (*Beat.*) Don't suppose you fancy popping in for a cup of tea?

Pete   That's lovely, but I can't.

Housewife   He won't be back for a bit, the old man. (*Beat.*) Ain't been back for a couple a nights. I don't –

Pete   I've got to get on. Thank you though.

Beat.

Housewife   Another time.

Pete   Yeah.

Housewife   Ta for clearing that lot up. Right eyesore it was.

Pete   It's my pleasure.

She disappears back into the house, muttering to herself.

Housewife (*muttering*)   Bloody BNP clearing up the streets, dunno what the world's coming to . . .

Pete *carries on his work, putting a couple more things into the bag.* **Clint** *walks past.*

Clint   Fucking hell, look who it ain't! What you doing here?

Pete (*hurriedly stuffing leaflets back in his pocket*)   Clinton! Alright son! This ain't your normal way home.

Clint   Nah, had a shufti at this gaff they want me to put in a bid on.

Pete   Anything good?

Clint   Not worth my while. Where the fuck you been? Tash thought we might have fell out or something, she ain't seen you for so long.

Pete   Yeah, sorry about that.

Clint   Nah, it's all good, busy people, busy people. So's this it then? The new job?

Pete   It is, yeah.

Clint   Clearing up rubbish and that?

Pete   It's community outreach, mate. This is just one part.

Clint It's good you're getting your hands dirty, anyway. Most of them council bods couldn't tell one end of a shovel from the other.

Pete No.

Clint Effing useless, council. Waste of bloody taxpayer money. Still, least they got you out here.

Pete Yeah.

Clint Step in the right direction.

The **Housewife** *comes back out, head down, reading the leaflet.*

Housewife Here, I wanna ask you summink . . . (*Catches sight of* **Clint**.) Fucking hell! You got them an all??!!

Pete It's not a great time.

Housewife Darkies an all!

Clint Who the fuck are you calling –

Housewife Sorry love, I didn't mean it in a racist –

Clint What other fucking way –?

Pete Just call the –

Housewife (*to* **Pete**) How long have you lot –?

Pete Just call the number on the leaflet and they can answer any queries, alright?!

Beat. She turns and stomps back into the house, muttering again.

Housewife (*muttering*) Pulled the rug right out from under my feet, that has. Dunno what the world's . . .

Clint Bitch. Like she's never seen a black man working for the council.

Pete It's not the council.

Clint I'm not, but she don't know that . . . That's got me right fucking . . . You know what I'm like, you pulled me off fellas in the factory nuff times.

Beat.

Pete   I'm sorry, Clint.

Clint   Not your fault, is it? (*Beat.*) Fuck it. Let's go for a pint. There's this mad job I got offered the other day. I know you'll say knock it on the head, specially after that, but it's tight as a gnat's arse at the mo –

Pete   I can't, mate.

Clint   If I wanna keep Mark on, I've gotta find –

Pete   Another night.

Clint   Fair enough. Come round for dinner then. How's next Tuesday?

Pete   Yeah, good, yeah.

Clint   Sorted. Good to see you, old son. We'll have a proper chinwag and you can catch me up on the rest of what you're doing. (*Beat.*) I'm glad for ya, mate. You look happy.

Pete   I am happy.

Clint   Good. You deserve that. You're worth more than some decorating job, Pete.

Pete   Thank you, Clint.

Clint   See you Tuesday.

He starts to make his way off.

Pete   Clint?

Clint   Yeah?

Beat.

Pete   You're a good mate.

Clint   Always. (*Beat.*) See you Tuesday.

He leaves. **Pete** *carries on with his work.* **Gina** *enters.* **Pete** *brightens.*

Pete   You got the message then?

Gina   Yeah.

Pete   Good day? I've had a good day.

Gina   Long day.

Pete   Where were ya?

Gina   What's all this?

Pete   I told ya, it's the Pete Case master plan.

Gina   Picking up rubbish?

Pete   Why do people think that's all . . . This is politics, Gina. The theory and the ideas, that might mean something to us, but to people out here, this is what politics means. Go see some panel beater and discuss the appropriation of surplus labour, you get a bang in the face. Tell him how to get a week's more holiday, he's right there with ya.

Gina   The factories are closed, Pete.

Pete   But the principle's the same. In the last words of the immortal Joe Hill, 'Don't Mourn. Organise.'

Gina   Who?

Pete   Who?! Joe Hill was leader of the Wobblies, American union mob, turn of the last century. He got stitched up for murder by the bosses: they stuck him in front of a firing squad and shot him. His absolute last word was 'Fire!' I like that.

Gina   Me too.

Pete   'Don't Mourn. Organise.' Useta think I'd have them words on my gravestone.

Gina (*smiling*)   What d'you think you'll have now?

Pete (*grins*)   I'm not thinking about it right now, Gina. Have a gander at this lot.

He passes her several lists of names.

Gina   What are all these?

Pete   Sign-up lists.

Gina   You got all these in one day?

Pete   Going back tomorrow.

Gina   You diamond!

She gives him a big hug.

Pete   I had my doubts when I started, but it's you on the leaflet. The number of people who don't wanna take one and you show 'em your picture –

She kisses him deeply. He hesitates, then responds. They kiss for a while.

Gina   Come to mine.

Beat.

Pete   I don't –

She kisses him again.

Gina   Come to mine.

Pete   Alright. Yes.

She smiles. Beat.

Gina   You're something, you know.

This moves him – how long has it been since someone told him this?

Pete   You're . . . more than I let myself expect.

She takes his hand and they start to leave.

Gina   I did have one idea. About what you just said.

Pete   Go on.

Gina   The thing everyone mentions, apart from housing, is education. How their kids don't get enough time in school cos the immigrant kids need basic English.

Pete   I've heard the same, yeah.

Gina   What about a campaign 'Local Children, Local Schools' something like that? Saying it's not racist for people to want equal treatment, it's what they deserve.

Pete   Sounds good.

Gina   Couple of photogenic local kids on the posters. (**Pete** *nods in agreement.*) I was thinking of Ella for one of them.

Pause.

Pete   I dunno, Gina.

Gina   She's perfect. She's pretty, she presses all the right buttons . . .

Pete   Black but not too black, you mean.

Gina   Don't be silly. (*Beat.*) We can use that photo you've got in your wallet.

Pete   I'd have to ask Mark.

Gina   Of course. I'm sure he won't mind though. After what we did for him?

Beat.

Pete   She liked you, Ella.

Gina   I liked her.

Pause. He hands over the photo.

Pete   Look after her.

Gina   I will. (*Beat.*) Come on then. Or have you changed your mind?

They leave, his arm around her.

Mark *out on the streets with* **Zenobia**. *They are handing out leaflets.*

Zenobia   Stop the Academy!

Mark   Scrap the Academy!

Zenobia   Axe the Academy!

Mark   Er, knock the Academy on the head!

Zenobia   Refute the Academy!

Mark   Sod the Academy!

Zenobia   Repudiate the Academy!

Mark   Bollocks to the Academy!

Zenobia/Mark Fuck the Academy!

Mark   Let's go home now.

Zenobia   Not until we've got rid of this lot. You've got loads more left than I have! Go on, get that man there.

Mark *approaches a white man walking quickly. He holds out a leaflet.*

Mark   Excuse me, mate, it's about this new school they wanna build –

White Man Got no kids, mate.

He disappears.

Zenobia (*imitation*)   'Excuse me, mate!'

Mark   What? Easier for girls, innit.

Zenobia   And why's that?

Mark   You got certain assets.

Zenobia   Yeah. A brain. (*She approaches a black man.*) Hello sir. Did you know that the new Academy school will be weighted in favour of Muslim children?

Black Man   What? They get everything, don't they?

Zenobia (*handing over a leaflet*)   There's a concerned citizens' fightback meeting, next Thursday, Town Hall?

Black Man   Ta for that, darling. I'll take a look, yeah.

He walks off reading it.

Mark   You can't say that!

Zenobia   Sssh. (*She approaches an Asian woman.*) Hello madam. Did you know –

Asian Woman   Very sorry, can't stop.

Zenobia   The new Academy school will be weighted in favour of Christian children?

Asian Woman   No-one told me that.

Zenobia (*handing over a leaflet*)   There's a concerned citizens' fightback meeting, next Thursday, Town Hall?

Asian Woman   Thank you. I never heard that, are you –

Zenobia   If you pop along next Thursday you can find out more.

Asian Woman   I'll certainly try, thank you.

She leaves.

Mark   You're right out of order! You can't be telling 'em lies to get 'em to come!

Zenobia   Once they get in the door, they'll find enough to piss them off.

Mark   Yeah, that the reason they came was bollocks!

Zenobia   The head of the Council is a director of the developers! How fair is that?!

Mark   That don't mean –

Zenobia   So we have to be goody-goodies while they stitch up the 'independent' decision? Do you want Ella's school to survive or not? (*Beat.*) Mark, on its own the truth is not gonna be enough for us to win. We have to give it a little helping hand.

Beat. He puts his hand on her hips. She does the same to him.

Mark   Created a monster, didn't I?

Zenobia   A flesh-eating monster.

They kiss. Eventually she lets him go.

Zenobia   Go on. I know it's the Arsenal game tonight.

Mark   You sure?

Zenobia   On yer bike. Slacker.

Mark   See you at mine later?

Zenobia (*grinning*)   I'll think about it. (*He leaves.*) Scrap the Academy! Block the Academy!

McDonald *appears. He watches her.*

Pete *in the office, listening to the radio with growing concern* '. . . *with reports of attacks on the Asian community in which at least one man has been hospitalised. Some have linked the violence to a new campaign by the British National Party, advocating discrimination by local schools against immigrant children.*'

Pete   It's not *against* anyone, it's *for* us . . .

He turns, cup of coffee in hand, and almost walks into **Clint**, *who is carrying a bag with his decorating stuff.* **Clint** *drops the bag. They stare at one another. Long pause. The radio goes on* 'In a recent poll, 62% of whites said they agreed with the policy, and almost half said it would make them more likely to vote BNP in the upcoming general –'. **Pete** *switches off the radio. Beat.*

Clint (*grabbing bag*)   No, fuck this.

Pete   Clint, stay –

Pete *grabs* **Clint**. **Clint** *violently shoves him away, sending his coffee mug flying.*

Clint   Get your hands off me! Don't you fucking touch me, you traitor! You *traitor*!

Clint *shapes to punch* **Pete**.

Pete   It's me, it's me, it's me . . .

Clint *slams his fist into his palm. He doesn't know whether to run, hit or cry. Pause.*

Clint   Thirty seconds. Thirty fucking seconds you *cunt*.

Pete   It's housing. It's hospitals. It's schools. That shit where they're gonna close down your little one's school, Ella's school, we'd never allow that.

Clint   We.

Pete   Yeah, we. You and me and the people that've put the fucking graft in, whatever their colour.

Clint   Colour already.

Pete   I don't give a fuck about that, you *know* I don't. But *we are here*, we've been here generations and how come that don't count for anything?

Clint   Listen to yourself.

Pete   I have *nothing* against the new people. But the ones what's put their time in, we are *owed* something.

Clint   You know what you sound like?

Pete   It's different with Gina. She's not gonna let them go back to –

Clint   You sound like the bosses. 'Do yer time, stand in line, don't you get ahead of the man in front cos he's been here longer.' You sound like the bosses, Pete.

Beat.

Pete   It's only what's fair.

Clint   You're going after the wrong people. It ain't those down the bottom taking from us, it's them at the top.

Pete   How many times've I heard you going on about 'fresh off the boat Africans'?

Clint   Yeah, cos of something in the fucking *Sun*, but I'm talking about. . . (*He makes a big frame gesture with his hands.*) You was the one showed me. How we'd be squabbling so much over a few crumbs, management'd drive by in their new Bentleys and we'd let 'em go. Divide and rule. This is the same thing, mate. (*He repeats the gesture, starting small and opening his hands wider. Beat.*) You was the only one treated me as a straight up human my whole first year at school. I'll never forget it.

Pete   I don't want nothing to come between us, Clint.

Clint   Then you shouldn't have joined the *BNP*, Pete! (*Beat.*) Why didn't you tell me?

Pete   Cos I knew it'd be like this. That you wouldn't understand.

Clint   Why wouldn't I understand?

Pete   Look at ya. You're alright.

Clint   How the fuck am I alright? I'm that fucking brassic I was seriously thinking of putting in a tender on the BNP offices! (*He screws up a piece of paper and throws it at Pete.*) You can stick that where the sun don't shine.

Pete   New car.

Clint   So fucking what?

Pete   Nice extension on the house.

Clint   And? I haven't worked for it?

Pete   Foreign holidays.

Clint   You of all people should know I've worked for it.

Pete   I've worked too! I've worked too, and where's all that for me?

Clint   I ain't took it.

Pete   But I ain't got it!

Clint   Are you jealous of me, Pete?

Pete   Of course not.

Clint   Are you *jealous* of me, is that why you're doing this?

Pete   I want something of my own! (*Pause.*) You're the people I'm doing this for, Clint. You and me and Mark. Locals.

Clint (*softly*)   Where am I from? (*Beat.*) Where am I from, Pete?

Pete   Dagenham.

Clint   Originally.

Pete   Hornchurch.

Clint   What does it say on my passport for place of birth, dickhead? What woulda happened to my folks and me if your lot had been in charge then? You're telling me we shouldn't be here, Pete. (*Beat.*) They was always gonna go back to Yard, my folks. Always 'Nex' year, nex' year we reach.' But we chose to stay. When you *choose* a country, you choose being less than you should be. You choose eating other people's shit, washing their streets and emptying their toilets and having them question your right to everything you get. You eat that shit for the sake of your children. He had a degree, my dad, you know that?

Pete   I didn't, no.

Clint   Engineering degree. He had a degree and he drove a bus. Never complained about it. It's the way it was. (*Beat. With deep sadness.*) It's divide and rule, old son, it's the oldest trick in the bloody book. You're so much smarter than me, how come you can't see that?

Pete   I don't know what else to do. What else can I do, Clint?

Clint   I don't know. (*He picks up his bag.*) Don't come Tuesday.

He leaves. **McDonald** *approaches* **Zenobia**. *She goes to hand him a leaflet.*

Zenobia   Hello sir, did you know –

Another white man, wearing a balaclava, emerges from the shadows. They flank her. She falters. Beat.

McDonald   What you doing?

Zenobia   I'm . . . it's a campaign . . . against the –

He rips the leaflet from her hand. She gives a little involuntary gasp.

McDonald   Let's have a look then.

Zenobia   Don't –

McDonald   Sssh. I'm reading. (*Beat.*) This looks like shit.

Zenobia   No, it's –

McDonald   Are you saying I can't read? Cos I'm reading this and it looks like a load of nigger-loving, mongrelising shit. 'Protect the rich diversity of our community.' (*He tears up the* *leaflet with deliberate slowness.*) But I don't like the rich diversity of our community. I want all the rich – interesting choice of word, seeing how much you lot sponge off the fucking state – diverse parasites to fuck off back where they come from. Can you explain to me why this *isn't* a load of mongrelising shit, darling?

Zenobia *can hardly speak from terror.*

Zenobia   I . . . please . . .

McDonald   You see, this is the thing with coons. They're very chatty when they've got the whip hand, but get 'em one on one and they generally struggle. (*He pulls out a large hunting knife and opens it slowly.* **Zenobia** *starts to hyperventilate. To* **Zenobia**.) Did you know it's scientifically proven that blacks are on average fifteen to twenty per cent less intelligent than white people?

Zenobia   I . . . I . . .

McDonald   She can't even speak. You're pulling your average right down, love.

Zenobia (*whispering*)   I'll call the police . . .

McDonald *puts the knife close to her cheek. She shrieks. The other man holds her fast.*

McDonald   I want you to give whoever you're working for a message. (*Beat.*) The message is, 'Fuck off you spear-chucking African cunt. This is the white man's country.' Can you remember that? (*Beat.*) Then I'll give you something to help you.

He runs the point of the knife gently down her cheek, then suddenly cuts the straps of her top so she has to clutch it humiliatingly to her. She hunches in on herself, face averted, as **McDonald** *deliberately folds up the knife, puts it away and as the two men leave, pats her on the head. She is left in a tearful, shell-shocked, terrified heap.*

Pete *makes his way to his front door. As he puts his key in the lock,* **Mark** *appears out of the shadows. He clutches several documents and a can of beer. He is considerably drunker than he realises, but the alcohol fuels not sloppiness but a tight, focused rage.*

Pete   Jesus, you nearly gave me a heart attack! (*Beat.*) What are you doing here?

Pause.

Mark   Good night?

Pete   It was alright.

Mark   Where'd you go?

Pete   To this woman's place, as it goes. Why?

Mark   Quite late back.

Pete   Yeah, time got away from us, you know.

Mark   But you had a good time, yeah? That's the important thing. As long as you had a good time, Dad.

Pete   What are you doing here, Mark?

Mark   I brought you a bit of reading. Cos I know what a thinker you are. 'Countering the Smears', by the British National Party.

Beat.

Pete   I was gonna tell you but I didn't know how.

Mark   Question 'Why do you disapprove of mixed marriages?' Answer 'We believe in human diversity, and in preserving the individuality of different ethnic groups.' (*Holding the can out.*) Beer?

Pete   Come inside.

Mark   'Environmentalists are always keen to preserve unique animal species in the wild, so why shouldn't the same principle apply to people?'

Pete   Why don't you come inside, son, eh?

Mark *crushes the can and slings it away with such ferocity that* **Pete** *jumps a little.*

Mark   Two of your environmentalists attacked my girlfriend with a knife tonight.

Pete   *What?*! Is she alright, is she −?

Mark   No. She's not. And when she sees *this*, she's never gonna talk to me again.

Mark *holds up a BNP campaign poster showing* **Ella***'s face, with 'Local Children, Local Schools' written above it along with 'Vote British National Party'. Pause.*

Mark   Question: 'Do you accept or deny that blacks and Asians born in Britain are totally British?' Answer: 'Blacks and Asians born here are *legally* British, but they are not *genetically* British. Species − *species* − which move into a new area and become established are called colonisers.'

Pete   Come inside and I'll try to explain −

Mark   MY DAUGHTER IS NOT A SPECIES. (*Beat.*) Tell me what Ella is, Dad.

Pete   She's my granddaughter.

Mark   Some science mishmash? A freak experiment gone wrong?

Pete   She's my granddaughter who I love very, very much.

Mark   How can you read this and look at her the same way?

Pete   Listen to me −

Mark   How can you expect me to let you touch her?

Pete   I don't do any of that.

Mark   Then what do you do?

Beat.

Pete   They've done things for me.

Mark   What've they done, Dad?

Pete   You don't need to know that.

Mark   I think I do.

Pete   They've give me a job −

Mark   Fuck off.

Pete   A sense of purpose, a reason to get up in the bloody morning –

Mark   FUCK OFF.

Pete   Your flat! They gave me your flat! I got your flat from them, Mark, OK? (*Pause. Mark sways for a second, seems on the verge of falling over.*) Come inside.

Mark   You stupid old man. You stupid clueless old man. What did it cost you, Dad?

Pete   Nish, it's a council gaff.

Mark   You don't know the price of fuck all, do ya? What did you have to do for it?

Beat.

Pete   I'm organising the election campaign.

Mark (*holding out poster*)   You *organised* this?

Pause. **Mark** *pulls another can out of his pocket, drinks and looks away. Long pause.*

Mark   D'you think less of me cos I didn't make it as a footballer?

Pete   What?

Mark   Do you think less of me because I didn't make it as a professional footballer?

Pete   Why are you asking me that?

Mark (*looking away again and drinking*)   There's an answer.

Pete   No, of course not.

Mark   Are you ashamed of me, Dad?

Pete   *Ashamed* of you?

Mark   Are you ashamed of me because I'm a failure?

Pete   You're not a failure, Mark.

Mark   I didn't make it, I'm a failure, simple as.

Pete   It weren't your fault you got hurt.

Mark (*sharp*)   No-one is talking about fault.

Pete   You're not a failure, Mark.

Mark   You are though. You're like an old toy you remember was brilliant when you was a kid, but then you get it out the attic and it's gone dusty and cracked and rubbish. Tell me I disappoint you.

Pete   You don't disappoint me, Mark.

Mark   Tell me, Dad. Say it. Say I disappoint you. (*Beat. Raging.*) *Say it*! I'm a failure. I had our future in my hands and I pissed it away, I shoulda had you in a nice big house in Epping or Loughton but I failed, I'm a fucking useless failure of a cunt.

Pete   Mark –

Mark   You think that everything I've done has been a mistake, that Ella is a mistake, a warped twisted little fuck-up –

Pete   Please, son –

Mark   Couldn't even get that right, had to embarrass myself and embarrass you, that I'm not your son, Dad, not the way you wanted him to be. Tell me that's what you think of me.

Pause.

Pete (*gently and full of love*)   That's not what I think of you.

Mark   Then why have you *done* this?!

He pulls out the keys to the flat.

Pete   Don't leave the flat.

Mark   Give me some fucking respect at least! Stay in *that*?

Pete   I worked for that flat, Mark.

Mark   Are you really that thick to think, *really* that thick to think, that if we did mug 'em all off, the immigrants and the asylum seekers and whoever else, if we did put 'em in vans or shove 'em behind barbed wire or send 'em off to the fucking abattoir, that after all that there'd be more left over for people like us? Are you stupid? Didn't you learn nothing from all them days on the picket line?

He throws the keys at **Pete***, turns and runs away.*

Pete   Mark! MARK!

Sounds the breaking of glass, the wailing of car alarms, shouting, pitched battles in the street. An assault voices taunting, pleading in a foreign language, scuffling, muffled blows. A terrified cry for help. The sharp crack of head on stone. The wail of a siren and the sounds of running feet.

In amongst this, the radio cuts in and out. '. . . prepares for the general election, pollsters are predicting a first ever parliamentary seat for the British National . . . escalating violence continues to plague . . . three more assaults on Asians, including on an eighty-seven year old . . . say they wish to interview members of the BNP on suspicion of incitement . . .'

Backstage at **Gina***'s election press conference. The bustle of TV cameras and expectant journalists out front.* **Gina** *in a smart suit with* **Coleman***.*

Coleman   Nervous?

Gina   Not really. You?

Coleman   Am *I* nervous?

Gina   Yes, Rick. Are you nervous?

Coleman   I have done this a few times before, Gina.

Gina   Then you've nothing to worry about.

Beat.

Coleman   So the Islamification of Britain, the cost to the welfare state –

Gina   I know what I'm going to say.

He looks hard at her. Pause.

Coleman   I won't be able to stay for the election itself.

Gina   That's fine.

Coleman   Got to get back up North.

Gina   That's absolutely fine.

Coleman   So it's all in your hands, Gina. If it goes wrong.

Beat. A low whistling the tune of 'Camptown Ladies'. **McDonald** *appears.*

McDonald (*singing*)   'Don't Unpack, You're Going Back, doo dah, doo dah. Don't Unpack, You're Going Back, doo de doo da dey.' Sing it with me, Rick.

Coleman   You're barred.

McDonald (*to Gina*)   Your big day.

Gina   What do you want?

Coleman   You are no longer a member of this Party.

McDonald   I thought you might like some input on your speech.

Gina   Thoughtful.

McDonald   I think a lot.

Gina   Of Hitler with his cock out, I expect.

McDonald   I think about purity. How the littlest drop of filth spoils it, makes it worthless. My job is to preserve the purity of England for generations yet unborn. That means a long, lonely job of elimination. And nobody likes the exterminator, nobody loves the ratcatcher. But at the end of the day, most people, if they're honest, they're glad he's out there all the same. (*Beat.*) I want you to resign.

Gina   And why would I do that, Tony?

McDonald   I want you to go out and say it was all a big mistake and you got in over your little shit-brown head.

Gina   But I'm not going to do that.

McDonald   How many more of your people do you want to get hurt?

Gina   They are not my people.

McDonald   Because I can arrange that.

Gina   I'm sure you can.

McDonald   Not just before the election but afterwards too. Every day another three, four, five, ten Pakis go down.

Coleman   Oh dear.

McDonald (*explosion of rage at* **Coleman**)   FUCK OFF. FUCK OFF. FUCK OFF. (**Pete** *enters, unseen. Calmly, to* **Gina**.) It won't be hard. The anger is out there. I just have to direct it. (*Beat. A note of urgency.*) Are you listening to me?

Gina   No, Tony.

McDonald   It won't work, Gina. Look at the streets out there.

Gina   That'll pass, when you do.

McDonald   People don't want to mix.

Gina   They already have. They will more. Your world is gone, Tony.

Beat.

McDonald   Look at you. You can't keep discipline, you can't keep your people safe. What the fuck can you do?

Coleman   Get attention. Thanks to you. (*Pause.* **McDonald** *is thrown.*) When she started, Gina was a bit of a joke. The Asian bird standing for the BNP, a snigger for the ruling classes. Now, she's for real. Look out front: TV, broadsheets, tabloids. Because of her, people have an opinion of us they've never had before: Reforming. Courageous. Electable. The only thing those people used to think about the British National Party was that it was full of people like you. The people we are now seen to be purging. So thank you, Tony. Well done. I couldn't have choreographed it better myself. Because it's not the policies that's got the attention. It's not even the novelty brown girl – no offence, Gina, you know what I mean. It's the violence.

Beat. **McDonald** *snarls.*

McDonald   Clever.

Coleman   You can always rely on a little bit of violence to tickle the jaded palate of middle England. And where would we have found such a compliant group of inbred, Paki-bashing knuckle-draggers without your help?

McDonald   You clever cunt.

Coleman   It's just a shame you can't stick around to enjoy the fruits of your labours. But on the bright side, you've helped make the BNP a mainstream political force. So if you love the party like you –

McDonald *grabs* **Coleman** *in a headlock and punches as* **Coleman** *flails his arms uselessly.* **Pete** *lunges out of the shadows and inflicts a terrible rage-fuelled beating on* **McDonald***, eventually dragging him to the door, throwing him out and turning to face* **Gina** *and* **Coleman***, who adjusts his suit and tries to regain his dignity. Pause.*

Coleman   My God. What a man. What a man. Who is this, Gina?

Gina   This is Pete Case.

Pete   Don't.

Gina   Pete is my election co-ordinator.

Coleman   Gina told me about you, Pete. What a fantastic –

Pete *grabs* **Coleman** *by the cheeks with a single strong hand, squeezing his mouth closed. Eventually he lets him go. Pause.*

Coleman   What can I say? It's a contact sport, democracy. (*He straightens his clothes one last time and makes for the exit.*) I'll be waiting, Gina.

Coleman *leaves. Pause.*

Gina   I didn't know –

Pete   Yes you did.

Beat. She can't refute it.

Gina   Come out there with me, love. I'm going to do something wonderful.

Beat.

Pete   You've still got my picture.

Gina   What picture?

Pete   The one of my granddaughter. Can I have it back?

Gina   Now? I'm about to do the biggest event of my life –

Pete   I'd like my picture back.

Gina   I don't have your picture on me, I –

Pete *presses his hand into* **Gina***'s face and mashes it back and forth, driving her to the floor where she sits open-mouthed with shock.*

Gina (*like a hurt little girl*)   What did you do that for?

Pete   Who are you?

Gina   My name is Gina White.

Pete   No it ain't. Your dad was Pakistani, you said. Not many Whites in the Karachi phone book, are there? What's your proper fucking name?

He takes a step towards her.

Gina   Begum. My birth name is Hafsana Begum.

Pete   Why are you doing this, Hafsana Begum?

Gina   Does it matter?

Pete   Course it matters, it –

Gina   What difference does it make? It's all bollocks, the explanations, the *reasons*. It matters what I'm *doing*.

She scrambles to her feet. Beat.

Pete   Is that all this was? A way to get attention?

Gina   No.

Pete   Is that all I was?

Gina   I want you to come out there with me.

Pete   My son won't talk to me. My best mate won't talk to me.

Gina   It'll pass, when –

Pete   No it / *won't*.

Gina   When I win. When all this gets washed away.

Pete   You're just like all the rest.

Gina   When I make things *clear*.

Pete   Using us and moving on.

Gina   Trust me, baby. Please.

Pete   I believed you.

Gina   Keep believing me.

Pete   What about the people that got hurt?

Gina   Gandhi tried non-violence. He got shot. I'm going to win.

Pete   And that's all that matters?

Gina   This is about more than you and me and a couple of Pakis getting a slap now. All the things you believe in, the things you want your society to be – how else are you going to make them happen? How else are you gonna make the world you want to see?

Pete   Not through you.

Gina   Then *how else*?

Beat.

Pete   Do you care about me, Gina?

Gina   Yeah. I do.

Pete   Then don't go out there.

Pause.

Gina   Don't make me do this.

Pete   You care about me, don't go out there.

Gina   I've gone through too much, Pete.

Pete   *You've* gone through . . . You put my granddaughter on a BNP poster knowing people would get hurt.

Gina   I've gone too far now.

Pete   For me, Gina. Stop this for me.

She kisses him. He doesn't respond. Eventually he pushes her away. Pause.

Gina   I've got to go.

Pete   See ya then. Hafsana.

Gina   It's a waste. It's such a waste. (*Beat.*) Call me. Any time. Please.

She leaves. Hubbub outside. **Pete** *stands rooted. Long pause. He strides after her.* **Gina** *at the press conference with* **Coleman**. *Journalists facing them. Flashing bulbs.*

Gina   Dignity. History. Togetherness. A British nationalism based on Britain's greatness, not on skin colour or place of birth. What makes me different from the rest is that I have *faith* in the British people, black, white, brown, all of us. Anyone that's here now and wants to be British first and foremost, I salute you. I believe that once you get the dead weight off your back, you'll make this country *Great* Britain again.

Pete *stands up at the back of the room.*

Pete   Liar.

Gina   But that is what it requires you have to be British first and foremost. No more special treatment. No more subsidies for mosques where hatred of Britain is –

Pete   What about the violence?

Gina   It's a choice you have to make. I made it.

Pete   Like you chose to have those people beaten up?

Journalist   Could you shut up please?

Gina *starts to falter.*

Gina   I am . . . the future of . . . the future of British politics –

Pete   Explain the violence, Gina.

Journalist   Can we get this guy out of here?

*A security guy moves over and takes **Pete** by the arm. He resists and raises his voice.*

Pete   I can show you Gina White deliberately –

Gina   Pete, don't . . .

Coleman   We know this man.

Pete   Deliberately caused the violence in our streets –

Coleman   This man has a long-standing grudge against the / British National Party –

Pete   To raise her profile –

Gina   Please . . .

Pete   And to get you here today.

Journalist   And how do you know that?

Pete   Because I'm her campaign manager. I organised the whole thing. Everything that's happened out there, every beating, every attack, it was all done through me.

*The light narrows to a beam on **Pete**, then blacks out.*

Mark *and* **Clint** *working on another flat, wrestling a cistern into place.*

Mark   So the stepdad chases the kid off and the kid's all upset and crying . . . Next day, the dad hears this massive racket coming out the old granny's room –

Clint   Here we go.

Mark   So the stepdad goes in and what does he see but the kid grinding away on top of the granny, who's having the time of her life. And the kid looks up, sees the stepdad and goes, 'Not so fucking funny when it's *your* mum!'

Amidst their laughter, **Pete** *enters. He stops near the door. The laughter fades. Pause.*

Pete   That's nice work, that. (*Beat.*) Nice finish. I never could get that right.

Pause. **Clint** *rises.*

Clint   I'll leave you two to it.

Pete   I came to see both of you.

Clint   I'm not the one you need to sort things out with, Pete.

Pete   I need to talk to you, mate. Please.

Clint   I don't have anything to say to you.

Clint *leaves. Pause.*

Mark   It's funny, he ain't shut up about ya for the past week, in that weird way of his.

Pete   Every compliment sorta half a criticism, you mean?

Mark   You know the one. Out the corner of his mouth, 'Least he stopped the fucking BNP bird.' 'Least he done the right thing in the end.' (*Beat.*) Give him time.

Pause.

Pete   I went in the pub last night and nobody would talk to me. Lifted their pints and turned their backs. Half of 'em cos they think I did what I said and the other half cos they think I didn't.

Mark   Finally managed to unite the community then.

Pete   I'm a stupid, stupid fucker, Mark. (*Pause.*) How's Zenobia?

Mark   She's alright. (*Beat.*) She gets flashbacks. There's a proper word for it.

Pete   I'm sorry to hear that.

Mark   Yeah.

Beat.

Pete   Her campaign's going well, looks like you might win.

Mark   Yeah, we are. I can see why you used to do it now. It's beautiful, as it goes.

Pete   I'm very, very proud of you. I hope you know that. (*Beat.*) Are you two –?

Mark   Rocky.

Pete   Where are you kipping, Mark?

Mark   Mate's place.

Pete   With Ell?

Mark   It's only for a bit.

Pete   Come home, son.

Mark   I can't, Dad.

Pete   I miss you round the place.

Mark   I really want this thing with Z to work.

Pause.

Pete   Yeah. OK.

Beat.

Mark   I can't look at you in the same way. I really want to, I keep trying, but I can't.

Pete   I'm not any different than –

Mark   I know what you thought you were doing, and I know why, and I love you for that –

Pete   Mark, I –

Mark   And I know what you did to try and make it right, she lost because of you, but I don't feel the same way about you. (*Beat.*) Something in here has shifted or gone cold and I'm trying to make it warm up again, I am, but it won't.

Beat.

Pete   You're my only son.

Mark   And I don't know if it ever will and that terrifies me, Dad, it makes me feel sick. I want it to come back. I'm waiting for it to come back. (*Beat.*) Will you wait with me?

Beat.

Pete   I don't have a choice, do I?

Mark   I'm sorry, Dad.

Pete   You've got nothing to be sorry about.

Pause.

Mark   I need to fetch Clint. We're behind as it is.

Pete   Can I see Ella?

Mark   In a bit. (*Beat.*) Do us a favour? Don't be here when he gets back.

Mark *makes to leave. He places a hand on* **Pete**'s *shoulder. Pause. He leaves.*

Pete *stands alone, staring out. He pulls out his phone and stares at it. Lights gradually down.*

If You Don't Let Us Dream,
We Won't Let You Sleep

Introduction

So this is where I think we are, at the start of the second decade of the twenty-first century, on this fascinating and infuriating small wet island that firmly believes it's approximately 3,000 miles further west than it actually is:

AUSTERITY WAS NEVER ABOUT FIXING THE ECONOMY
Or we wouldn't be in triple dip recession. Not even Gideon Oliver Osborne, heir to the baronetcy of Ballentaylor and Ballylemon and thus the ideal embodiment of Tory attacks on 'entitlement culture', is that inept. Austerity is about fundamentally reshaping not just government but our basic understanding of what it means to be a member of society, in order to serve the needs of financial markets.

KILL THE ZOMBIE
The austerity boys get away with it because hardly anyone understands financial capitalism, but mainly due to a killer zombie. The 'market knows best' paradigm, born in the seventies amidst the uncollected rubbish of the three-day week, died in spectacular fashion in the 2008 banking collapse, which proved financial institutions to be as trustworthy and productive as one of their NINJA loans. But like in the George A. Romero films, the zombie won't die! In fact the zombipocalyptic idea of the infallible private sector is chomping away on ever more of the real economy and people's lives . . .

KEYNES IS DEAD
In large part because the zombie's traditional foe has expired too. The Keynesian idea of the state as the moral and economic alternative to the private sector, which animated the Left for most of the twentieth century (not the Blairite 'left', obviously, which was animated by non-executive directorships and black cod miso) looks far gone when the private sector now runs the state and soaks it for bailouts and subsidies. All political parties cringe before the market. The result is that,

in an era that touts 'choice' as its cardinal virtue, politically we have none.

POST-PARTY POLITICS

And yet in a way that's great – we're starting to leave the old corrupted dichotomy of Labour and Tory behind, and look for new forms of political engagement. The political lesson of the twentieth century is that concentrated power, whether fascist, corporate or vanguard of the proletariat, produces catastrophes. So the question for the twenty-first century is what shape our new political forms will take. The most immediately exciting stuff is grassroots action, of which Occupy was one type and the riots another.

RADICAL OPTIMISM

What turns people off conventional politics is a sense that it won't make a difference, and direct action gives you that feeling of making a difference back. It also gives you a sense of optimism and excitement, and optimism is about the most radical quality you can possess right now. But on its own, can grassroots action control financial flows? Can it reconfigure institutions and structures to serve people instead of speculative capital? Unlikely. So our paradoxical relationship to institutions of power, who only listen to us when we make it clear we reject them, is what we need to think about next.

So that's the intellectual chain of thought that made me write this play. But it's only one part of why I wrote it.

I wrote it because a few years ago I was teaching in prison, and my friend Esther Baker put on a version of *Accidental Death of an Anarchist*, which I rewrote to be about the Stephen Lawrence case. Prisoners are a loud group of people and not easily inclined to silence, but (apart from the bits where we had to physically remove large men from the stage as they argued with the characters about various plot twists) they were spellbound. That was my first real experience of the theatre, and of the joy of storytelling in particular.

I wrote it because I love the feeling in a room of an audience and a cast feeling and creating something collectively. It's a microcosm of a good society.

I wrote it because at its heart this system of finance that now dominates us is quite simple under its impossibly convoluted technicalities, and I want to help people understand it. What they do with that knowledge is up to them.

I wrote it because now's the time for the return of proper political theatre. Not old-style agitprop, but 'anti-prop' that takes on the overwhelming reality of 2013: the propaganda of markets that they're indispensible. What if we put up taxes and the bankers threatened to leave? Well, (a) they wouldn't, because there's nowhere else with such lax regulatory and tax regimes, where their kids can be poshly educated and they speak English and have Michelin-starred restaurants and nobody bothers you. The people who love London the most are the twenty-year-old Italian kid escaping Mama and the fifty-year-old hedge-fund manager escaping tax, both for the same reason: nobody's watching them. But (b), we'd be much better off, because we wouldn't be paying trillions in bailouts, because our whole society wouldn't be under the sway of a tiny interest group, and because we are capable, talented people who'd find more productive ways to make a living. You want to leave? Enjoy Russia. Say hi to Gerard Depardieu and tell him I burnt every DVD of *Cyrano de Bergerac* I could lay my hands on.

I wrote it to make you feel, and therefore to think. Hope it worked.

Anders Lustgarten,
January 2013

Acknowledgements

It takes a lot of people to write a good play. Laurence Lustgarten, Donna Dickenson and Chris Britton got me to adulthood (more or less). Esther Baker and Simon Stephens got me into theatre. Nick Hildyard is a political inspiration. Angela Debnath a personal one. Joseph Rochlitz provided a place to write. Neil McPherson took the first theatrical chance on me. Chris Campbell and Dominic Cooke took the biggest one. There are dozens of people who've made this play possible in some way, but I'll go all Gwyneth Paltrow if I list all of you. Thank you.

This play is dedicated to Louise-Mai Newberry, who knows it better than I do. Bu Ru! TBFC!

If You Don't Let Us Dream, We Won't Let You Sleep was first performed at the Royal Court Theatre on 15 February 2013 with the following cast and creative team:

Joan	Susan Brown
Thacker/Thomas/Ross	Ben Dilloway
Kelly/Nurse/Teacher 2/	
Lucinda	Laura Elphinstone
Ryan	Daniel Kendrick
Workman/Jason/Ray	Damien Molony
Taylor/McDonald Moyo	Lucian Msamati
James Asset-Smith/	
Zebedee	Ferdy Roberts
Administrator/Teacher 1/	
Karen McLean/Jen	Meera Syal

All other parts were played by members of the company.

Director   Simon Godwin
Design Consultant   Lucy Sierra
Lighting Designer   Jack Williams
Sound Designer   David McSeveney
Shona Translation   Lucian Msamati and Denton Chikura

Characters
in order of appearance

McLean
Taylor
Thacker
Asset-Smith
Lucinda
Joan
Workman
Ryan
Man
Nurse
Administrator
McDonald
Jason
Ross
Teacher 1
Teacher 2
Thomas
Jen
Kelly
Zebedee
Ray

Part One

Prologue

Darkness. The sounds of smashing glass and an alarm wailing. Running footsteps. Shouting. Laughter. A police siren in the distance. KRS-One's 'Sound of Da Police' starts up: 'Woop woop, that's the sound of da police/Woop woop, that's the sound of the beast . . .'

Lights up on: a group of people in pinstriped suits and balaclavas robbing a bank, taking not just cash but paperwork, the office plants, the lot. Caught for a moment, they freeze, then get in formation and do a little dance to the music. The music stops. They rip off the balaclavas and assume a professional attitude round a table.

Scene One

Department of Home and Business Affairs. An expensively abstract logo on the wall.

McLean   Karen McLean, Department of Home and Business Affairs.

Taylor   Simon Taylor, Empathy Capital.

Thacker   Mick Thacker, Competitive Confinement Ltd.

Asset-Smith   James Asset-Smith. I believe you all know where I work.

Lucinda   Hi, I'm Lucinda, I make Delightful Chocolate. I mean, I don't make it, other people do, you know?

McLean   Good. Simon, it's your baby, why don't you christen it?

Taylor   Social dysfunction. Addiction. Depression. Violent crime. They cost this country tens of billions every year, expenses we simply can't afford in these austere times. The endless futile trek through courts, prisons, social workers, rehab and A&E. The pointless cycle of deprivation and dependency.

McLean   The *culture* of dependency. That's what we want to eradicate.

Thacker   Mmm. That 'I-want-something-for-nothing' disease.

Taylor   But what if there was a way to turn those burdens into opportunities? (*Holds up papers.*) Unity Bonds. Unity Bonds transfer the costs of social repair from the taxpayer to the private sector at a healthy return. Problem families can now be monetised, at a profit to investors and no cost to the public.

McLean   It's an incentive structure. The fewer people receive treatment for the problems, and/or the greater the reduction in offences, the higher the returns.

Taylor   It really is a game-changing solution.

*They all subtly look at **Asset-Smith**. He leafs through the papers. Beat.*

Asset-Smith   And investors bear the brunt of the costs?

McLean   With government underwriting. The usual arrangement.

Asset-Smith   What are the IRRs?

Taylor   Seven and a half per cent.

Asset-Smith   Seven and a half.

Taylor   To start with. At a minimum.

McLean   Capped at fifteen.

Asset-Smith   I've got Indian infrastructure and Chinese mines bringing in two or three times that.

McLean   Come on, James, we're talking about something *useful*.

Asset-Smith   And highly illiquid.

Thacker I've got no problem with monetising social behaviour. It's the principle the private prison system is based on. My concern is if we were saddled with the impossible cases, the hard nuts. What does that do to our profit margins?

McLean I think in order to get schemes like this off the ground, we can see our way clear to a certain number of exemptions.

Asset-Smith I'd need no caps on profits, baselines on losses –

McLean James –

Asset-Smith You're up against private equity here. The pursuit of alpha returns. You either engage with that reality, or forget it. (*Beat.*) We'd also need bail-out guarantees and a controlling stake in how the bonds are administered.

McLean That isn't the purview of the private sector –

Asset-Smith Come on, Karen, you're not exactly bargaining from a position of strength, are you?

Pause.

McLean I'm sure the model has space for development. Simon?

Taylor Absolutely. It's all about commonality of interests.

Beat.

Asset-Smith In which case I think it has considerable possibilities.

McLean Excellent. Then let's proceed.

Lucinda Sorry, I just . . . I know it's . . . What actually is a bond?

Taylor What *is* it? What do you mean?

McLean Lucinda is one of our Regenerator Innovators.

Taylor Ohhh.

Lucinda (*gesturing at* **McLean**)   We're donating some money to –

Taylor   I've heard of the scheme, yes.

McLean   She's at 'Trailblazer' level, no less.

Lucinda   Once you've made a bit of money you want to do something with it, don't you? Something you can be proud of.

Taylor   I think that's how we all feel, yes.

McLean   A bond, Lucinda, pays off when a certain threshold is achieved. If the number of people who commit crimes or receive treatment for drug addiction goes down to a certain level, investors get a return. If not, they don't. It's all about harnessing the incentivising power of the market.

Beat. **Lucinda** *nods.*

Lucinda   I see. No, that sounds very . . . sensible.

They start to gather their papers.

Why doesn't the state pay for it?

McLean   Sorry?

Lucinda   From, you know, taxes.

They politely suppress their collective amusement. Beat.

Thacker   Delightful Chocolate? That's you, is it?

Lucinda   It is, yes.

Thacker   I've had the lemongrass and chilli. It's very nice.

Lucinda   Thank you.

They rise and go. As they leave, a quote is scribbled on the wall, then fades:

> Fascism should more properly be called corporatism, because it is the merger of state and corporate power.
> *Benito Mussolini*

Scene Two

An old woman, **Joan***, sits. A* **Workman** *installs something behind her. Pause.*

Joan   I don't know how you can do it. (*Beat.*) I don't know how you can –

Workman   Nearly finished.

Joan   Like going back in time, it is. Be bringing back rationing next. Poorhouses.

Workman   Won't be long now.

Beat.

Joan   Fought a war for this. Fought a war for our rights.

Workman   You don't have a Phillips-head, do you?

Joan   Not the Germans. After that. A war against our lot. The elite.

Workman   Think I left mine in the van.

Joan   To be treated as human beings. To think of ourselves as human beings. We weren't used to it, y'see.

Workman (*holds up a screwdriver*)   Tell a lie. It was here all the time.

Joan   A place to call home. Food on the table. Why shouldn't we have them things? What's a society for unless to make sure people have them things? (*Beat.*) It's the way we treat each other now. Like threats. That's what I can't bear. We treat one another like threats. (*Beat.*) You probably aren't listening to a word I'm saying, are you?

Workman   Be out of your hair any minute now.

Joan   Have you got a granny? I said, have you got a – ?

Workman   I heard you.

Joan   Well?

Workman   It won't make it any easier on you, you know.

Joan   Answer the –

Workman   I have got a granny, yes.

Joan   And are you doing the same to her?

Workman   They're not, no.

Joan   Why not?

Workman   Because she pays the tax, as it happens.

Joan   Does she now?

Workman   She does, yes.

Joan   And how does she afford that?

Beat.

Workman   She lives with us.

Joan   Well, isn't she the lucky one?

Beat. He leans towards her.

Workman   Pay it.

Joan   Not mine to pay.

Workman   Everyone else is.

Joan   Didn't cause it, not paying for it.

Workman   It's only a one-off, they reckon.

Joan   For now.

Workman   Just pay it.

Joan   With what?

Beat. He fiddles for a short while then steps away. It's an electricity meter.

Workman   Right.

Joan   Done, is it?

Workman   It is, yeah.

Joan   Right-oh.

Workman   You put the money in here. It takes coins or notes. When you're about to run out, there's a beep and a red light starts to flash. (*Leafing through papers.*) Right then, Joan –

Joan   Mrs Thompson.

Workman   Your debt tax has been set at –

Joan   Five hundred and thirty-three pounds and sixty-three pence.

Workman   When that's paid –

Joan   Ninety-six pound fifty.

Workman   I'll be –

Joan   That's my pension. Ninety-six fifty a week. I was forty-two years a nurse. Looking after people.

She stares reproachfully at him. Beat.

Workman   When that's paid, I'll be right back to take the meter off again. Quick as you like. Call any time.

Joan   What if I don't pay?

Beat.

Workman   Please call. Number's on here, look.

Joan   Mind how you go.

He makes to leave, hesitates.

Workman   Eighteen months. Eighteen months tramping in the rain and standing in line, nothing. There's a way people look at you now when you're out of work, you'd think with more of us there'd be more solidarity, but it's the opposite. My nan with us. Three kids. My wife looking at me angle-eyed. Then this come up.

The meter beeps and a red light starts to flash.

You got any change?

Joan   You run along.

*The **Workman** digs in his pocket and pulls out some change.*

Workman   There's two quid, look. Get you started.

Joan   I don't want your money.

He puts the money down in front of her. Beat.

Workman   I'll be late for the next one.

He leaves. Pause. The red light flashes violently and the beep becomes a drawn-out screech.

Blackout. Silence.

Scene Three

Prison holding-cell. A young boy, **Ryan**, *seated at a table. A large* **Man** *sits across from him holding a file. He wears a black leather jacket with the logo 'Competitive Confinement Ltd' across the back of it. The man flicks through the file. Pause.*

Ryan   It was nothing to do with me.

The **Man** *flicks through the file again. Beat.*

Ryan   It was nothing to do with me.

The **Man** *looks up and around the room.*

Man   There's an echo in here.

He eyeballs the boy. Pause.

Tell me what happened, Ryan.

Beat.

Ryan   There's this protest. Against these cunts trying to kick away the ladder –

Man   Leave the politics out of it, there's a good lad.

Ryan   And it gets a bit out of hand. People are fucking angry, you know what I mean, and there's one or two not there for the right reasons.

Man   Like Jason.

Ryan   He comes out JD's with a few boxes and hands 'em to me and says he'll be right back, he needs some size-fives for this yat he's got a ting with. I told him I didn't want nothing to do with it. There's a hand on my shoulder and I'm in here. No word of a lie, mate, that is what happened.

Pause.

Man   Bit of a prick. Jason.

Ryan   He's a mate of mine.

Man   He's done it before? Thieving?

The boy looks uncomfortable. Beat. The **Man** *flicks through the file.*

Man   Not a bad lad, are you? Not been inside before, no record with the police. Bright lad as well. Were you hoping to go to university?

Ryan   I am going to university.

Man   Are you, son? Good on you. Might be difficult now.

Ryan   I'm not that kind of person.

Man   No. You're not. The thing is, Ryan, that's why you're here.

Beat.

Ryan   What?

Man   Our job, what they pay us for now, is to reduce rates of reoffending. Your mate Jason, as you just admitted, is a serial offender. No chance of him stopping.

Ryan   Hang on a sec.

Man   Why should we be punished for that? For his moral turpitude?

Ryan   But he's the one –

Man   You, on the other hand, you're the decent type. You're not gonna do it again, are you?

Ryan   I didn't fucking do it this time!

Man   If you plead guilty –

Ryan   They weren't my –

Man   If you plead guilty, bearing in mind the relatively minor nature of the crime, I'd see you getting a very short custodial sentence. Three months maybe.

Ryan   Fuck off! Three months –

Man   In return for which we'd write you the most glowing reference you can imagine. After all, we have what our website calls a 'commonality of interests'. If you come back here after you get out, we don't get paid.

Beat as the boy gathers himself.

Ryan   One more time, mate, yeah: they weren't mine.

Man   Or you can put that claim to a judge. It's quite a hostile environment out there at the minute. They were in your hands when you were arrested, Ryan. (*Beat.*) You don't have to decide now. I'll see you again in the morning.

He gets up and starts to leave. He stops and puts his hand on the boy's shoulder.

One more thing. If you do take up our offer and I see you back in here, I will come to your cell one night when you are sleeping, and I will pour battery acid over your face. OK? (*Beat.*) There'll be someone along to take you upstairs in a few minutes.

He leaves. The boy stares into space. Blackout.

Scene Four

Joan *in A&E. Strip lighting, plastic seats, dirty linoleum floor. A hubbub of languages and screaming kids grates on her ears. She holds her arm close. Blood seeps through a dressing. A harassed* **Nurse** *enters and attends to someone else.*

Joan   Nurse. (*Beat.*) Nurse. (*Beat.*) Nurse.

Nurse (*not looking*)   Sorry, I'm dealing with another patient.

Beat.

Joan   Nurse. Excuse me, nurse?

Nurse   What is it?

Joan   How much longer?

Nurse   We're very busy at present.

Joan   Half an hour? An hour?

Nurse   I couldn't say. A couple of hours maybe.

Joan   It hurts.

*The **Nurse** gets up and leaves. She returns a short while later with an aspirin, a plastic cup of water and a sheaf of papers.*

Nurse   There you go.

Joan   Thank you. (*She takes the aspirin with the water.*) What are these?

Nurse   Forms you need to fill in.

Joan   I filled in a load before.

Nurse   Different lot. That was Unity, this is the care trust.

Joan   Why do they need different lots?

Nurse   Efficiency.

She goes to another patient. The old woman writes but it causes too much pain.

Joan   It's this bloody bandage is the problem. It's not on right, I can tell. Can you have another look at it, nurse? It's . . .

*The **Nurse** comes and fiddles with the bandage. The old woman moans.*

Nurse   How'd you do it?

Joan   Trying to fix something. Smash something, more like.

Nurse   Should know better at your age.

Joan   Smash that bloody box off my electricity them thieving parasites put on.

*The **Nurse**'s manner changes abruptly. She drops **Joan**'s arm.*

Nurse   That's the best I can do for you, I'm afraid.

Joan   What d'you mean, that's the best you can do?

Nurse   It's not my area.

Joan   Not your area? What kind of a nurse are you, can't do a simple bandage?

Nurse   I'm not a nurse, as it happens.

Joan   Not a . . . ?

Nurse   I'm a volunteer. I don't have to be here. I'm trying to do my bit.

Joan   What are you then, if you're not a nurse?

Beat.

Nurse   I work for an electricity company.

An administrator enters, holding papers.

Administrator   Joan, is it?

Joan   Mrs Thompson.

Administrator   I'm afraid we can't make provision for you at this hospital, Joan.

Joan   Why not?

Administrator   It's an insufficiently serious injury to justify –

Joan   It's a laceration with subcutaneous hematoma –

Administrator   What I mean is, given our exceptionally high –

Joan   I've always come to this hospital.

Administrator   – *exceptionally* high patient volume, you'd be better off looking –

Joan   I used to *work* in this hospital.

Administrator   We can't make provision for you.

Joan   Why not?

Beat.

Administrator   Unity rejected your application.

Joan   I didn't make an application. I didn't *make* an 'application'.

Administrator   I'm very sorry, Joan. Please accept my sincere –

Joan   Why'd they turn me down?

Administrator   I couldn't say, it's a matter of commercial –

Joan   Tell me that. Tell me that and I'll get out of your hair.

Beat.

Administrator   Unity incentives are based on the reduction of waiting lists. One rather effective way to achieve that is not to let people on them.

Joan   I see.

Administrator   I really am sorry, but I am going to have to ask you to leave.

He leaves. She stews. An African man, **McDonald Moyo**, *enters leaning on the nurse, bleeding heavily. She sits him next to* **Joan**. *The* **Administrator** *enters.*

Administrator   Papers? Do you have insurance papers? Doesn't seem to speak much English. Insurance? (*French.*) Assurance?

Nurse   *Seguro?*

Administrator   *Assicurazione?*

Nurse   *Bima?*

Administrator   *Страхование? (Strakovanye?)* ؟تأمين؟
(*Tamin?*)

McDonald *pulls some papers from his pocket and hands them to the* **Administrator**, *who looks them over briefly and nods.*

Administrator   He's next.

He leaves. **McDonald** *leans back, clutching his side. Pause.*

Joan (*to* **McDonald**)   Bet you think you're clever. Bet you think you're right clever. Coming in waving them around. (*Beat.*) What gives you the right to jump over me? What gives you the right to bloody be here at all?

He says something placatory.

Don't you talk back to me! Don't you talk to me, you sod! Parasite! Why don't you piss off back where you come from, get them to look after you? Go on, piss off. (*She stands. Beat.*) I hope you bloody die.

Blackout.

Scene Five

A Wetherspoon's in a satellite town. **Ryan** *and two of his mates,* **Jason** *and* **Ross**, *quite drunk, screaming at a screen with WKD alcopops in front of them.*

Jason   You *cunt*! You useless fucking cunt!

Ross   Two yards out!

Ryan   Fucking spastic!

A whistle on screen. Groans of disappointment from the punters around.

Jason   FUCK!

Ryan   That's two points thrown away.

Ross   I told you he was shit when we signed him.

Jason   FUCKING BLACK CUNT.

He lunges for a WKD and knocks it to the floor. Somebody shouts 'Wahey!'

Ross   Call Autoglass, somebody's smashed.

Jason   Your round.

Ross   What? I just –

Jason   Your round.

Beat. **Ross** *gets up and goes.* **McDonald** *pushes on a mop and bucket and starts to clean up the mess.* **Jason** *watches him. Beat.*

Jason   Here's another one, look.

Ryan   For fuck's sake, Jase.

Jason   Oy, mate? Mate?

McDonald *looks up at him.*

Jason   Be a top African and get some water for the boys? Wa–ter. Yeah, be a top African and fetch us some.

Beat. **McDonald** *takes a step towards the bar.*

Jason   Not from there. Do like you usually do. (*Kicks bucket.*) Put that on your head and take it to the watering hole.

Ryan   Jase.

Jason   What? I'm only having a bit of banter with him. I'll have mine without any AIDS in it, please mate. And no hippo shit. Yeah? Nice one.

Ross *returns with three more WKDs.* **McDonald** *cautiously returns to the mess.*

Ross   What's he on about?

Ryan   Gone off on one again.

Jason   Mate, mate, listen to this: I adopted an African child, yeah? I was worried he wouldn't adapt to our way of life, so I installed a treadmill in front of the sink.

Ross   Got that one off Sickipedia.

Jason   Laugh then, ya black cunt.

McDonald *gets up and leaves.*

Ryan   Fuck's sakes, John Terry.

Jason   What? I wouldn't complain if someone called me a white cunt.

Ross   Cos it's true.

Jason   So what's he complaining about?

Ryan   Cos maybe it's –

Jason   I knew you was gonna say that. It's not fucking 'racist', it's a *description*. Like Ross just got a round of drinks in, Africans go get a bucket of water in.

Ross   Fair play.

Jason   How d'you kill a hundred flies? Smash an African in the face with a shovel.

Ross   Alright, Farmer Giles.

Jason   Eh?

Ross (*making 'milking cow' gestures*)   Fucking milking it now.

Ryan   Fucking Gold Top.

Ross   Get a float, mate.

Jason   What are you laughing at? It's cunts like him that's why you're here.

Ross   Mate, I'm here to get battered and watch the footie.

Jason   You know what I mean. (*To* **Ryan**.) He's got your job.

Ryan   I don't wanna wash floors.

Jason   You wanna fucking do something. Thumb up your arse all day like −

Ryan   I'm going to universi −

Jason (*slamming down his WKD hard on the table*)   *Don't* fucking −

Ryan   I am −

Jason   Stop with that shit. Stop it.

Ross   Ah, let him −

Jason   You're deluding yourself. You are, Ryan. Nobody fucking wants you.

Ross   'Ckin hell, Jase, that's harsh.

Jason   They don't though. Who wants him? Nothing kid, been inside, *English*, who gives a fuck about him? What they want, son, is cunts like him.

Ryan   He's washing floors, mate.

Ross   He is right though, Ryan.

Jason   Go up London. Africans in big headdresses swanning out of Harrods. Chinks in fucking suits and ties, stuffing their faces in the posh restaurants. Arab cunts with their postbox birds mincing up and down King's Road with ten shopping bags in each hand. Go up London, that's all you see. Everyone, *everyone's* got a piece of the pie except for us and I am sick and fucking tired of it. I am sick and fucking tired of −

Ryan   I am going to uni −

Jason (*in his face*)   You fucking get a grip. You *fucking* get a grip. (*Beat.*) It is us against them. Nobody in this world gives a flying fuck about you apart from the people round this table. That's the truth, Ryan. The sooner you get your thick head around that, the better off you'll be.

McDonald *appears with the bucket on his head.*

Jason   Oy oy!

Ross   Oy oy!

He walks towards them with an exaggerated servility, limping and cringing.

Ryan   Oh my days!

Ross   Yes, my son!

Jason   That is a top African. That is one who knows his place.

Ross   Get in!

Jason   That is a nigger who knows his –

McDonald *throws the bucket of water over* **Jason**. *A beat of calm before the storm.*

Ryan   Oh shit.

Blackout.

Scene Six

A nursery. Brightly coloured scribbles on the walls. A teacher stands with a piece of paper. Pause. Another teacher enters. Beat.

Teacher 1   How is she?

Teacher 2   She's fine. Playing.

Teacher 1   Does she . . . ?

Teacher 2   I don't think so, no.

Teacher 1   What's she saying?

Teacher 2   Not saying anything. Just playing. Peppa Pig.

Teacher 1   Did you get through?

Teacher 2   The phone's still off. Been off for the past hour.

Teacher 1   Shit.

Teacher 2   Did you speak to Social Services?

Beat.

Teacher 1   I mean, there's quite a few you can tell are struggling. Kim's mum.

Teacher 2   Mmm. Hair.

Teacher 1   Danielle's. Crying in the street the other day about the state of Danielle's coat. But not her. Never late. Make-up always nice.

Teacher 2   Bit tarty for me, to be fair.

Teacher 1   Always polite.

Teacher 2   Fancies herself a bit.

Teacher 1   Always time for a chat.

Teacher 2   How d'you reckon she chose?

Beat.

Teacher 1   Chose?

Teacher 2   She's got three, doesn't she? So how d'you reckon she chose? (*Beat.*) Read it again. Doesn't say about the other two. Just says about Anna.

Teacher 1 *reads the note again.*

Teacher 1   Call her again.

Teacher 2   Her phone's off.

Teacher 1   And go check up on Anna. Please.

Beat. **Teacher 2** *leaves.* **Teacher 1** *reads the note again. Pause.* **Teacher 2** *re-enters. She shakes her head.*

Teacher 2   How do you tell a three-year-old girl she's the one her mother left behind?

Beat.

Teacher 1   Where's the dad?

Teacher 2   Gone with her, I expect. Lost his job, didn't he? He was fitting those debt tax meters.

Teacher 1   Alright, this is what we're going to do. You stay with her. I'll pop out to the shops –

Teacher 2   The thing is, Jess –

Teacher 1   Get her a change of / clothes

Teacher 2   I've got a date.

Beat.

Teacher 1   *What?*

Teacher 2   With that guy. Jason. I told you about it.

Teacher 1 (*pointing at the room*)   There's a – !

Teacher 2   Call Social Services –

Teacher 1   And you're talking / about

Teacher 2   They'll –

Teacher 1   I called them. I called them, OK?

Teacher 2   And? What'd they say?

Teacher 1   They won't take her.

Teacher 2   They've got to, don't they?

Teacher 1   Apparently not.

Teacher 2   Why not?

Teacher 1   She'd put them over their incentives.

Pause.

Teacher 2   I've got to go.

Teacher 1   You're not / serious?

Teacher 2   I've done my job, my job finished an hour ago, and this is not my fault –

Teacher 1   She's three years old, Rachel.

Teacher 2   It's not my fault, OK? I do my job bloody well for hardly nothing and I never meet anyone and he's really nice. I got a dress special. (*Beat.*) I'm sorry, love. He's really nice. You'll like him.

Scene Seven

Asset-Smith *behind his desk in his spacious office. A trader,*
Thomas, *in front of him. Over them plays Cameron's speech after the*
2011 riots:

Cameron (*recorded*)   'There is a complete lack of responsibility
in parts of our society. People allowed to feel that the world
owes them something, that their rights outweigh their
responsibilities and their actions do not have consequences.
Well, they do have consequences.'

Pause.

Asset-Smith   We short rape.

Beat.

Thomas   What?

Asset-Smith   Senior rape, mezzanine rape, junior. We
short all of it.

Thomas   But –

Asset-Smith   Crime, depression, illiteracy. All the Unity
stuff. Set up new markets in all of them. OTC derivatives
should do it. I've already reached out to a few pension funds,
institutional investors. Lots of interest. (*Beat.*) Problem?

Thomas   What's the pitch?

Asset-Smith   Say it's a hedge. We're long the initial
investment, we're hedging.

Thomas   What kind of volume?

Asset-Smith   Start with a couple of bill and go up from
there.

Thomas (*whistles*)   That's not a hedge, that's a twelve-foot
ornamental shrubbery carved into the shape of a giant fucking
peacock.

Asset-Smith   Alright?

Thomas   Yeah, fine.

Beat.

Asset-Smith   You don't understand.

Thomas   Course I do.

Asset-Smith   But you don't want to admit it.

Beat.

Thomas   We put all that time and money into setting them up, I just –

Asset-Smith   A rape bond, or a crime bond, or an addiction bond, Thomas, pays out when the number of rapes or crimes or addictions is reduced, am I correct?

Thomas   I don't need a lesson in –

Asset-Smith   Sorry, did you make partner recently? Congratulations. Someone should have told me. (*Beat.*) In other words, Unity bonds are a bet on social harmony. Look out of this window. Do you see a rise in social harmony on the horizon? Is that angry roaring noise in fact the sound of an enormous number of colourful butterflies?

Thomas   I get the point, James.

Asset-Smith   Social discord seems the safer bet. An almost guaranteed bet, in fact. It would be a dereliction of my duty to shareholders not to make that bet. Short fucking rape.

Thomas   What about the . . . ?

He trails off. Beat.

Asset-Smith   What about the what?

Thomas   Nothing. (*Beat.*) The social utility factor. You're basically asking for a rise in –

Asset-Smith   I'm not asking for a rise in anything. I'm responding to simple reality. If we could make sufficient returns on a reduction in crime, I would do it. That is why I invested in the initial scheme. It would appear we can make better returns on an increase in crime. It's not the job of markets to shape the world. (*Beat.*) It's nothing personal, Thomas. I hope you understand that.

Thomas   We invented Unity. Do we not have a responsibility to – ?

Asset-Smith   Markets are not responsible to anyone. That is their peculiar beauty. It's what makes them free. (*Beat. Looks at his BlackBerry.*) I'll see you in the pub later, Thomas.

Blackout.

Scene Eight

Ryan *in a prison cell. Pause. His door opens and the* **Man** *in the black leather jacket fills it. In his hand is a bottle that looks like it contains chemicals. Pause.*

Man   Evening. (*He holds up the bottle.*) Thirsty?

Ryan   Get out of my cell.

The **Man** *sniffs the bottle and recoils.*

Man   Wouldn't wanna drink that. Use it to clean your toilet, maybe.

He jerks the bottle at **Ryan**, *who flinches.*

Man   I told you I'd see you again. Didn't I?

Ryan   Don't.

Man   Here I am. And I brought you something.

Ryan   Don't!

The **Man** *throws some of the contents of the bottle over* **Ryan**, *who screams in fear. Beat. The* **Man** *sips from the bottle and holds it out to the boy.*

Man   Mineral water. The water in here is very hard. (*Beat.*) You're a lucky boy, Ryan. You fucked up. I asked you to do one simple thing and you fucked it up. Luckily for you, priorities have changed.

Ryan   You lied to me.

Man   Not too bad in here, is it? You'll get used to it soon.

Ryan   You lied to me!

Man   The thing you've got to understand, Ryan, is the public won't wear it. Very little appetite out there right now for hard-luck stories. A lot of people are having a tough time, but *they're* not stabbing hardworking immigrants in unprovoked attacks, being a burden on the state, costing taxpayers' money. You should see the polls. Very much against you. Very much against you, Ryan.

Beat.

Ryan   What do you *want*?

Man   I want you not to have any hope. (*Beat.*) I want you not to lose yourself in any delusions. It's important that one sees oneself for what one truly is. One of the hardest things to achieve in life. To cut through the fog of delusions and aspirations and dreams, to really plant your feet on the hard rock of reality. Hardly any of us manage it. We're away with the fairies, living in the future, a world of things to come that probably never will. In that sense, Ryan, you're quite lucky. Here, within the rough concrete embrace of these four walls, you truly know who and what you are.

Beat. He moves back to the door.

Good talking to you.

Ryan   You lied to me.

Man   I'll be downstairs if you ever want to chat again.

Ryan   You told me if I went guilty you'd –

Man   The thing is, Ryan: priorities have changed.

Blackout.

Scene Nine

Department for Home and Business Affairs. **McLean***, better dressed.*
Lucinda *enters.*

Lucinda   Karen, hi!

McLean   Lucinda, good to see you. Thanks for coming in.
The others should be here any minute.

Lucinda   You look different.

McLean   Really?

Lucinda   Mmm.

McLean   It's the diet, I expect. Managed to stick to it for a
change.

Lucinda   How much have you lost?

McLean   Only half a stone, but it's how you carry it, isn't it?

Beat.

Lucinda   This should be fun.

McLean   Fun?

Lucinda   Exciting. To hear people's opinions.

McLean   Oh, I think I know what they're going to say. I
mean it's been an enormous success.

Lucinda   Has it?

McLean   Hasn't it?

Lucinda   Oh no, I didn't mean to suggest –

McLean   We've exceeded all initial expectations. The
returns have been quite spectacular. And there's an absolute
deluge of interest in the new offerings.

Lucinda   The new . . . ?

McLean   The second phase. (*Beat.*) It was always the intent
to extend Unity into more abstract realms. Biodiversity.

Reproduction. Areas that are inherently more difficult to monetarise.

Lucinda   I'm not sure I –

McLean   It's more difficult to put a price on clean air or children, to establish a monetary value for happiness or truth. But not impossible. With the right model.

Lucinda   But they've failed, haven't they?

McLean   I'm sorry?

Lucinda   The bonds have failed.

Beat.

McLean   You have a rather odd definition of failure, Lucinda.

Lucinda   They didn't actually bring down crime. Or depression. Or rape.

McLean   Saving the state, and therefore the taxpayer, billions in payouts.

Lucinda   Those things have gone *up*.

McLean   And generated, via the derivatives market, a cascade of new revenues to deal with those issues. Simon, for example, is planning to make four or five new investments off the returns generated by the last one. The sky's the limit.

Beat.

Lucinda   I think I'm being thick.

McLean   I mean, these *are* complex financial models.

Lucinda   No, it's . . . But then it goes round and round for ever and you –

McLean   – turn social problems into an endless motor for growth. Correct. You spin the grubby cotton of common lives into golden thread. You give ordinary people, most of whom, let's face it, have no future as consumers in this society, let alone as workers, you give those people a purpose.

Lucinda   To get arrested. To drink. To fail.

McLean   You give people back their productive role. And thus their *dignity*.

Lucinda   You're making human weakness into raw material for financial speculation.

McLean   Well, what else can you do with it? At least it's not costing us money. (*Beat.*) It's when you give the market its head that you really start to see a difference, Lucinda. That you have, in your words, something to be proud of.

Pause.

Lucinda   You have to do something.

McLean   No.

Lucinda   Review it. Stop it.

McLean   I'm not in any position –

Lucinda   Of course you are, you're the government, none of this –

McLean   You misunderstand me, I –

Lucinda   This financial wizardry –

McLean   I'm –

Lucinda   – can work without public money.

McLean   I'm no longer in government, Lucinda. An opportunity arose in the private sector that I felt was . . . Where I felt I could do more good.

Lucinda   What are you – ?

McLean   I've replaced James. He's moved on to bigger things.

Beat.

Lucinda   I want my money back.

McLean   That's entirely your prerogative. I will just say that times like these, difficult times, are when we can least afford grandstanding.

Taylor *and* **Thacker** *enter.*

McLean   Good. Come in. Coffee on the left, tea on the right. Before we start, I believe Lucinda has something she wants to share with you. Over to you, Lucinda.

Pause.

Lucinda   I brought everyone some chocolate.

She holds out some bars of chocolate.

Blackout.

Scene Ten

Joan's *flat. In darkness, lit by a few guttering candles. Obviously cold –* **Joan** *and her companion,* **McDonald***, are wrapped heavily in tatty blankets. They hold mugs of tea. Over the top, Cameron again, his speech of January 2012:*

Cameron (*recorded*)   'I believe that open markets and free enterprise are the best imaginable force for improving human wealth and happiness. They are the engine of progress, generating the enterprise and innovation that lifts people out of poverty and gives people opportunity. And I would go further: where they work properly, open markets and free enterprise can actually promote morality.'

Pause.

Joan   Comfy?

Beat.

Another blanket?

Beat.

I'm sorry about the cold. There's wood for cooking and there's wood for heating but not always enough for both.

Beat.

Could be worse. Could be downstairs. In the basement. I was born in a basement.

Beat.

You have to be grateful, I suppose. Small mercies.

Beat.

You're very easy to talk to. A good listener. I'm glad of that.

Beat.

Took me a long time to find you. That terrible place. Wetherspoon's.

Beat.

I just wanted to say: I'm not that kind of person. That's all I wanted to say, really. They made me so angry in that hospital they made me not myself. It burned me acid inside like a digested penny after. What I said to you.

Beat.

Thank you, then. For letting me apologise.

Beat. **McDonald** *stirs.*

McDonald   *Zvinoshamisa! Haisi nguva refu yapfuura pandanga ndive ne mukadzi wangu ne vana vangu - ndiinawo mumaoko angu – ndiinawo ndichi va fema. Iye zvino, handi chambo gona kuvafunga. Rangariro yavo yangove se chiutsi, se bhayiscop ye upenyu we mumwe munhu. Handichaziva zvakaita vana vangu, handichaziva hwema hwe mukadzi wangu. Murume anokanganwa hwema we mukadzi wake sei? Vana vaakarera mumaoko ake. Pane zvinhu zvino nyanyo nyadzisa mu nyika muno, ku kokotama ne kupemha serombe zvinhu zvinofanira zviri zvangu se nhaka! Ku kanganwa chinhu chakabva mumapako angu, chiri muviri wangu, ndizvo zvino ndi sisimutsa.*

[It's very strange. Only a short while ago I was with my wife and children, I held them and breathed them. And now I can only remember them through a haze, as if they were images on screen from someone else's life. I cannot remember what my children feel like, what my wife smells like. How can a man forget his wife's smell? What he has held in his hands? Of all the humiliations here, the stooping and the begging for things that should be mine by rights, to forget the feeling of something that came of my body, that is my body, is the worst.]

Joan   You're talking about your wife and kids.

McDonald   You speak Shona?

Joan   It's obvious. The way you move your hands.

Beat.

McDonald   I am a structural engineer. BSc (Hons) from the University of Zimbabwe.

Joan   That's very impressive.

McDonald   BSc (Hons)!

Pause. His anger subsides into sadness.

This is the first time any English person has invited me into their home.

Beat.

Joan   I'll make you a new cup of tea.

Beat.

McDonald   Thank you.

Blackout.

Part Two

A beautiful wood-panelled courtroom – judge's bench, witness stand, jury – in a state of serious disrepair. A light hangs by wires, floorboards are loose and there's junk all over the place. A solid oak door, locked, guards the entrance. Above the bench hangs a banner in massive black letters:

THE COURT OF PUBLIC OPINION

Jen, *a veteran activist in her forties, sits with a mug of rooibos tea, bleeding from a head wound.* **Kelly**, *early thirties, new to the movement, cleans and bandages it.*

Kelly   Keep still.

Jen   Aah.

Kelly   Sorry.

Jen   'Salright.

Kelly   Nearly finished.

Beat.

Jen   I was on trial here.

Kelly   Serious?

Jen   Twyford Down, I think it was. '91?

Kelly   I was nine.

Jen   Or Reclaim the Streets. We were the last batch before they shut it down.

Kelly   How long did you get?

Jen   Three months. 'Assault on a policewoman'.

Kelly   Did you do it?

Jen   I did, yeah.

Kelly   Why?

Jen   Because she'd been stamping on my face. Two big buggers held me down in a chokehold and she stamped. For a good few minutes. Broke my nose in four places. When they let me go, I got up, wiped the blood off my face, and smacked her in the teeth.

Kelly   Wow. OK.

Jen   It was all worth it for the surprise in her eyes.

Kelly   I've never hit a girl.

Jen   She wasn't a girl.

Kelly   What did the judge say?

Jen   He didn't believe me. Nobody ever believes what the police do until (a) they've been battered on a demo, or (b) they've seen footage of someone else being battered on a demo.

Kelly   That's what got me into it. Watching the Tomlinson killing on YouTube.

Jen   The best protection against pro-corporate police violence isn't Amnesty International, it's a mobile phone with a camera in it. Made by a corporation. The world, Kelly, is a complex place. Ow.

Kelly   There you go.

Jen *springs to her feet.*

Kelly   How do you keep going?

Jen   How'd you mean?

Kelly   Twenty years of this.

Jen   And the rest.

Kelly   How do you do it?

Jen   Easy. You keep plugging away and you never give up and you keep fighting. I'm not special, Kel. Anyone can do it.

I'm just lucky I enjoy it, I suppose. (*Twigs.*) The Criminal Justice Bill, that was it. 'A succession of repetitive beats'.

Kelly   Eh?

Jen   Bloody hell, you are young, arentcha?

Kelly (*grinning*)   No, you're old.

Jen   The Criminal Justice Bill wanted to ban all music characterised by a succession of repetitive beats.

Kelly (*indicates* **Jen**'s *head*)   Ironically, what the police just did to you.

Jen   I'm thinking of opening a Met Police-themed health spa.

Kelly   Isn't all music characterised by a succession of repetitive beats?

Jen   The 'Ian Tomlinson' head-and-body massage. The 'Jean Charles de Menezes' special acupuncture.

Kelly   Slogan: 'You'll think you died and went to heaven.'

Jen   That's good, I'll have that. (*They smile at each other.*) Right, enough wittering: where are we?

Kelly   Al-Jazeera's coming.

Jen   I would expect no less.

Kelly   Someone from *Guardian* 'Comment is Free'.

Jen   I *hate Guardian* 'Comment is Free'. Particularly the comments. They drain me of the will to live.

Kelly   And the *Mail* is coming, 'to see if we're the dirty layabouts everyone says we are'. I *think* she meant it ironically.

Jen   Al-Jazeera, the *Guardian* and the *Mail*: together at last.

Kelly   There's a good few others showing interest. You lot getting battered can't hurt. Metaphorically speaking. Loads of retweets, blog hits . . . It's building up.

Jen   How many people coming, do you reckon?

Kelly (*shrugs*)   Couple of hundred, maybe.

Jen   Then we'd better crack on.

She stares at her fingers. There is blood on them. Beat.

Kelly   Are you OK, Jen?

Jen'*s façade slips a little and distress peeks through. She stifles it. Beat.*

Jen   My own fault. You'd think I'd know better after all these years. Never turn your back on the cunts.

Enter **Zebedee**, *a 'professional' activist wearing an Anonymous mask (the Guy Fawkes one from* V for Vendetta.) *and* **Joan**, *the old woman from the first part.*

Zebedee (*muffled by the mask*)   Toilets are done.

Jen   Take off the mask.

Zebedee (*muffled*)   The point of the mask –

Jen   I'm aware of the point of the mask, Zeb. It's to maintain anonymity and enhance the power of the collective. No one else is wearing one right now, which isn't doing wonders for your anonymity. I've got a headache. Take off the mask.

Zebedee *takes his mask off.*

Zebedee   Fucking disgrace.

Joan   I still think you should report it.

Jen   Who to? If you're gonna say 'the police', there's a tiny flaw in your plan.

Joan   The press? I don't see why they should get away –

Jen   Can we stop talking about it? Please? Hazards of the trade. If you can't take it, don't be here. Where are we?

Zebedee   Toilets are done.

Joan (*wrinkling her nose*)   Done as they'll ever be.

Zebedee   Fair point.

Jen   Lights?

Zebedee   No.

Jen   Floorboards?

Zebedee *kicks a loose floorboard.*

Jen   Come on! We've got no time!

Joan   We're waiting for Ray to bring the tools.

Jen   Well where is he?

A knock on the big wooden doors.

Ray (*off*)   It's me.

Kelly (*with some affection*)   Speak of the devil.

Zebedee (*calls out*)   'It's been a long time, I shouldn't have left you.'

Ray (*off*)   It's me.

Zebedee   'It's been a long time, I shouldn't have – '

Ray (*off*)   Open the fucking door.

Jen   Let him in.

Zebedee *opens the door to let in* **Ray**, *an Irishman in his twenties, followed by* **Ryan**, *the young boy from Part One, and an unexpected arrival:* **Thomas**, *the former trader, dressed down. He looks about in amazement.*

Zebedee (*to* **Ray**)   The correct response is, 'Without a strong rhyme to step to'.

Ray   Who made that shite the password anyway? (*To* **Ryan**.) 'Ne'er-do-well'. That was the horse.

Ryan   Fair play.

Jen   Let's get to work.

Ray *starts chucking hammers, screwdrivers, etc. to people while recounting his tale to the room. People grab the tools and start fixing the walls and flooring.*

Ray   Who wouldn't back a horse called Ne'er-do-well? It's a plain double bluff. Twenty to one, dead fucking cert.

Ryan (*grinning*)   Standard.

Ray   I plonk down twenty pound, the fucking thing goes down like a sniper's hit it five yards from the line. I says to the bookie, I'm willing to take a fifty per cent haircut on that bet. 'Excuse me?' says your man. I says, I'm a core investor in your firm, let's diversify risk, give me ten quid back and we'll say no more about it. The eedjit calls over security! You clearly don't understand how the global economy functions these days, my son.

He spots **Jen***'s face for the first time.*

Ray   Jesus, what happened to you?

Jen   They cleaned us out of the square.

Ray   Are you fucking serious?

Jen   Get to work, Ray.

Ray   But –

Kelly *pulls at his arm and he goes quiet for a moment. The rest work for a few beats.* **Thomas** *wanders, hammer in hand.* **Ryan** *and* **Joan** *working together.*

Ryan   You seem to know what you're doing, Joanie.

Joan   I've always loved work. It's the thing that makes me feel most real.

Ryan   You're good at it.

Joan   My father was a carpenter.

Ray   Tommy, over here, son.

Tom   Sorry, mate. It's mad here. I've not seen anything like it.

Ray   Everyone, I've news.

Joan   You seem to have the knack yourself.

Ryan   Done a coupla courses.

Ray   There's good news and bad news. Or good news, good news and bad news. Or is it good news, bad news and good news?

Joan   College courses?

Ryan (*uncomfortable*)   College, yeah.

Ray   The good news is we've been declared terrorists.

Jen   What?

Ray (*unfolds a piece of paper*)   Leak from the plod: terrorism update for the City of London Business 'Community'. High-level terror threats to the City of London: the Revolutionary Armed Forces of Colombia, who last I heard were mainly known for their exploits in *Colombia*, thus the name; Al Qaeda; and us.

Jen   Fuckers. *Fuckers*.

Kelly   How is this the good news?

Ray   Shows we're doing our job, getting under their skin. They can't get rid of us so they have to call us names.

Ryan   Trust.

Ray   Solve some real crimes, ya fat plod fucknuts! The true crimes of the modern world, the ones that rob millions of people not just one or two, take place in the big shiny glass towers down the road. LIBOR-rigging. Gas-market rigging. Google and Vodaphone dodging billions in taxes. Mubarak depended on the City of London. So did AIG and Lehman Brothers. Every non-dom dictator and Russian klepto-plutocrat rinses their filthy money clean through the London

Stock Exchange – the Jordanian army is listed on the London Stock Exchange, for fuck's sake! – but oh no, *we're* the terrorists, get the armed response unit down the protest camp pronto in case someone gets stabbed with a sharpened lentil.

Kelly   So what's the bad news?

Ray   The bad news is I've decided not to be the defence.

General hubbub.

Jen   *What?*

Zebedee   We voted you the defence, Ray.

Ray   The good news part of the bad news is I've found the perfect replacement.

He pushes **Thomas** *gently forward.*

Tom   What?

Kelly   What?!

Ray (*innocent*)   What? You said you wanted to help.

Tom   No, I'm not –

Zebedee   You can't just decide –

Ray   Ah, it's grand –

Jen   It is not 'grand' –

Ray   Tell 'em where you're from, Tommy.

Tom   I'm just here –

Kelly   You can't do this, Ray.

Zebedee   We *voted* you –

Ray   Tommy used to work for Goldman Sachs.

Zebedee   Oh, fucking brilliant.

Ray   He's the perfect fella to defend them.

Tom   Defend who from what?

Zebedee   A spy? You've brought in a fucking spy?

Tom   I'm not a spy. What kind of spy says who he's spying for?

Zebedee   A fucking . . . clever spy? A double-bluff spy?

Tom   Look, I just came down here to see what all the fuss was about.

Jen (*to* **Ray**)   You will do your job.

Ray (*gesturing at* **Tom**)   Your man here is ten times better qualified –

Jen   You will do your fucking job, Ray. For once in your life you will do something that isn't whatever you want to do.

Ray   Don't fuckin' tell me –

Jen   You swan about like it's all a bit of a laugh –

Ray   You don't even know me, Jen.

Jen   Terrorism is not a laugh. It's how they fucked us before. Ten, twelve years ago, we had them running. I honestly thought the world was never going to be the same. J18, Seattle, Genoa: the anti-globalisation protests, hundreds of thousands of people looking for something new, beyond the old dead lies of nation and state and market. A radically new world. And then came 9/11.

Ray   Jen, I respect what you've done in the past, but –

Jen   And it all died. People got scared, and every fucker was suddenly an expert on the evils of Islam, and all the old dead ideas grabbed us by the throat again. It's taken ten years to get the poisonous lie of terrorism out of our bloodstream. So what's the first thing they try to do? I will not let them shut us up this time. And that means, Ray, that we take this seriously.

Beat.

Ray   Have you been to Ireland?

Jen   No, but I –

Ray   Sitting here drinking your rooibos fucking tea –

Kelly   Ray –

Jen   I'm not trying to –

Ray   D'you know what the worst of Ireland is, Jen? It's not the joblessness. Nor the rake of never-to-be-finished houses looming over you like scaffolds. It's the guilt. The giving in and the guilt. Ireland was bankrupted by fifteen men. There's fifteen property speculators owe Anglo Irish half a billion apiece and all the rest of us'll be choking on that for life and nobody says a thing because, for some literally insane reason, *we* feel guilty. Like somehow it's *our* fault we got robbed, because we had the temerity to want a little happiness. We had something beyond the cold creak of the church door, just for a moment, and then the greatest theft since Cromwell, and now every family of four is carrying two hundred thousand euros of someone else's debt and how in God's name are they supposed to pay it? There's a loss of life, a whole world of what could have been that's being strangled and *nobody will fight back*, and I'm as committed to this thing as anyone but if you think I'm going to say a single word in defence of those murderers you'd better think again, long and hard.

Pause.

Zebedee   Coffee, anyone?

Ryan   I'll come with ya.

Tom   I'm gonna head off I think.

Kelly   Ryan, can you go?

Ryan   Alright.

He slips away.

Kelly   Tommy . . . is it Tommy?

Tom   Tom.

Kelly   Please stay. Just for a few minutes. We could really use you.

The rest gather into a circle. **Tom** *hesitates a moment, then decides to see what's going to happen.* **Ray** *refuses.*

Ray   A meeting? Another fucking meeting?

Kelly   Shut up and sit down.

Ray   I did not join a revolutionary autonomist organisation to sit in fucking meetings.

Kelly   You are making a twat out of yourself.

Jen   Right, so the first question is: do we still want to do the trial?

Zebedee *and* **Joan** *make the signal for agreement: fingers up, palms out, hands waved from side to side.*

Tom   What's with the jazz hands?

Joan   It's how you say yes without saying 'yes'.

Tom   It makes you look like a Marcel Marceau tribute group.

Joan   It gives everyone a chance to speak. Not just the men with the loudest voices.

Zebedee   Changes the power balance.

Tom   In favour of those with a degree in circus skills.

Jen   In favour of equality. Probably not much like where you came from, is it?

Tom   I'm not mocking –

Jen (*to* **Tom**, *making a fist*)   This is 'veto'. (*Holds up her two index fingers.*) This is 'direct response' – I want to reply directly to that point. (*Makes a 'T' with her hands.*) This is 'technical point', if you want to propose say breaking into smaller groups.

Tom   Smaller groups? There's only four of us.

Jen (*to the group*)   So we're still agreed on the trial?

Zebedee and **Joan** *show agreement.* **Tom** *does 'hands on an invisible glass wall'.*

Jen   Tom?

Tom   I don't even know what you're talking about.

They lean into a discussion.

Ray   Are we not having . . . you know, a thing, Kelly?

Kelly   We are having a 'thing', Ray, it's called sex.

Ray   Do we not have a thing more than just that thing?

Kelly   Are you getting romantic with me?

Ray   Why are you not supporting me then?

Kelly   OK. Right. Supporting you.

Ray   Backing me up.

Kelly   I like you, Ray. The last thing I expected when I came down here was a holiday romance with extra tear gas, but you're funny, you're charismatic, I'd even say in the highly unlikely event I wanted to be impregnated and Olivier Giroud wasn't returning my calls, I'd put you on my initial shortlist –

Ray (*blushing*)   Well now, Kelly, you don't need –

Kelly   But you are also a fuckwit.

Ray   I am not –

Kelly   You stomp about shouting and yelling and refusing to make any compromises whatsoever, totally contradicting the fact that what you really want, more than anything else, is to belong to a *group*. Don't you? (*Beat.*) And a group has to be *worked at*. Solidarity isn't born, it's built up, layer by layer, out of the tedious sediment of discussion.

Ray   I fucking hate meetings.

Kelly   Real democracy is boring, slow, probably the most inefficient way to achieve social progress – and, it's the thing that makes us different.

Ray   I won't do it, Kel. I'd rather go and chuck a Molotov.

Kelly   Anyone can chuck a Molotov. Only a genuine revolutionary can make it through an affinity group.

She gestures at the group. **Ray** *puts his hands on his hips and exhales heavily.*

Ray (*muttering*)   Fuck's sakes . . .

Kelly   Come on.

Beat, then the two of them join the circle.

Jen   Why won't anyone hold the bankers to account? Thirteen trillion in bailouts, six million people made homeless in the US alone, and has anyone been arrested? Has anyone even been fired?

Tom *holds up his index fingers.*

Zebedee   Quick learner.

Tom   Me.

Zebedee   Really?

Tom   Yeah. There's been a lot of layoffs, actually. We're not all Fred the Shred. Carry on.

Jen   So we decided to do it ourselves. Put it on trial: not just bankers, the whole system. First thing was to find a proper courtroom. I remembered this place.

Kelly   I've been past it out clubbing a hundred times and never knew it was here.

Zebedee   So we found a way in.

Joan   That was the fun part.

Kelly   Fixed up the toilets and the electrics.

Joan   Clambering up trees, over walls. I haven't done that since I was a little girl.

Kelly   It's in a lot better nick than when we arrived.

Jen   The council tried to have us chucked out so they could do, um, absolutely nothing with it, but we got a court stay in our favour.

Kelly   Which is why the police charged us out of the square. (*Points at* **Jen***'s head.*) Can't let us get on top, can they?

Zebedee   We have a prosecutor –

He mock-bows and pulls out a sheaf of notes.

We have a defence lawyer –

At **Ray***, who rolls his eyes.*

Zebedee   We even have a judge –

Joan   Real judge, retired, coming down from Wolverhampton. He sounds quite excited.

Tom   But no bankers? Nobody physically on trial?

Jen   No.

Zebedee   We invited them. They told us to fuck off.

Tom   But –

Zebedee   If you don't agree, you should do the disagreement gesture.

Tom   Right. What's the disagreement gesture?

The group do the disagreement gesture – hands wave, fingers down, palms inward.

Tom (*muttering*)   Fuck's sakes.

He does the disagreement gesture.

What's the point? You don't actually have them in the room, what's the point?

Kelly   Because it's not for them. They have their say all the
time: it's called government policy. It's for the rest of us.

Ray   Everybody thinks austerity is necessary because we're
told it is, over and over again. If enough people repeat a lie
enough times, it becomes true. Boris Johnson is a harmless
clown. John Terry is a legitimate member of the human race.
Austerity is necessary.

Kelly   No one puts that idea on trial. They quibble at bits of
it, but no one takes it on head-on, in a public forum.

Tom   A public forum of people like you?

Joan   We're not 'like us'. Like what others think we are.
Shouty. Here to burn things down.

Ray   Speak for yerself, Joanie.

Joan   I do.

Kelly   A lot of people, maybe most people, have a very
strong sense that things are wrong, but they don't know
what's right. And nor do we. That's the point. That's what
makes it exciting.

Tom   It sounds a little self-indulgent maybe.

Jen   Not if we take it seriously. That's why we voted for Ray
as defence –

Ray   Nothing like elections to put you off democracy.

Jen   Because he's our most persuasive speaker. He's the guy
we most want to believe. And so he's the one who has to
express what we don't want to believe.

Tom *looks at* **Ray** *with an expression of 'That makes sense.'* **Ray**
shrugs grumpily.

Tom   I still don't see what it's going to change.

Joan   My late husband used to say that life was a process of
narrowing down, of casting people off, till you ended on a
small dark island, alone.

Tom   Cheery fella.

Joan   I'd have divorced him if he hadn't died first. Always had to have the last word, the sod. Thing is, he proved himself right. Because people do leave you. They die, or they retire to Spain, same thing. He died because he was afraid, and because it was the easiest thing to do. It was easier to give up and fade away than make himself vulnerable to the possibility of something better. And so he pulled his own coffin lid closed. I won't do that. I'll keep my eyes open to the bitter end. (*Beat.*) And with that, I don't half need a wee.

She gets up and heads to the toilet. A knock at the door.

Zebedee   'It's been a long time, I shouldn't have left you.'

Ryan (*off*)   'Without a strong rhyme to step to.'

Zebedee *opens the door.* **Ryan** *enters with several Starbucks in a cardboard carrier.*

Ryan   Classic tune.

He touches fists with **Zebedee**.

Ryan   I dunno who likes cappuccino or latte so I got some of each.

Zebedee *looks horrified.*

Ryan   What?

Zebedee   Starbucks!

Ryan   And?

Zebedee   Nobody in this movement drinks Starbucks!

Ryan   I spent my own fucking money on these!

The circle gets up and comes towards **Ryan**.

Jen   How much did you spend, Ryan?

Ryan   I dunno, tenner?

Jen   That's ten pounds more tax than Starbucks have paid in the last three years.

Ryan   Where I'm from, Jen, this is all there is.

Ray (*reaching for a cup*)   It is actually quite cold in here, isn't it though? Actually?

Zebedee   Are you seriously gonna – ?

Ray (*offering* **Zebedee** *one*)   Actually quite cold actually?

Zebedee   I'd rather gargle with Michael Gove's urine. Thanks though.

Ray   Ah, go on, it can't be that – (*He takes a drink and spits it out.*) See if you can get your money back.

Ryan   Fuckin' will do.

Zebedee   There's a fair-trade place round the corner. Come on, I'll show you.

Ryan   Fucking fair-trade . . .

They leave. **Ray** *shuts the door.*

Jen   Do you wanna help out, Tom?

Tom   How? I'm not going on trial if that's what –

Kelly   You know the system. Challenge us.

Jen   Tell us when we get too fanciful.

Beat.

Tom   Look, I don't . . . At the risk of sounding like a patronising ex-banker: I don't know if you really understand what you're dealing with. I live in a block of flats in Bow, and from my balcony you can see the City, squatting like a spider atop the town, daring anyone to take it on. And when you're in there, that's how you feel: where the fuck else would you want to be? I did an internship before my last year at uni, I'd never given a thought to finance before, but when you walk in, you're just like, 'Holy fuck. I want to work here.' Miles and miles of chrome and glass and a billion flickering numbers that pile up around you like snowdrifts . . . And you can press a button and change the value of the currency in Argentina. Press another one and a thousand people in Mumbai lose their jobs. Do you have any idea how good that feels? How seductive it is to know that people know you can do that to them, and are afraid of you? And even when you don't understand one fucking word of what is going on, Exhibit A, the derivatives market, which is why we had the financial crisis and are going to have another one, the outside world doesn't know that. Or have any idea how to change it. Do you really think you're going to stop all that, change the real rulers of this country, the system that keeps politicians on their knees, with (*gestures round the room*) this?

Beat.

Kelly   I don't know.

Tom (*urgent*)   Well, why not? Because they will eat everything.

Jen   We know that.

Tom   They will never ever ever change, because that is the most well-oiled machine for the extraction of value since the Roman Empire, and if a part malfunctions or starts to play up (*raises his hand*) they will have it out before you can blink. Nothing personal. (*Beat.*) I came down here because I would very much like to feel my contribution to this life was something more than making money out of pain. But if you're going to raise our hopes that things can be different, you have to give us an alternative. (*Looking around.*) Don't you?

Kelly   All my mates ask me that. And when I tell them we don't have one, yet, they look all smug. Like I failed the test, so they're allowed to keep their shit facial hair and retro T-shirts and ironic hipster detachment that masks an abyss of emptiness. Like they don't have to think.

Tom   I'm not trying to be a dick. I just . . . I need this.

Kelly   Before I came here I was a student. Anthropology. In terms of making a living you'd be better off burning twenty grand's worth of scratchcards, but totally fascinating. One of the books we read was about debt. The writer was talking to this woman about the IMF and the horrible shit it gets up to, and after he laid out that people *die* in the name of austerity, have been doing in Africa for quite some time, she just looked at him and said: 'But they have debts. They have to pay them.' And he was amazed by this, that debt has such a powerful hold on us that a perfectly reasonable woman can think it's better for people to die than for financial imbalances to be corrected. And he started to dig into why. And he concludes, five hundred pages later, that it's because our deepest social ties and obligations – to our ancestors, to the society that birthed us – we express in terms of debts. That at its deepest level, debt is our word for love.

Tom   Hah. That's quite . . . I never thought of it like that.

Kelly   Debt is our word for love. And love is the thing we're most frightened of. And you can't take on a deep, atavistic, millennia-old thing like that without a new space and a new language. It's not the answers right now, it's the questions. We are trying to learn to ask the right questions, ones that don't start with money, that start with people. Asking those questions: that's the alternative, Tom.

Jen   And it's the action. The action of doing this, of *doing* something, not just moaning. Things change because people *do things*. Ideas come mainly from actions. It's *actions* that give people the sense things can be changed.

A knock at the door.

Ray   Some rap shit.

No answer. Another knock. They look at each other.

Jen   Ryan?

A third, more insistent knock. **Jen** *nods to* **Ray** *to open the door. It opens to reveal* **McDonald Moyo** *in hi-vis jacket, hard hat and clipboard.*

McDonald   Good afternoon. Health and Safety.

Jen *goes very still.* **Ray** *is amused.*

Ray   Health and Safety?! Em, I think you've the wrong place, fella.

McDonald (*checks his clipboard*)   I don't think so.

He steps inside and begins to take stock of the place, kicking a loose floorboard and making notes. **Ray** *goes to* **Jen** *with a wry expression. She looks worried.*

Ray   The fuck is this shite?

Jen   If we fail Health and Safety they can have us out within the hour.

Ray   You serious?

Jen   It's the quickest and least violent way to dispose of an occupation.

Ray   I cannot believe, as a revolutionary autonomist movement, that we have to abide by Health and Safety legislation.

Jen   Clever bastards.

She approaches **McDonald***.*

Jen   Hi, I'm Jen.

McDonald (*not stopping his work*)   Pleased to meet you.

Jen   Can I get you a cup of tea or anything?

McDonald   No thank you.

Beat.

Jen   You know we have the right to stay?

McDonald   That's nothing to do with me. I'm here to ensure your safety.

He moves around the room, taking notes. **Jen** *and* **Kelly** *look on with concern.*

Ray   It's like *Strictly*, is it?

McDonald   Excuse me?

Ray (*nods at clipboard*)   The notes. A few friendly suggestions on improving our style. How's my cha-cha? So to speak.

McDonald *pushes past him.* **Ray** *steps in his way.*

Ray   Would you see yerself more as Bruno or Darcey, I wonder, fella?

McDonald (*looks at him*)   Excuse me.

He gestures at the other side of the room. Beat. **Ray** *steps aside.* **McDonald** *moves past him, taking more notes. Pause.*

Kelly   Listen, can we – ?

McDonald   You intend to use the venue for public gatherings?

Jen   Yes, we do.

McDonald   That adds to your responsibilities.

Kelly   How so?

McDonald   It brings into play workplace legislation. The Health and Safety at Work Act of 1974.

He kicks a loose floorboard.

Kelly   We've been –

McDonald   The Workplace (Health, Safety and Welfare) Regulations 1992 . . . (*He pulls down a wall panel.*) Dear oh dear, what kind of cowboy has done this?

Jen   Us.

Kelly   We're fixing up the place. To hold this trial.

McDonald   May I ask what qualifications you possess?

Kelly   We've made it loads nicer since we got –

McDonald   Construction qualifications.

Jen   We're building a new world, if that's any good to you.

Beat. **McDonald** *shakes his head and makes another note on the clipboard.* **Joan** *enters, wiping her hands on a rag.*

Joan   Toilets are still in a terrible state, I've been trying to – McDonald?

McDonald *stares at her and stiffens. Beat.*

McDonald   Hello.

Joan   It's me, Joan. Do you remember –

McDonald   I remember you. Yes. Hello.

Joan   You came to –

McDonald   You made me a cup of tea. Yes. Thank you. Now if you don't mind . . .

Joan *steps back, hurt.* **McDonald** *continues his work. They watch. Pause.*

Tom   Growth industry. Health and Safety.

Beat.

McDonald (*not looking at them*)   Is it?

Tom   It is, yeah. Health and Safety, prostitution and repossession.

Ray   There's a shocker.

McDonald (*looks up at* **Ray**)   Meaning?

Ray   The only way to make money these days is fucking people.

Jen   Helpful.

McDonald   Health and Safety is not fucking people. Health and Safety is helping people. It is duty of care and the protection of workers' lives. Not that people like you would know much about working.

Kelly   We've been fixing this place up for a week.

Jen   'People like you'?

McDonald   Excuse me?

Jen   'People like you', you said. What did they tell you?

McDonald   It was an expression.

Jen   The police, before you came in here. What did they tell you?

McDonald   Nobody told me anything. Just that it was an old building, and unsafe for –

Kelly   About us.

Beat. **McDonald** *flicks a look at* **Joan**. *He goes back to his work.*

Joan   McDonald –

McDonald   Please don't talk to me.

Joan   But –

McDonald   My first job, OK? This is my first job –

Joan   Just let us tell you why –

McDonald   Please, Joan.

A knock at the door.

Ryan/Zebedee (*off*)   'Think of how many weak shows you slept through – '

Ray *opens the door.* **Zebedee** *and* **Ryan** *come in with coffees, which they start to hand out.*

Ryan   'Time's up, sorry I kept you.' Got my money back from Starbucks.

Tom   How?

Ryan   Told 'em otherwise we'd occupy the shop.

Jen   Would you like a coffee?

McDonald   No, I . . .

Ryan   They even gave me some free muffins, look.

Ryan *is talking over his shoulder as he approaches* **McDonald**. *He throws out a couple of muffins, turns his head and they come face to face.* **Ryan** *drops a coffee.*

Kelly   Shit, I'm so sorry, let me…

She starts to clean up the spilled coffee. **Ryan** *is first to break away.*

Ryan (*to the group*)   Fucking come on then.

Ray   What?

Ryan   Fix up these fucking floors. Standing around like cunts. Come on!

He grabs a floorboard and a hammer and starts to beat it into place. **McDonald** *stares at him, icy cold. Beat. He turns calmly to the group.*

McDonald   As I was saying: the application of workplace legislation.

Ryan *bangs louder to try to drown him out.*

McDonald   The Provision and Use of Work Equipment Regulations 1998, the Management of Health and Safety at Work Regulations 1999, the Fire Safety Order of 2005 –

The floorboard splits. **Ryan** *holds the broken end in one hand. Beat.*

McDonald   And the adequate provision of toilets. Where are they, please?

A couple of hands point dumbly in the direction of the toilets. **McDonald** *marches off.* **Ryan** *throws the broken piece of wood viciously away.*

Zebedee   What the fuck is going on? Ryan? What –

Ryan   Don't fucking talk to me. Don't fucking talk to me, you hippy cunt.

He turns his back on them, distraught.

Kelly   Ryan, will you please tell us what's going on?

Ryan *doesn't look at them. Pause.*

Joan   I'm going to get him a cup of tea.

Ray   Oh, that should make all the fucking differ.

Joan   He likes tea. I'm going to get him a tea.

She stops by a distraught **Ryan** *as she leaves and speaks quietly into his ear.*

Joan   I don't know what you're afraid of, but I know what fear looks like. I was married to it most of my life. Don't give in.

She leaves. The rest helpless. **Zebedee** *kicks a plank in futile rage and sulks. Pause.*

Kelly   All to waste.

Tom   Where would you start?

Zebedee   What's the fucking point?

Tom   Because this will get done.

Kelly   But not here. Not in the place that's perfect for it, in front of the media, of hundreds of people who might not come back if –

Tom   But it will get done. Won't it? Or what are you doing here? If you can get knocked off course by a . . . (*Beat. Insistent.*) Where would you start?

Jen   We're starting with debt.

Ray   The debt they're always telling us we have to pay back. We don't.

Tom   Course we do.

Kelly   No, we don't. Tell him, Zeb.

Zebedee   Oh, fuck off.

Kelly   I'll do it then.

She grabs a piece of paper from his back pocket and reads from it.

'The "a government – '

Zebedee (*unsuccessfully grabbing for it back*)   Oy! That's my –

Kelly   We're a collective, aren't we?

(*Reads.*) 'The "a-government-is-like-a-family, it-has-to-balance-its-books" metaphor is a devious lie. Family debts are nothing like national debts. When times get tight – '

Zebedee   Yes, alright, alright. (*To* **Tom**.) When times get tight a government can print more currency. A family can't go up in the loft and bang out more money.

Ray   Unless your name is Harry Redknapp.

Zebedee   All an indebted government has to do to get out of trouble is make sure its debt grows more slowly than its tax base. The tax base grows, the debts fade away. It's what the Americans did after the Second World War.

Kelly   Which makes Osborne letting corporations off billions in tax, plus making people unemployed instead of taxpayers, even more insane.

Zebedee   But the main reason we don't have to pay these debts is they're not ours to pay. There's a thing called odious debt. Odious debt was legalised by the Americans after they stole Cuba from the Spanish. They didn't fancy paying Cuba's debts, so they cast around and found a fella called Alexander Nahum Sack. Sack had this doctrine of odious debt, which held that . . . Hang on...

He leans over **Kelly**'s *shoulder to consult the notes.*

Ray   Spit it out son, as the priest said to the altar boy.

Kelly   Ray.

Tom   Yeah, but the international markets –

Zebedee (*holds up a hand*)   Held that if the debt was incurred for specific rather than national interests, and the lenders knew that, 'This debt is not an obligation for the nation; it is a *regime's* debt, a personal debt of the power that incurred it.

The creditors have committed a hostile act with regard to the people.'

Jen   Sound like anywhere you know?

Zebedee   'Legally, the debts of the State must be incurred for the needs and in the interests of the people.'

Kelly   That *doesn't* sound like anywhere I know.

Zebedee   If the bank bailout was used for the benefit of a tiny clique at the expense of ordinary people, we don't have to pay it back.

Tom   Bollocks.

Zebedee   It's quite clear under international law. The UN Charter states that full employment and social and economic welfare take precedence over all other obligations, including debt repayments. The UN Human Rights Council states that 'The exercise of the basic rights of the people of debtor countries to food, housing, clothing, employment, education and health cannot be subordinated to economic reforms arising from debt.'

Tom   Yeah, but international law is largely hortatory, isn't it?

Ray   It's what?

Tom   It's there for encouragement. It's not binding.

Ray   I'll use that next time. 'Well, officer, I wasn't going to smash the bank windows in, but then I remembered that the law is largely hortatory.'

Zebedee   The principle of *force majeure* allows for cancellation of international debt on grounds of financial necessity. Under the internationally established principle of the State of Necessity, quote, 'a State cannot be expected to close its schools and universities and courts, to disband its police force and to neglect its public services to such an extent as to expose its community to chaos and anarchy, merely to provide the wherewithal to meet its moneylenders, foreign or national'.

Jen   'No democratic government can bear the long-lasting austerity exacted by international institutions.' Henry Kissinger, would you believe.

Zebedee (*scribbling the quote down*)   Where'd you get that one?

Jen   Wikipedia.

Zebedee *stops writing and grimaces.*

Jen   Ah go on, fuck it, no one'll know the difference.

Tom   If you tried that in any serious way, the markets would rip you apart. A run on the currency, bond spreads go up, cost of borrowing through the roof –

Ray   Not necessarily. I give you the case of Ecuador.

Tom   Give me the case of Ecuador.

Ray   So the Ecuadorians took a squizz round and thought, 'Funny, all this "aid" all these years and the president is covered in gold leaf and we've one spare pair of undies for the entire country,' and decided to carry out a debt audit. They came to the conclusion that seventy per cent of the debt had disappeared up a fat man's nose, and they wrote it off. They offered their creditors thirty cents in the dollar. What's that they say on the pension adverts? 'The value of your investment may go down as well as up.'

Zebedee   And ninety-five per cent of the creditors took it. Because that's how you deal with markets. You bully them. You do not let them bully you.

Kelly   In Mesopotamia, three thousand years ago, they held a Debt Jubilee every seven years. The clay tablets recording the debts were publicly smashed and the slate wiped clean. Because even the Mesopotamian equivalents of George Osborne had enough sense to realise that the repression of an ever growing percentage of the population can't, in the long run, be sustained. And out of self-interest if nothing else, they let the debt go.

Jen   There's a beautiful thing happening right now called the Rolling Jubilee. People are pooling money, buying up poor people's debt for pennies on the dollar, and abolishing it. Just poof! Letting it go, getting their fellow citizens out from under the thumb. Look it up online.

Pause.

Tom   Why don't I know all this stuff?

Ray   The point of an Oxford education, old boy, is not 'to learn', it's 'not to learn'.

Tom   I was at Cambridge.

Jen   You know it now.

Tom   But if all that's true . . .

Jen   Yes?

Tom   And we don't have to pay this money back?

Jen   Yes?

Tom   Then why are we doing it?

Jen   Oh, well that one's easy.

Ray (*making his fingers into guns*)   Stick 'em up! It's a robbery!

Zebedee   Austerity doesn't 'work' because it's not supposed to 'work'. Or rather, it's not supposed to fix things. What it is supposed to do, and this it's doing rather well, is to transfer an overwhelming amount of money and power to a tiny elite. It's a coup, mate. It's the same thing they did to Russia, to Latin America, the same thing the World Bank's been doing to Africa for decades and calling it 'development'. It's a *heist*: the greatest heist in the history of the modern world.

Pause.

Jen   You see the alternative now? (*Taps her head.*) Starts up here.

Kelly (*to* **Jen**)   I see how you do it now.

Tom   But . . . you have such an obvious agenda, it makes it hard to –

Ray   An agenda?! Of course we have an agenda. Everybody's got an agenda. You think *The King's Speech* didn't have an agenda? 'How tough it is to be the king. Aaaah. Kings are people too.' Fuck off. If it's so fucking hard to be the king, I've an idea for you: r-r-r-r-r-resign. a-a-a-a-a-abdicate. And while you're at it, d-d-d-d-d-dissolve the fucking monarchy, ya cunt.

Tom   It was a shit film.

Ray   *Downton* fucking *Abbey*: 'Wouldn't it be nice if we all went back to the nineteenth century, when men were men and poor people were raped in the scullery?' There's nothing without an agenda, Tommy.

Jen   That is where they wanna take us, Tom. Back to the Victorians: an aristo elite giving charity to the deserving poor and incarceration to the undeserving poor. The basic project of the people in charge of this country is to undo the twentieth century, and we are not going to let them do that. We are going to fight them, brick by brick and bone by bone.

McDonald *enters, writing on his clipboard. He looks over his notes. Turns over a page. And another. And another. And another, for effect. There's a lot of notes.*

McDonald   Well. Thank you for your co-operation.

He starts to move towards the door. A knock. He stops.

Joan (*off*)   'It's been a long time, I shouldn't have left you. Without a strong rhyme to step to.'

Ray *opens the door, giggling a bit despite the situation.*

Ray   You're a one, aren't you Joan?

Joan   There is a code. I used the code. (*Hands* **McDonald** *a cup of tea.*) Tea.

McDonald   I don't want –

Joan   Two sugars.

Beat. He takes the tea. She gestures at **Ryan**.

Joan   We'll leave you to it.

McDonald   I don't –

She shrugs at him, gestures to the group and they slip away, leaving **McDonald** *and* **Ryan**. *Pause.*

Ryan   You're waiting for my apology.

McDonald   I don't give a fuck what you say.

Ryan   You do though. Or you'd be gone.

They make eye contact for the first time.

It's not just me, you know. Lot of people have put a lot of work into this.

McDonald   So what?

Ryan   You can't punish them for what I did.

McDonald   I can do whatever I want. I can do *whatever* I want.

Ryan   Then go. Door's open.

Beat. He nods towards where the group has gone.

They're alright, these.

McDonald   I don't care.

Ryan   They're brave. They stand up and say, 'This is what I want.' I've never said that to anyone.

McDonald   You want me to feel *sorry* – ?!

Ryan   It makes you vulnerable. Gives people something to hurt you with. We'd do anything not to be hurt, most of us. (*Beat.*) I am sorry for what I did to you.

McDonald   If that is your apology, I do not accept it.

Ryan   That's up to you.

McDonald   In any form I do not accept it.

Ryan   Up to you. (*Beat.*) This is what I want: I want this thing to go ahead. Please.

McDonald *pulls back his shirt to reveal a colostomy bag. Beat.*

Ryan   Is that permanent?

McDonald   They don't know. (*Beat.*) Do you know how much work I lost? This is my first job and now you, *you* of all people want me to . . . My child was barred from school because –

He shoves **Ryan** *aside and makes for the door.* **Ryan** *grabs him.*

Ryan   Just listen, please.

McDonald   No! Why should I? Who listened to me, who cared for me all those nights in the hospital, all those mornings in the freezing rain clearing up other people's shit and puke and blood? Why should I care about this godforsaken country when it has never, for one moment, cared for me? (*Beat.*) *Why?*

Ryan   You don't know these people.

McDonald   What do they know?

Ryan   Why don't you ask them?

McDonald   What do they know about life? About suffering?

Ryan   Is it a competition? What's the prize?

McDonald   Every day now I look over my shoulder. I sweat and I shudder in crowds. I look at everyone, every man, every white man, as an enemy, because of you. You have ruined this country for me. You have narrowed my world.

Ryan   I'm sorry.

McDonald   I do not accept it.

Ryan   Then let me give you something else.

McDonald   Ccch! I won't take your money.

Ryan   The chance to do to me what I did to you.

Beat. **McDonald** *stares at him.*

McDonald   I don't carry a knife.

Ryan   I'm on probation. Anything kicks off, I'm back to bang up. You can say I assaulted you, abused you, whatever, they'll believe it.

McDonald *moves away.* **Ryan** *grabs his arm.*

Ryan   Alright. Listen. *Please*. If you shut this place down, where do you think I go?

McDonald   I don't *care* –

Ryan   You know where I go. You've been there.

McDonald   Where you belong.

Ryan   Where I belong. Yes. The people I know. The things I know how to do. What you said: a narrow world. If I go back to that pub, I am never coming out. If there isn't something else, if I can't *imagine* something else whether it's this or something different but the *possibility* of something else, I am never coming out. I'm asking you, one man to another, not to send me back there. (*Beat.*) There it is. I'm in your hands, mate.

Long pause.

McDonald   What is it you want to do?

Ryan   A trial.

McDonald   A trial?

Ryan   Yeah. (*Beat.*) Can I tell you about it?

Beat. **McDonald** *sips his tea. The others creep tentatively into the room.*

Lights slowly down.

Blackout.

Black Jesus

This play is dedicated to Louise-Mai Newberry,
who understands love despite the harshness
of the past like nobody else.
And has a lot of feist.

Acknowledgements

This one took some time and even more than most plays, a lot
of people to make happen. Thanks first of all to Gilbert Douglas
and Tumbuka Dance Company, the brilliant Zimbabwean
dance crew I met in Malawi in 2008, who gave me my first
real insights into Zim. That autumn the Tristan Bates Theatre
gave Chipo Chung, David Thacker, Nat Martello-White and
me a week to devise the rudiments of a play. Phil Clark
organised a showing of that early effort at an Oxford University
conference on post-conflict societies. Miles Tendi provided
insight and a copy of his excellent book before it was published.

In 2010, the British Council flew me to Zimbabwe to develop
the play further and take it to the Harare International
Festival of Arts (HIFA). Fay Chung generously gave me both
her remarkable knowledge and a place to sleep, and Chipo
took me to meet a range of people from government figures to
peace and reconciliation groups. Zimbabwean company Fourth
World Productions added extra material to my existing text
and took it, entitled *You Cannot Escape Our Love*, to HIFA that
year, directed by Jonathan Holmes.

At that stage my intent was to use the play and the relatively
safe space of HIFA to bring up a lot of heavy and horrible
things that had happened in Zimbabwe, things Zimbabweans
themselves lacked the opportunity to talk about. The show
provoked incredibly powerful reactions, not so much because
of the skill of the play but because the suffering people had
been through was acknowledged. The problem was that made
it a pretty tough play to watch! It was David Mercatali, the
director, who encouraged me to revisit something I'd put away.
Black Jesus is still quite unflinching in its look at the effects of
violence, but is a little more philosophical, thinking through the
human complexity of damaged societies and how any of us deal
with the failures and traumas of the past. It's got a resonance
beyond Zimbabwe now, though with a bit of luck it's also
pretty accurate about Zim too. And most of all, it's hopeful.

Anders Lustgarten, September 2013

Black Jesus was first performed at the Finborough Theatre, London, on 1 October 2013 with the following cast and creative team:

Eunice   Debbie Korley
Gabriel   Paapa Essiedu
Rob   Alexander Gatehouse
Moyo   Cyril Nri

Director   David Mercatali
Set and Costume Designer   Max Dorey
Lighting Designer   Howard Hudson
Sound Designer   Max Pappenheim

Characters

Eunice
Gabriel
Rob
Moyo

The action takes place in Zimbabwe, 2015.

Scene One

Zimbabwe, 2015. A battered interview room in a high-level detention centre. A worn table with a pot plant on it. On one side sits **Gabriel Chibamu**, *mid-twenties, with a powerful presence developed from years of keeping his guard up in jail. He stares at* **Eunice Ncube** *on the other side of the table.* **Eunice**, *same age, has files and a bottle of water in front of her. She is flustered, intimidated by* **Gabriel** *and the situation.*

Beat. She moves the pot plant to one side to get a better look at him. He moves it back. Beat. She moves it. He moves it back. Beat.

Eunice   Mr Chibamu –

Gabriel   My name is Gabriel. Like the angel.

Beat. She moves the pot plant.

Eunice   So I can see you.

He shrugs. She looks at her files.

There is a lot of material here.

Gabriel   We were busy.

Eunice   So I see.

Gabriel   Busy and hard-working.

Eunice   I would like to begin by asking you about the killing of –

Gabriel   I am not allowed visitors.

Eunice   I am aware of that.

Gabriel   For their security.

She takes a quick involuntary peek over her shoulder for a guard, but there is none. He smiles.

But they made me see you.

Eunice   I have explained why I am here.

Gabriel   I know why you are here. For the same reason the police always come.

Eunice   We are a completely independent body. Nothing to do with the police.

Gabriel   You will not share our little chat with them?

Eunice   I don't talk to the police.

Gabriel   What did you bring me?

Eunice   I'm sorry?

Gabriel   Cigarettes, money, what did you bring me?

Eunice   I'm not allowed to give you anything.

Gabriel   And who told you that?

Beat.

Eunice (*reluctantly*)   The police.

He sits back, knowing he's on top. Pause.

Eunice   I want to ask you about the killing of Lloyd Musiwa –

Gabriel   Give me the water.

Eunice   Mr Chibamu –

Gabriel   Give me the water.

Beat. She passes him the bottle of water. He swigs greedily from it.

We get one cup of water a day.

Eunice   I'm sorry.

Gabriel   No. You are not.

Eunice   The killing of Lloyd Musiwa.

Gabriel   Lloyd Musiwa was an MDC sell-out whose fate was earned.

Eunice (*reading from notes*)   Mr Musiwa was attacked on the night of 4 June 2008 by a group of four men, commanded by you.

Gabriel   What is a pretty girl like you doing in a place like this?

Eunice   You entered Mr Musiwa's house by force at 10.30 p.m. In the course of the struggle, Mr Musiwa was tied to a chair and his eyes were gouged out using a sharp implement, in all probability a hunting knife. His jugular vein was severed and –

Gabriel   Put a little life into it, for God's sake. You read it like you are reading a car repair manual.

Eunice   We are talking about a man's death.

Gabriel   But why are we talking about it, Miss . . . ?

Eunice   Ncube. My name is Eunice Ncube.

Gabriel   Why are we talking about it, Miss Ncube? That is my question to you.

She leans forward.

Eunice   The Truth and Justice Commission is an unprecedented event in the history of Zimbabwe. It is our first real opportunity to confront the violence and bloodshed which blighted our past, to establish responsibility for the human rights violations –

Gabriel   They said if I talk to you I can get out.

Eunice   The Truth and Justice Commission is a golden chance for real justice, for we Zimbabweans to confront the past so we no longer have to live in the past. You are in a unique position to help because of what you know about the operations of the youth militia, better known as the Green Bombers, and who ordered and co-ordinated –

Gabriel (*forcefully*)   They said if I talk to you I can get out.

Beat.

Eunice   There is a possibility that in return for your co-operation –

Gabriel   A *possibility* – ?

Eunice   That the courts will look upon your case with greater leniency. I cannot guarantee that.

Beat.

Gabriel   Are you quite mad?

Eunice   I do not have the authority to –

Gabriel   You come to me with nothing, no cigarettes, no promises, only windy talk of 'justice', and you think I will dig my own grave for you?

Eunice   You will go on trial one day.

Gabriel   And I will give them *nothing*.

Eunice   It is likely the courts will look favourably on your co-operation –

Gabriel   I am not a warbler or a bulbul bird, to sing sweetly for others' pleasure.

Eunice   Things are not the same as before. You have the chance to do something for yourself, to give yourself the possibility of hope –

Gabriel   Do you know who I am, Miss Ncube?

Eunice   You were called Black Jesus.

Gabriel   And do you know why I am called by that name? Because I decided who would be saved and who would be condemned. I took that responsibility for others and now I take it for myself. I am Black Jesus. I do not crawl.

Beat.

Eunice   If not yourself, then I hoped you might want to help your country.

Gabriel   Why should I help my country when my country has never helped me? How many generals, how many politicians are in this place with us? Can you name them?

Eunice   That is why I need your assistance.

Gabriel   There is only us, the dirty boys, the high-density filth they used to do their bloodwork and then hung up in the streets to say 'Look how much better we are now! Give us money!' But even so *we* are the ones who must help our country! (*Beat. He looks away.*) When the hour is up you will leave. But until then let us be silent, Miss Ncube. Where I live, it is never silent.

He enjoys the silence. Pause. She starts to collect her things, then looks up at him.

Eunice   How long have you been here, Mr Chibamu?

Gabriel (*irritated*)   Look in your file.

Eunice   Five years. No trial. No prospect of a trial.

He shrugs.

The world outside has changed very much in that time. The politicians you speak of, the men who ordered you to do what you did, no longer talk of sell-outs and puppets. Now they speak of constitutions and 'free and fair' elections. They are burying you alive, Mr Chibamu. You did their bloodwork, just as you say, and now they are leaving you here to rot.

Gabriel   And you think they will let your Commission do anything? Intellectuals are the stupidest people.

Eunice   They are the ones who set it up. To prove to the world they are 'reformed'. They don't think it can harm them. I think differently.

She gets through to him for the first time. He studies her for a long moment.

Gabriel   Who is behind you?

Eunice   How do you mean?

Gabriel   Who pulls your strings, Miss Ncube?

Eunice   It's not like that now. You are out of date.

Gabriel   Answer my question.

Eunice   The Commission has the support of the government, the international community –

Gabriel *breaks into a broad grin.*

Gabriel   Aaah, it is the whites! I knew it! They do not give up, the colonialists, is it?

Eunice   This is nothing to do with –

Gabriel   They are like cell cockroaches – very persistent, no matter how much you smash them.

Eunice   This is for we Zimbabweans –

Gabriel   Your boss in this Commission: is he white? (*Beat.*) I thought so. Ask him something. Ask him if he thinks truth and justice are the same thing.

Scene Two

Eunice *in the office of her boss,* **Rob Palmer***, a good-looking white Zimbabwean only a decade or so older than her. He is watching the news on television.*

Rob   It's a bloody good question.

Eunice   The man is far from stupid.

Rob   Maybe we should hire him. Black Jesus, Truth and Justice Commissioner.

Eunice   Please don't call him that.

Rob   It's no weirder than some of the others we've got on board.

His phone goes. He glances at it, rejects the call and waves at the TV.

You make a halfwit sidekick with a thirst for power your junior partner, you dump all the shitty policies on his head, and bingo – five more years in charge. Do you think Mugabe got the idea from Cameron or the other way round?

Eunice   Chibamu is a no-go.

Rob   Maybe Mugabe and Cameron are the same person. Similar attitudes to democracy. You never see them at the same time, do you?

Eunice   He's too angry and suspicious to tell me anything.

Rob   Go back and see him again.

Eunice   It's pointless.

Rob   You think I'd do any better?

Eunice (*smiling*)   Probably not.

Rob   There's always a way in. Ego. Vengeance. Guilty conscience. Keep trying different wrenches till the nut pops free.

Eunice   I'm not a plumber, Rob.

Rob   That is exactly what we are, Eunice. The plumbers of the new Zimbabwe, flushing away the accumulated shit of the past. Gotta get your hands dirty sometimes.

Eunice   He scares me.

Beat.

Rob   I got a phone call today.

Eunice   Who from?

Rob   A man with a scratchy voice.

Eunice   What did he say?

Rob   That I had a green Mazda.

Eunice   OK.

Rob   A green Mazda with a flat front tyre. And I should check it the next time I got into it. To make sure it was safe. I asked him should I check it every time. 'Your system of car maintenance I will leave up to you, Mr Rob Palmer.' I hung up, and I went outside and checked it, and sure enough it was stone flat. Which was odd, because I drove it here not ten minutes before and it was absolutely fine.

Beat.

Eunice   Weren't you scared?

Rob   Of course I was scared, I was bloody shitting myself! I was sweating like a paedophile in a playground.

Eunice   I'm sure the head of a respected human rights organisation isn't supposed to say such things.

Rob   And if I meet the head of a *respected* human rights organisation, I'll tell him so. Chibamu is the key here. If we're going to push this thing beyond the boundaries they want to put on it, he's the one who'll take us there. We know it and they know it.

His phone goes again. He guiltily rejects the call again.

Eunice   Who is it?

Rob   It's, er, it's Thandekile.

Eunice   What does she want?

Rob   She's my wife, she's entitled to call me.

Eunice   I wasn't saying she –

Rob   Tonight's our seventh wedding anniversary.

Eunice   Rob, it's 8 p.m.!

Rob   I've been working. It's . . . I don't know. We're ships in the night these days, you know?

Beat. He grabs his coat and stands.

You're right, I should go.

Eunice   I didn't say that.

Beat. He doesn't go. **Eunice** *nods at phone.*

How is she? Thandekile?

Rob   She doesn't like it here. She says Zimbabweans are too full of themselves.

Eunice   Ha! She should know about that, she's South African.

Rob   You know what she asked me the other night? If I was trying to get my brother's farm back.

Eunice   Ouch.

Rob   Ja. My brother of course wants to know why I'm helping the thieving kaffirs.

Eunice   The burdens of the white liberal.

Rob (*grins*)   It's a hard life.

Eunice   You don't have to go home.

Rob   No, I –

Eunice   We could go somewhere.

Beat.

Rob   It's my seventh wedding anniversary, Eunice.

Eunice   So you said.

Rob   I can't . . . with you . . . on my seventh –

Eunice   Fine, go then. Go home to your wife.

Rob   Don't be like –

Eunice   I'm not –

Rob   We said –

Eunice   I know we did. It was my idea to stop. (*Beat.*) I shouldn't have . . . Get her something nice.

Rob   I will. I have, actually.

Eunice   Oh? What did you get?

Beat.

Rob   Look, take this for what it's worth, bush radio and all that, but Endurance Moyo is sniffing around the commission.

Eunice   What?!

Rob   The shifting sands of Zimbo politics.

Eunice   They can't let *Moyo* be involved! He should be in there with the rest of them!

Rob   What I've always said: a bad commission is worse than no commission at all, because if you raise people's hopes and then dash them, they're ten times as angry. (*Beat.*) Go say howzit another time to Chibamu, will you? While we still can.

He leaves. Beat. Blackout.

Scene Three

The interview room. **Gabriel** *is slowly eating the leaves of the pot plant one by one.*

Eunice   Next case. The abduction and torture of Constance Chimwanda.

She looks at him to gauge his reaction but there is none. Beat. She reads from a file.

Constance Chimwanda was taken from her home in Gweru on 18 June 2008 –

Gabriel   I am glad you came back.

Eunice *looks up, her face full of hope.*

Gabriel   The prison diet is lacking in green vegetables. This plant is much appreciated. Would you care for a leaf?

He holds the plant out and laughs to see her scowl. She continues.

Eunice   Constance Chimwanda was abducted by a gang of men, again led by you, and taken to a remote farmhouse, where she was systematically raped, beaten –

Gabriel (*singing*)   'The Blair that I know is a toilet!'

Eunice   Beaten and tortured, including the pouring of boiling plastic –

Gabriel   'The Blair that I know is a toilet! The Blair that I know is a toilet!'

Eunice   The pouring of boiling plastic into her vagina.

Gabriel   That was my favourite of all the election jingles.

Pause.

Eunice   Why did you do those things, Mr Chibamu? Were you ordered to do them?

Gabriel   Are you married, Miss Ncube?

Eunice   Who gave you the orders?

Gabriel   You do not have the look of a married woman. You look like the girls I met coming through the villages with a hundred men at my heels – afraid, but excited too.

Eunice   This is not –

Gabriel   Soon to give in. Despite themselves.

Eunice   This is not the place for personal affairs.

Gabriel   What are you asking me?

Eunice   I am asking you about professional matters, not personal.

Gabriel   They are personal to me.

Beat.

Eunice   How do you decide to pour hot plastic into a woman's body?

Gabriel   My job was to get people to tell me things. I was the best at my job.

Eunice   Really?

Gabriel   Yes! The best! Many many subversions were stopped because of crucial information I found.

Eunice   I see. What did she tell you, Constance?

Gabriel   Many things. Very many useful things.

Eunice   Useful enough to make *that* worthwhile?

He shrugs.

Somehow I doubt it.

Gabriel   Constance Chimwanda was organising the MDC to steal the election –

Eunice   Not according to her file. It says here she was married to a senior member of the MDC but she herself had no political involvement.

Gabriel   Your papers do not know.

Eunice   She spent her days on shopping and shoes. So what could she tell you?

Gabriel   I know. I was there.

Eunice   People misunderstand torture. They think it's to get information. It's not, it's the opposite. Torture is to destroy information, destroy the ability to think or understand, and to replace them with frozen terror and obedience.

Gabriel   How would you know this? What have you ever done?

Eunice   That was your job, Mr Chibamu.

Gabriel (*contemptuous*)   Intellectual.

Eunice   You weren't a gatherer of information.

Gabriel   Intellectual!

Eunice   You were a bludgeon. A set of human electrodes. One step up from a dog.

Gabriel   'We Zimbabweans!'

Eunice   What?

Gabriel   'We Zimbabweans,' you said last time. 'A process for we Zimbabweans!'

Eunice   I am from Zimbabwe.

Gabriel (*in Shona*)   'But not from my part of Zimbabwe. Mufakose. The poor part.'

Eunice   I do not speak Shona. That does not mean I am not −

Gabriel   I said, you are not from my part of Zimbabwe. Mufakose. The poor part.

Beat.

Eunice   You are a clever man, Mr Chibamu.

Gabriel   Thank you. Yes, I am.

Eunice   Since you are so clever, tell me: how will the rest of us, those who are not from Mufakose, understand you if you do not tell us about what you did?

Gabriel   Why should I care? You will not understand.

Eunice   Because I am not a 'real' Zimbabwean? But I know why you do not sleep. Why you have the haunted look. Hmmm? *Ngozi.*

He jerks back in his chair.

Who haunts you at night, Gabriel? Is it Constance Chimwanda? Does she come through the door screaming?

He hurls the pot plant at her. It crashes against the door. She shrieks and jumps up.

Gabriel   You will not understand! Nobody will ever understand!

Eunice   Why did you pour the plastic?

Gabriel   Do not harass me!

Eunice   Why did you cut the eyes?

Gabriel   You do not think! This is a knife, these are eyes, the two must meet! (*Beat.*) Sometimes the orders were quite vague. Some of the senior commanders had a taste for metaphor. They said he had seen too much and should see no more. I . . .

He slumps back, rage gone. Pause. She cautiously retakes her seat.

Eunice   Tell me about them. The senior commanders.

Gabriel   No.

Eunice   You say they gave you orders. In which case these events are not wholly your fault, the responsibility for them should be shared –

Gabriel   You will not take my pride away.

Eunice   I don't –

Gabriel   My father, from when I was a very little boy, he always told me to stand behind what I had done. Not to find excuses. 'Do not whine, Gabriel, be strong and accept your fate. It is a question of honour.'

Eunice   But when you talk to him now, he must tell you not to –

Gabriel   My father is long dead and you will not take away the thing he left me.

Beat.

Eunice (*to herself*)   And then he did this and ran.

Gabriel   Eh?

Eunice   Nothing. (*Beat.*) My father told me the same thing, that's all.

Gabriel   Who was he, your father?

Eunice   I told you, this is not the place for personal –

Gabriel   Some MDC intellectual, I am sure.

Eunice   My father was a member of Zanu-PF for many years, as a matter of fact.

Gabriel   Eh, is it?! So was mine! What was his name?

She makes a show of closing her files and capping her pen. Beat.

Eunice   Gabriel, I do not understand you, and I am one of maybe three people in the country who *wants* to understand you. The rest of the world thinks you are a monster and that you and all you did should be buried and forgotten as quickly as possible.

Gabriel   I am not a monster.

Eunice   I did not say you were.

Gabriel   I am a man. Like any other.

Eunice   The only way you can prove that is to talk to me.

Beat.

Gabriel   You want my horror stories, my monster's confession. Then you will leave.

Eunice   I want the truth. Unless you tell me the truth, they will bury it, and you, for ever. Please. Talk to me.

Pause. He nods. Blackout.

Scene Four

Rob's *office. He is bloodied and bruised and drinking a beer.* **Eunice** *rushes in.*

Eunice   Rob, I made a real breakthrough with Chibamu. He –

She stops dead as she sees him. Beat.

Rob   On the bright side, I don't have to worry about driving that fucking car again.

Eunice   What happened?

Rob   Side-swiped. Coming down the Avondale Road. Big Jeep with tinted windows pulls out of a blind bend and hits me before I can blink.

Eunice   Who was it?

Rob   They didn't leave a card. If they send me a Facebook friend request I'll let you know though.

Eunice   Was it deliberate?

Rob   Who knows? They didn't have plates, I saw that. (*He swigs.*) Fuck it, I can use the insurance money anyway.

She gently inspects his injuries.

Eunice   Are you OK?

Rob   Whiplash, scratches, nothing serious.

Eunice   I mean, are you OK?

Rob   Eunice, all my life these fucking people have been trying to write me out of the history of my country. I am African, I am Zimbabwean just as much as them.

Eunice   You don't have to prove anything, Rob.

Rob   I may not have been 'bloodied in the bush', but I can be bloodied now if I have to be.

Eunice   That's not what our job is about.

Rob   I won't be run off. I *belong* here.

His hand shakes involuntarily and he spills some of his beer.

Rob   Jesus, this fucking hand, it won't stop –

Eunice   You're in shock, we should get you to –

Rob   Tell me about Chibamu.

Eunice   Forget Chibamu, it can wait –

Rob   It can't wait –

Eunice   You need medical –

Rob   It can't wait! (*Beat.*) It's worth it, right? All this?

Eunice   How can we say? It's *necessary*.

Rob   Because it has to be, doesn't it? To make all the shit we've gone through, all the stuff we, I've, got wrong, it has to be worth it. Because if it's not I don't know what I'm going to do –

She puts a finger very gently to his lips. They're almost in each other's arms.

Look, I know it's not . . . But . . . I don't suppose that offer still stands, does it? (*Beat.*) I need you, Eunice.

Beat. She nods. Lights slowly down as they begin to kiss.

Scene Five

In the interview room.

Gabriel   I joined the Green Bombers for an education. I got the best marks at school and my mother hoped I could go to university. But at that time it was impossible for a boy from Mufakose unless first you passed the Green Bombers. So I went to camp.

Eunice   How did you find the camp?

Gabriel   I enjoyed it.

Eunice   You *enjoyed* it?

Gabriel   Why would I not?

Eunice   Others have mentioned beatings, rapes –

Gabriel   There were girls there, yes, many of them. They gave us food. We had parties.

Eunice   Parties?

Gabriel   The *pungwes*.

Eunice   The indoctrination sessions.

Gabriel   Indoctrination? This is the sell-outs filling your head with rubbish again. I loved the *pungwes*. They lasted all night and they would give us *dagga* and alcohol and teach us about the history of Zimbabwe. It was very educational.

Eunice   I can imagine.

Gabriel   For example, did you know the white Rhodesians are working with the British to take control of Zimbabwe again?

Eunice   I did not know that. That is because it is not true.

Gabriel   Psssh! Why did the British not pay us the compensation they promised?

Eunice   Because of what Zanu-PF was doing, the land seizures, displacements –

Gabriel   Seizing the land that was stolen from us in the past! But we are supposed to pay the thieves to get it back? If I steal your car, will you pay me for it?

Eunice   If you steal twenty cars in the name of the people and keep them while the people ride the bus, I'll call you a thief, because that is what you are.

Gabriel   You went to university?

Eunice   I did.

Gabriel   No camps for you, is it, Miss Ncube?

Beat.

Eunice   No camps for me. Please continue.

Gabriel   After a time the crowd at the *pungwe* would become very whipped up, you know, very intense, and those were the times that anything could happen. A boy would accuse another boy of being a supporter of MDC and both of them would go into the circle. The crowd was the judge. The atmosphere was like a summer storm – so hot and you never knew which way the electricity would strike!

Eunice   Were you in the circle?

Gabriel   Many times! Often I would knock the other boy down even before he opened his mouth. I was the strong man when I went in there.

Eunice   To keep yourself safe, keep trouble away?

He shrugs.

And that worked? Because I was told the camp instructors made an example of the strong ones.

Beat.

Gabriel   You do not know what you are talking about.

Eunice   In what ways did they make an example –

Gabriel (*hissing*)   That is all I will say to you about that. (*Beat. Pained.*) You rake my ashes to find things to burn me with.

Eunice   Tell me about your first mission. (*Beat.*) I need you to tell me about your first mission, Gabriel.

Pause.

Gabriel   They load you into a truck without your normal cohort, with older, more experienced men, and they blindfold you. You bump and twist along the rutted roads, your mind running through all the possibilities of where you will go, what you will be asked to do, but when they shove you from the truck and take off the blindfold, at first you do not recognise the place they have taken you. It comes to you in pieces. That is where my grandmother would prepare the *sadza* and relish, and the smell would make my stomach jump. That is where for the very first time I and a girl . . . (*Beat.*) Your first mission is to your home, to your family. I had an uncle who was an MDC sell-out and I had to beat him right there in the yard, in front of all his relatives, under the baobab tree where I cut my knee when I was five years old. He screamed from humiliation more than the pain. After that there was no going back. You have only one family, and it is the family of the Green Bombers.

Pause.

Eunice (*gently*)   Who gave you the order for your first mission?

Gabriel   The captain's name was Matongo. Josephas Matongo. After my initiation we became friends. He said I had an intuition.

Eunice   But he was not the key man.

Gabriel   No. There were others above him.

Eunice   Like who?

Blackout.

Scene Six

Eunice *enters the interview room. She stops in shock as she sees not* **Gabriel** *but* **Endurance Moyo**, *government minister. He greets her warmly.*

Moyo   Hello, Eunice!

Eunice   Where – ?

Moyo   Chibamu will not be attending today's session. An incident in the prison yard.

Eunice   Is he – ?

Moyo   I saw bodies but did not have occasion to inquire whose. Look at you! Is not the unfolding of life a beautiful thing? When last I saw you, you were no more than a little bud, your true colours only peeping through. And now you have blossomed.

Eunice   Zimbabwe is rich in fertiliser. At the top if not at the grass roots.

Moyo   How are you, my dear?

Eunice   I am well, thank you, Minister Moyo.

Moyo   No need to be so formal, Eunice. I am here to see you in a personal capacity.

Eunice   You are here to see *me*?

Moyo   My dear friend's daughter? Why else would I be here? Please. Take a seat.

Beat. She sits. He observes her. Beat.

How are you finding the Black Jesus? They say he is a tricky customer.

Eunice   Compared to some, I find him quite straightforward.

Moyo   I hope you will not suffer from, what do they call it, Stockholm Syndrome, where you start to identify with the wrong people.

Eunice   Minister Moyo, with respect, I'm not sure it's proper for you to be −

Moyo   The Commission is a government-sponsored process. So it is wholly proper for the government, in the person of myself, to take an interest in it. Is it not?

Eunice   I don't identify with anyone. I am here to do my job.

Moyo   And a most valuable job it is. You know, Eunice, you are wasted at this level. With your qualifications. I could use someone of your renowned acuity in my office.

Eunice   Thank you, Minister, no.

Moyo   A policy director. A shaper of the country's future.

Eunice   I am happy here.

Moyo   As you wish. (*Pause. He ruminates.*) Truth. And justice. My son Josiah – You remember little Josiah, you used to play kiss-chase with –

Eunice   I remember Josiah.

Moyo   He is at Princeton now. Big strapping boy. He is studying political science. They have him reading comic books. *Batman*, you know?! For his university studies! I am thinking of asking for my money back.

Eunice   I don't –

Moyo   'Signs and signifiers', some such nonsense as this. They do not believe in the truth any more, you see. In the West. Where they are always telling us we must 'deal with the truth of our violent history'. But for themselves, no. Only in symbols, shadows, approximations of the truth. Is it any surprise that the Chinese are kicking their bottoms?! Are you a post-modernist, Eunice?

Eunice   No, Minister.

Moyo   Neither am I. You get on an African bus, there are no post-modernists. It's hot or it's not. The fucking bus gets where it is going or it does not. There is no room on it for Foucault!

Eunice *can't suppress a slight smile. Moyo smiles back.*

Moyo   I also believe in the truth. Like you. The question for me is how it is used.

She's caught off-guard.

To what ends do you foresee the Commission's report being applied?

Eunice   I don't understand.

Moyo   Who has asked to read the report before it is even published? The British, the Americans, Amnesty International . . . Why do you think these people want to be involved in the internal affairs of the new Zimbabwe?

Eunice   A belief in human rights, in holding people to account –

Moyo   Ask the people of Iraq or Afghanistan about the West's belief in human rights. There were no human rights in this country for people like you and me until *we fought for them.* Until we ripped them from Western hands. Let me put it another way: why do they want to know what happened to us in recent years, but they did not want to know at the time of *Gukurahundi*? It is a nice touch, by the way, the Ndebele name.

Eunice   I –

Moyo   Why, Ms Ncube, when Zimbabwe took the West's Structural Adjustment Programme and protected their white farmers, we were Africa's shining light, but when we went our own way we were called a 'human rights disaster'? Why, after starving us half to death with sanctions, do they suddenly care about us, Eunice?

Eunice   Not everyone operates solely out of self-interest, Minister.

Moyo   Forgive me: we're talking about the *British*, yes? Zimbabwe now is a wounded man in a hospital bed: we need rest and healing. Too much picking at our wounds, by people whose medical objectivity may be in some doubt, could let in germs.

Eunice   Is that what you think of me? A germ?

Moyo   Eunice! Is that what you think of *me*? I have dandled you on my knee and cleaned the grass off your lollipop when you dropped it. Remember that.

Eunice   I was a child. I do not remember.

Moyo   But I do. I am talking to you as a friend. Knowledge is an explosive device designed to blow up somebody's building, somebody's bridge. The only question is whose.

Eunice   So you would rather we covered up everything? Let all the murders and rapes and beatings go unpunished, unacknowledged?

Moyo   What I'm asking you is, in whose interest is it for those things to be revealed?

Eunice   And what I am asking you, Minister, is in whose interest is it for those things to be suppressed?

Moyo   Are you not tired of reading only of Africa's failures, our massacres? Seeing white people tutting over their newspapers at endless black violence?

Eunice   I do not make the events. I look into them.

Moyo   When will Zimbabwe's face stop being a Black Jesus, the killer the world loves to think we are? When will we receive the praise and respect we are due?

Eunice   Perhaps when we stop torturing our political opponents?

Moyo   The events of 2008 were regrettable, no one is arguing that.

Eunice   Regrettable?!

Moyo   Yet history has proven us correct to take such measures.

Eunice   This mentality is why we need a real commission.

Moyo   The MDC, with its limitless longing for belongings, accumulated mountains of extravagances and lakes of luxuries once in power, just as we said they would –

Eunice   I wonder where they learned that.

Moyo   Their policies are neo-liberal and their leader would sleep with a goat if she wore enough Prada. Their bolt is shot. We won the last election freely and fairly.

Eunice   Twice as many police voted Zanu-PF as exist in the entire country.

Moyo   We introduced a constitution, brought in outside observers.

Eunice   Dead people voted. Some of them twice.

Moyo   We won overwhelmingly. Of course we tweaked the results a little, but that was only for enjoyment. A lovely little cherry on the top. We would have triumphed in any case. You are young, and urban, and you underestimate the love of our people, especially the older and the rural people, for the Liberation. Its roots go deeper than the baobab's, and its branches go higher in the sky. It is what makes Zimbabwe what we are. If you spoke to your father, he would tell you so.

Eunice   I – (*She catches herself. Beat.*) He told me. Often.

Moyo   Loyalty to the Liberation is why we will always win. Without it we would be South Africa. And now we are no longer the world's leper, our nose pressed forlornly against the glass. We are accepted. Do you know how important that is for us?

Eunice   For certain people, say those with assets abroad, I'm sure it's very important.

Moyo   Eunice, take off those close-tinted glasses and look around you. Five years ago our people had nothing: no jobs, no food, a worthless currency. They were running to the shops with armfuls of notes to buy a single loaf of bread, to find on arrival the money was no longer even worth that –

Eunice   Yes, they were, because of *your* policies –

Moyo   Now look at us. Land redistribution has sent agricultural productivity through the roof. Thousands of poor black families have a new stake in the future. There is a book, by an Englishman no less, proving as much. I have a copy in the car if you would care to borrow it? It is a very enlightening read.

Eunice   Thank you, Minister, another time.

Moyo   For the country and the people of Zimbabwe, the trajectory is up. Up, up, up. Why do you want to pull us down again? (*Beat.*) Do you know who will truly benefit from your work? Two entities. One, our erstwhile colonial overseers, galled to no end by seeing us succeed without the kindness and wisdom of the World Bank, and seeking a way to reel us back in. And two, men like him. The Black Jesus. Men who thrive on violence and disorder. Those are the only people you are helping.

Pause.

Eunice   You speak of healing, Minister. We cannot be healed until we are clear of the past. My job is to cut out the contamination so we can –

Moyo   I spoke to your father. He sounded unhappy. I do not know how an African can live somewhere so cold. I told him you and I would be working together, that I would be paying closer attention to your endeavours. I think there must be a fault in his phone, it went dead all of a sudden. (*Beat.*) You should come to the house, *Chimbwido*. It is the same old place. Miriam would love to cook for you again. (*Beat.*) Nobody is clear of the past, Eunice. The question is how you live with it. Do you understand me?

Eunice   I understand.

Moyo   For your sake, I hope you do. Your boss understands. Or, he was your boss.

Eunice   What do you mean?

Blackout.

Scene Seven

Rob*'s office. He is packing his belongings into a cardboard box.* **Eunice** *glares at him, simmering with rage, hurt and betrayal. He can't look her in the eye. Pause.*

Eunice   When do you start?

Beat.

Rob   Monday.

Eunice   Three days.

Rob   It's an urgent appointment. Lots to do.

Eunice   I bet.

Rob   I want us to keep working together.

Eunice   Oh, I don't think so. Minister.

Rob   We're aiming for the same goals –

Eunice   I have a job. Investigating the people you've chosen to work for.

Rob   As do you.

Eunice   I did not *choose* –

Rob   Well, Moyo's taking over the Commission tomorrow morning, so I don't see as you've got any choice.

Beat.

Eunice   Why, Rob? Right as we're about to make an actual difference.

Rob   Reconciliation and Unity is a *Ministry*. Totally new, all mine. We can requisition stuff, we can order people to appear in front of us. I can do a hell of a lot more than we ever could here.

Eunice   How many staff has it got?

Rob   It's early days.

Eunice   How many cars? How many computers? Where are its offices?

Beat..

'I need you, Eunice.'

Rob   For fuck's sake don't.

Eunice   Did you mean any of it, the other night?

Rob   Of course I –

Eunice   Have you ever meant any of it?

Rob   Don't be . . . You know you are very important to –

Eunice   Or was it all just to get a slice of the pie?

Rob   A slice of the . . . They followed my wife to our fucking home! In that same Jeep!

Eunice   So *I* may suffer, *I* may go alone into a room with killers, but as soon as precious Thandekile –

Rob   They sat outside with the lights off all night, the same night we . . . She called and called me and I . . . I can't let my wife be hurt, you must understand that?

Eunice   I take the risks, why can't she?

Rob   You chose to be here. She's alone, scared, in a foreign country –

Eunice   It's not enough I must have sympathy for Chibamu, now I must have sympathy for your fucking wife!

Rob   She'll leave me if I don't take this job, Eunice.

Pause.

Eunice   I admired you because you gave more of yourself than any man I knew. But it wasn't true.

Rob   Yes it was. It is.

Eunice   No it wasn't. You held something back. Something to keep yourself safe.

Rob   Ja, well some of us are safer here than others.

Eunice   What do you – ?

Rob   Who paid for your school fees? Your university fees? Your summer trips to South Africa?

Eunice   That's why I'm *not* safe.

Rob   You're in it up to the eyeballs.

Eunice   Moyo's taking over tomorrow?

Rob   That's right.

Eunice   And when did you accept the position in government?

Beat.

Rob   I've paid my price. I have paid my bloody price. My home burnt out twice, on the run, living in exile. I don't have to prove myself to anyone, least of all a scion of black fucking privilege like you.

Eunice   Don't. Don't let it end like this, Rob.

Rob   I've done my time taking the fall on principle, banging my head against a brick wall in the name of moral purity. I've been out there in the blood and guts of this country. I've been the sole white face with the miners or the farm labourers, helping to organise, ignoring the whispers and the threats from both sides. I've spent nearly forty years picking up the pieces of someone else's rage and I am tired of it.

Eunice   Life kills us all. That is no excuse.

Rob   I was the one who picked up my brother after they turfed him off his farm and made him eat his dog. They cut its throat and roasted it on his braai. The foreman who did it was the dog's best friend, he raised it from a pup.

Eunice   Good. I hate dogs.

Rob   It's a place, you know? I *belong*. That means something to me. Can you not understand that?

Eunice   Oh, you belong, Rob. You belong all too well.

Scene Eight

The interview room. **Gabriel** *has been badly beaten. He breathes raggedly and holds a wound in his side. Pause.* **Eunice** *stumbles in fearfully and slams the door, leaning on it without looking at* **Gabriel** *till she is sure no one is following her. Beat.*

Gabriel   You are late.

Eunice (*spinning round*)   They wanted to − (*She catches sight of him.*) Oh my God.

Gabriel   Five of them. It took five men to overcome Black Jesus.

Eunice   What did they − ?

Gabriel   And yet still I am here to tell the tale! I am too strong! Too strong!

Eunice *sinks into her chair, face in hands.*

Eunice (*to herself*)   I cannot do this.

Gabriel   If I had been in charge of that operation, the target would not be breathing air tonight! To rush me as if we were in the playground, as if I were some garden variety thief, a handbag criminal! Let them know who they are dealing with! Black Jesus! They must know my name!

Eunice (*standing*)   I cannot do this.

She gathers her stuff and makes to leave.

Gabriel   Where are you going?

Eunice   The guards wanted to rape me. As I came through the gate one guard said to the others, loud so I could hear, 'Those are the kinds of women we are supposed to rape.' Two of them followed me.

Gabriel   A threat only.

Eunice   I could hear their footsteps even when I could not see them.

Gabriel   It was only meant to scare you.

Eunice   Well, it worked!

Gabriel   There is a difference between a threat and a promise. Take it from one who knows.

Eunice   I cannot do this any more. The damage I have caused –

Gabriel   You cannot stop now.

Eunice   To you, to me, to others, it is too much, I –

Gabriel   You cannot stop now! (*Beat.*) Do you have any idea how much it hurts? To unfreeze myself, to melt the ice inside that allows me to forget the things I have done? To pull down the walls that protect the heart and let in the spirits that haunt the edges of my eyes, to tell them, 'Come in and do your worst'? My arms and legs and heart *hurt*, Eunice, as though the blood that was cut off for years runs through them again. Because of you.

Eunice   Then surely it is better to stop –

Gabriel   No. It is what must be done. What else can I do? To make it up?

Pause.

Eunice   Endurance Moyo has taken over the Commission.

Gabriel   Moyo?! But he –

Eunice   I know.

Gabriel   He will never allow –

Eunice   I have another –

Gabriel   All the things you told me, what you would do with the information –

Eunice   I didn't know Moyo would –

Gabriel   To rip this out of me, to make me feel so much pain, and it was all useless?!

Eunice   It wasn't useless, there is still something we can do with it, I have a −

Gabriel   You lied to me!

He rises from his chair, incandescent with rage, terrifying. He takes a step towards **Eunice**, *who shrinks back against the door. With a forceful effort of will,* **Gabriel** *controls his rage and retakes his seat.* **Eunice** *doesn't move from the door. Pause.*

Gabriel   You should know what kind of man you have been wasting your time on, Miss Ncube. How I have played on your sympathies. The murder of Constance Chimwanda.

Eunice   Gabriel.

Gabriel   The murder of Constance Chimwanda, who ordered it, you still want to know?

Eunice   You already told me. It was −

Gabriel   No one ordered it. Constance Chimwanda was not even a member of the MDC. She was a girl I liked at school who didn't like me. She made fun of me in front of the entire class and none of the other girls would talk to me for such a long time. She lived in a rich house on a hill and I would never have entered it had the Green Bombers not been ordered to arrest her husband after he fell out with some higher-up in Zanu-PF. It had been a long time, but when I saw her face I knew her straight away, and I knew what I would do to her.

Eunice   I don't believe you.

Gabriel   But it is the truth.

Eunice   You told me it was a direct order from −

Gabriel   I lied to you. Just as you have done to me.

Eunice   I don't believe you.

Gabriel   Because it is not the truth that suits your needs? That fits your story? She had a nickname for me that even now I cannot think of without my face burning with shame. I have killed and raped and mutilated and still I sometimes sleep at night, and yet a nickname from school brings colour to my face? What kind of man am I?

Eunice   It was a time of horrors, no one was in their right mind –

Gabriel   The gouging of Lloyd Musiwa's eyes.

Eunice   Stop it.

Gabriel   Lloyd Musiwa was a criminal and a thief and he cheated my best friend. One day we went round to where he lived and told him he would give the money back, and he said he could see no reason why he should fear us.

Eunice   This is just revenge, to get back at me because –

Gabriel   His lip twitched like a little maggot as he told us to leave. Without that maggot I might have left peaceably. But instead I tied him to a chair and I told him if he could see no reason to fear us then he would not see at all, and I took my serrated knife, the one I had sent specially for from South Africa, and I hacked his eyes out, one at a time. And then I went back to the camp and washed the blood from my boots, which took some time, and I had a beer. A Zambezi. It was cold and fresh and I had another. And then I went to sleep and dreamed of nothing.

Long pause.

Eunice   Are you afraid? (*Beat.*) I'm afraid.

Gabriel   I am not afraid of death.

Eunice   That's not what I asked you.

Pause.

Eunice   I have no way to tell for sure which of your stories is true, Gabriel. Maybe both. Maybe neither. What I do know is this: there is a judge in Masvingo. He is not part of the Commission, but he has read our initial submissions, and on his own initiative he has started to collect testimonies from people who were tortured, to file cases against the perpetrators in his court.

Gabriel   I hope he has good coffin insurance.

Eunice   There are others like him. Springing up around the country.

Gabriel   There are never too many to kill.

Eunice   There are organisations where victims and perpetrators sit together and talk and learn how to live.

Gabriel   I don't –

Eunice   What I am telling you is, you are not alone. We are not alone. We do not need to rely on government to do this. There are other ways. (*Beat.*) Let me know if you wish me to send your testimonies to Masvingo. And which ones. (*Beat.*) Goodbye, Gabriel.

She leaves. He sits, grimacing in pain, thinking.

Scene Nine

Eunice *enters the interview room, arms full of papers. She stops short as she sees* **Moyo** *sitting in* **Gabriel**'s *place.*

Moyo   Good morning, Ms Shamuyariwa.

Eunice   Where is Chibamu?

Moyo   Your work here is now completed. I intended to tell you at the office but I thought I would save myself the trip. Are those the Masvingo submissions?

Eunice   I need to talk to –

Moyo   You may leave them with me. (*Beat. Forceful.*) You may leave them with me. All of them.

Beat. **Eunice** *places the pile of papers in front of* **Moyo**.

Moyo   Thank you.

Eunice   You have no right –

Moyo   I have every right. You are the one who has no right, who speaks contemptuously to her elders, disobeys their direct instructions, goes behind their back. I should have you fired, but fortunately for you I am in a forgiving mood –

Eunice   Where is Chibamu? I need to –

Moyo   Chibamu does not wish to talk to you, Ms Shamuyariwa.

Eunice   That is not my name.

Moyo   He knows everything.

Her face falls.

Yes. Exactly. (*Beat.*) I told you, my child. You cannot run from the past so easily. You can change clothes, change names, yet the past follows you like a hungry dog you no longer love. It does not know you have cast it off.

Eunice   You seem to have managed it.

Moyo   Yes, but I am a special person.

Beat..

Eunice   Why do you do it?

Moyo   Why do I do what?

Eunice   Why do you cling on? You have all the money you need. You could retire to South Africa or Europe and live happily ever after. Why are you still here?

Beat. He ponders the question.

Moyo   It is what I know how to do. I have spent my time away in exile, like your father. It was calm and comfortable, no machinations, no intrigues behind the throne. But what was there to delineate the days? Where was the spice of life? It is a strange thing, power. When you have it, it feels as though it is not there. All the things you wish to do are blocked, hemmed in, frustrated. And yet when you do not have it, you are bereft. All you can think of is to get it again. It makes me think, in an ideal world, the best system is probably anarchism. (*Beat.*) Well. You will return to the office now, Eunice. Our report needs indexing and other such administrative matters.

Beat. He starts to tidy up the pile of papers in front of him.

Eunice   Look at the files.

Moyo   Excuse me?

Eunice   Look at the files in front of you.

Moyo   Don't push your luck.

Eunice   Look at the files of the things you had done. You've never looked at them, have you? You've never seen what actually happened.

She rushes to the pile of documents and pulls open a file.

Eunice   Look at this!

Moyo   Remove your hand!

Eunice   Look at this! And this! And this!

She spreads a series of photos in front of him. He cannot help but look at them. Pause.

Moyo   What is that?

Eunice   That is a child.

He grunts involuntarily.

These are the fruits of your labours, Minister Moyo.

He turns over a couple more photos. His face is ashen. Pause. He looks up.

Moyo   These were things which had to be done. They had to be done. What do you want me to do about them now?

Eunice   Look at them. Take them in.

Moyo (*gabbled*)   These were things which had to be done, I had no choice, they were not my orders, you cannot prove they were my orders.

Eunice (*quietly*)   Look at them. Do that for these people. Pay them that much respect.

He looks again. Beat. He can't look any more. He stands and hesitates for a moment, then makes his way to the door.

Eunice   Let me see Chibamu.

Moyo   Your work here is finished.

Eunice   I need to see Chibamu. There is something I must tell him.

Moyo *stops, dazed. He nods. For the first time he struggles to find the right words. Beat.*

Moyo   In another life I would have run a medium-sized accounts department and been a very happy man.

Beat. He leaves. **Eunice** *stares after him.*

Scene Ten

The interview room. **Gabriel** *standing, incensed.* **Eunice** *seated at the table.*

Gabriel   Your father is Daniel Shamuyariwa.

Eunice   Yes.

Gabriel   The inventor of the Green Bombers.

Eunice   Yes.

Gabriel   Your father did to me all the things I later did to others.

Eunice   Gabriel –

Gabriel   But in your pursuit of 'truth and justice', you did not have the courage to share that truth with me. You got the truth and I got the justice, isn't it, Miss Shamuyariwa? (*Beat.*) There is such a great part of me that would like to hurt you.

Beat.

Eunice   I came to tell you the story of my father. Will you let me tell you his story?

He glares. Pause. He nods assent.

Eunice   My father was a thinker.

Gabriel   It is always the intellectuals! Find a shit in the street and I guarantee an intellectual left it behind!

Eunice   He was a quiet, gentle man. Stiff in company, like new shoes. Warm and soft like old slippers with his children. I loved him very much.

He was a supporter of the revolution in the way he knew how. He could not live among the rats and steel bars of the imprisoned, nor the goats and wood smoke of the foot soldiers, but what he could do was think. He designed many of Zanu's best social policies. The Old Man took a shine to him.

As a child, the big men I saw on the television would come to my house and have tea. I thought this was normal, that every child shared a biscuit with Robert Mugabe, that it was something he did when he got bored of his office. He would ask me to fetch him the sugar, and he would let me take a cube from the bowl as a treat, and I felt special, not because I knew who he was but because an adult was paying me attention. My father watched me like a hawk every step of the way, and I will never forget the expression on his face – pride and happiness, but with a bilious green slick of fear over it. I always thought it was my fault, that I was doing something wrong that spoiled his pleasure. But I could never find out what it was.

Those were the good days of Zimbabwe, our days in the sun. Later on, the atmosphere changed and the house grew colder.

No more lines of black government cars in the street, their chauffeurs squatting in the drive to throw dice or dominos. No more shared biscuits with the Old Man. I went away to university, but whenever I returned it was to the sound of shouting matches, my mother's voice raised in anger and my father's in defence. Phone calls where the other man was very, very angry. A build up of pressure like before a thunderstorm. And then one day, a gap in the hallway where my father's coat lived. He had gone away for a few days, my mother said. Just a few days. And then a few more, and a few more, and more.

A month later, my father rang me, and told me the whole story. That one day the Old Man had called him into his study and asked him to undertake a new project. The mobilisation of unemployed youth. To give them something to do, to help them 'fulfil their potential'. A project called the Green Bombers.

Gabriel   He should have refused!

Eunice   He tried. He told the Old Man he did not think he was suited to the task. And he told him if he did not take it, the job would fall to Endurance Moyo.

Gabriel   And in the end it did! But with his fingerprints all over it!

Eunice   He never intended for you to be used in the way you were. He designed vocational training for you, jobs afterwards –

Gabriel   Excuses!

Eunice   It is the truth.

Gabriel   The truth is your father did not have the courage not to get our blood on his hands.

Eunice   He had a wife and children.

Gabriel   Excuses!

Eunice   When should you have walked away, Gabriel? When you went to the camp? When they drove you home with a blindfold on?

Gabriel   I do not claim excuses for what I did. I deserve punishment. What I want is for those who also deserve it to suffer with me.

Eunice   And is more suffering the best we can do?

Beat.

Gabriel   Where is he now? Dead?

Eunice   Canada.

Gabriel   The same thing.

Eunice   My mother died not long after. They would not let him back in, even for her funeral. He rang the house so many times a day, day after day, and I did not, I could not, pick up the phone. My last memory of that joyful house is the echoing of the unanswered phone through the empty rooms, throwing motes of dust into the sunlight.

Pause.

Gabriel   My father always had dirty hands. That is what I remember of him. Thick grime from the factory machines underneath his nails, all around his eyes. When he came home from work he would rub his hands into my scalp for fun and all the grime would come off in my hair. I *hated* it. I would always try to run away. (*Beat.*) After he died, once or twice I went to the factory and took some of the grime from his machine and I rubbed it into my own scalp. But it was not the same.

Beat.

Eunice   What happened to him?

Gabriel   He died when I was twelve. Of a wound he got in the war against the whites.

Beat.

Eunice   I brought you something.

She pulls a small bracelet made of wood from her wrist and puts it on the table. Beat. She gestures at it.

Eunice   Put it on.

Gabriel *picks the bracelet up and a slow smile creases his face. He puts it on his wrist, admiring it and showing it off.*

Gabriel   Eeeee! Watch out for me, you know?

Eunice   It's the season. The fragrant wood.

Gabriel   It is a shame, given Zimbabwe's problem of under-population, that I am currently in confinement!

Eunice   I just thought . . . To say –

Gabriel   Thank you, Eunice. It is a generous thing.

Eunice   It is nothing.

Gabriel   It is the most nothing I have had in a long time.

Eunice   They are gone.

He looks surprised. She smiles.

You still think I cannot see it! But it's obvious. The *ngozi*. Constance Chimwanda and the rest. They have gone.

Beat. He nods. Beat.

Gabriel   You should call your father.

Eunice   What?

Gabriel   A real Zimbabwean would call her father. Even after all he did. He is still your father.

She is moved. Beat.

Eunice   Gabriel, I did not come here only to give you an explanation. I came to give you a proposal.

Gabriel   And what is that?

Eunice   Minister Moyo will not permit the Truth and Justice Commission to complete its allotted task. He has, however, been prevailed upon to alter his recommendations for the treatment of certain victims and perpetrators.

Gabriel   What do you mean?

Eunice   We are introducing a new scheme. On a pilot basis at first. It is a kind of community justice. We ask men to volunteer to work the land of the families of those they have killed. To make up something of what has been lost.

Gabriel   How does this apply to me?

Eunice   One of the applicants is Lloyd Musiwa's mother.

Beat.

Gabriel   She has asked for me?

Eunice   She has.

Gabriel   She wants *me*?

Eunice   She does.

He is moved in wonderment.

Gabriel   Even after all I have done to her, all the pain I have caused, she wants me?

Eunice   It will not happen straight away, there is admin to be sorted out, bureaucracy, it may take a little time. But she wants you. (*Beat.*) What shall I tell her?

Pause.

Gabriel   Tell her . . . Tell her my answer is yes.

Lights slowly down.

End of play.

Shrapnel
34 Fragments of a Massacre

Introduction

'You're never alone with a drone . . .'

On his third day in office in 2009, Barack Obama ordered his first drone strike, killing nine civilians in Pakistan. Over the next five years, 390 US drone attacks killed more than 2,400 people in just three countries, Yemen, Pakistan and Somalia. Obama didn't initiate the use of drones as remote assault weapons – that honour goes to George W. Bush, under whom a US drone attack on a Pakistani madrassa killed sixty-eight children – but his regime has massively extended their use.[1]

Obama describes drone attacks as 'precision strikes' on terror suspects, but the thing about drones is they almost entirely kill innocent people, in massive numbers. It took seven strikes to kill Baitullah Mehsud, in the course of which 164 other human beings also died. Six attacks on Qari Hussain killed 128 people. Ayman al Zawahiri, al-Qaeda's 'second in command', is alive; the same can't be said for 105 people killed in drone strikes aimed at him. According to Reprieve, recurrent drone strikes on forty-one terror 'operatives' killed a total of 1,147 people.[2]

Obama's ambassador to Pakistan, Cameron Munter, quit in disgust at the number of civilians killed by drone strikes, telling the media, 'My feeling is one man's combatant is another man's chump who went to a meeting.'[3] But that hasn't stopped the rampant expansion of drone use. The US has authorised the export of armed drones, under pressure from the arms industry. Amazon is touting a drone delivery service, Prime Air (companies will do anything to reduce the number of actual humans they have to employ). There are now so many private drones in American airspace that the

1 www.thebureauinvestigates.com/2014/01/23/more-than-2400-dead-as-obamas-drone-campaign-marks-five-years/

2 www.theguardian.com/us-news/2014/nov/24/-sp-us-drone-strikes-kill-1147

3 www.independent.co.uk/news/world/americas/report-us-to-allow-widespread-export-of-armed-drones-after-lobbying-from-arms-industry-10052491.html

Federal Aviation Administration has started to regulate them, prompted by the crash of a small drone into the grounds of the White House.[4]

Drones epitomise one of the signal features of modern life: malice by proxy. Like so many functions of modern power, they let people do dirty things without getting dirt on themselves. Companies fire employees by email. Germany extracts billions from Greece not at gunpoint but via technocratic financial regulations. We let someone else fish the drowned bodies of migrants out of the Mediterranean instead of having an honest debate about immigration. We don't have the balls to do our own dirty work, so everything difficult or dangerous is outsourced to someone else, usually poorer. And we don't see the consequences.

Shrapnel, as I try to do with all my plays, wants to make you ask questions. What does it mean for human society that our internet-driven daily lives are becoming so virtual, so intermediated, that even killing can be done remotely? An army that won't risk its own soldiers in the course of military operations, that relies on drone operators thousands of miles away, surely seems to violate a basic code not only of warfare but of human interaction. If you're going to kill someone 'legitimately', in a 'just war', don't you have to see their face, or at least take some risk yourself? If you never see or feel the impacts of what you do, how can you understand or take responsibility for them? What are the parallels between drones watching our 'enemies', and the NSA and GCHQ watching us?

Shrapnel is a play about a drone-prompted strike, and the people who died and suffered as a result of it. But it's also a play about so much else: the wider elements that make such a strike possible. The things we don't immediately think of when we see the smoking aftermath of an attack, the people who escape responsibility, but without whom it wouldn't have

4 www.nytimes.com/2015/02/16/us/faa-rules-would-limit-commercial-drone-use.html?_r=0

happened. The politicians who can only inspire with fear. The fulminating, scapegoating media. The people in the defence industry who make a legitimate, morally acceptable career out of peddling weapons of mass destruction. Very often, of course, these groups cosily overlap: multiple executives from major British arms manufacturers are currently seconded to the Ministry of Defence.[5]

This is a play, most of all, about complicity.

Anders Lustgarten

---

5 www.theguardian.com/uk-news/2015/feb/16/dozens-of-arms-firm-employees-on-mod-secondments

Shrapnel: 34 Fragments of a Massacre was first performed at the Arcola Theatre, London, on 11 March 2015 with the following cast and creative team:

Ferhat	Tuncay Akpinar
Savaş	Josef Altin
Semira	Karina Fernandez
Bully Soldier	David Kirkbride
Hüsnü	Aslam Percival Husain
Raw Soldier	Ryan Wichert

Director   Mehmet Ergen
Designer   Anthony Lamble
Lighting and Video Designer   Richard Williamson
Music and Sound Designer   Neil McKeown
Dramaturg   Seçil Honeywill

Characters

Hüsnü, *a Kurdish man*
Semira, *Hüsnü's wife*
Ferhat, *Semira's brother*
Savaş, *Ferhat's son, nephew to Hüsnü and Semira*

Intelligence Officer, *in the Turkish army*
Voice of CIA

Columnist, *for a Turkish newspaper*

Bully Soldier, *a senior member of the Turkish army*
Raw Soldier, *a junior member of the Turkish army*

Reporter, *for a Turkish news channel*
Producer, *the Reporter's boss*

Steve, *a worker at an arms factory*
James, *another worker at an arms factory*

Executive, *at an arms firm*

Superior Officer, *a leading member of the Turkish army*

One

*The **Cast** recite 'Ne mutlu Türküm diyene', the 'Student Pledge' sung in Turkish primary schools until very recently.*

Cast   *Türküm, doğruyum, çalışkanım. İlkem, küçüklerimi korumak, büyüklerimi saymak, yurdumu, milletimi, özümden çok sevmektir. Ülküm, yükselmek, ileri gitmektir.*

Ey büyük Atatürk! Açtığın yolda, gösterdiğin hedefe durmadan yürüyeceğime ant içerim.

Varlığım Türk varlığına armağan olsun.

Ne mutlu Türküm diyene!

As they recite, the lyrics are translated.

I'm a Turk,
Righteous,
Hard-working,
My principle
Is to protect my juniors,
Is to respect my elders,
Is to love my homeland and my nation much more than my own self,
My law
Is to rise,
To go forward

O Supreme Ataturk,
I swear that I will always walk
On the path you paved,
Towards the goal you set.

My existence shall be dedicated to the Turkish existence.

Happy is he who calls himself a Turk.

As they finish the recital, they echo in English the last line.

Cast   'Happy is he who calls himself a Turk.'

There's something ominous about it.

Beat. Blackout.

Two

A spotlight on a single standing microphone. A **Cast Member** *steps to it.*

Cast Member   Nevzat Encü's birthday was on January 1st. His friends scraped together and bought him a cake and some cologne. They were going to give them to him on the first day of school.

On his birthday, they went to his grave and laid out his school uniform on it. They wrapped his school tie around his headstone. Then they left him his presents.

Nevzat Encü. Nineteen.

Three

A small mountain village in the Kurdish part of Turkey, close to the Iraqi border. **Ferhat** *digs his frozen garden. His sister* **Semira** *enters. He stops digging. Beat.*

Ferhat   A long time. (*Beat.*) It's good to see –

Semira   You're sending Savaş?

Ferhat   You want some tea?

Semira   Into the mountains? On his own?

Ferhat   He's not on his own. Hüsnü will be with him.

Semira   For a football match?

Ferhat   It's not a football match.

Semira   What is it?

Ferhat   It's the derby.

Beat.

Semira   You're a coward.

Ferhat   The boy can handle it. He's strong for his age. Good for him.

Semira   The way it was for you?

Ferhat   It's not only the game. These need planting.

Semira   It's December. What grows in December?

Ferhat   Plant now, harvest in spring. You know that.

Semira   You've always dumped what scares you on others. Always.

Ferhat   Not always.

Semira   Savaş is *fourteen*.

Ferhat   Come in and have some tea. Please.

Beat. She turns on her heel and storms out. He stares after her.

Four

The ghostly green glow of footage shot from a Predator drone, showing a column of men and mules trekking across barren highlands.

The crackle of static.

An army **Intelligence Officer**, *with a headset, is talking to someone else on the phone.*

Intelligence Officer   Yes sir.
I understand that, sir, but –
It's going to be hard to square that with the Americans, if I'm honest with you. They'll ask why we don't want to confirm the suspects' identities.

It *is* our land. Yes it is.
Fuck the Americans. Absolutely. Couldn't agree more.

The problem is the footage is pretty clear.
They're heavily padded because it's December, sir. There's no sign of weapons.

You can even see the mules' hooves.
The PKK don't travel with mules. Which means it's not likely
to be –

Maybe it *is* a bluff. Maybe it is a elaborate deception to bring
weapons in under our noses, you're absolutely right. The PKK
will stop at nothing, sir. I'm not arguing with you on that
score.

It's just . . .
They do it all the time, sir. The local villagers. It's their usual
smuggling route.

Diesel, mostly. Cigarettes. Small-scale.

Just villagers, sir. Kurdish villagers, yes, but village guards.
Our side, if you like.

I really don't see how –

Shouting down the phone. Pause. He is abashed.

I accept that, sir.
Absolutely.
You are, as they say, the boss.

No, I wasn't in any way –
There is no problem whatsoever.
I'll tell them now.

He hangs up the phone and speaks into the headset.

Sorry to keep you guys waiting. Chain of command.

The voice that comes back through the headset is American.

Voice   Tell me about it, brother.

Intelligence Officer   The answer is negative.

Voice   Huh?

Intelligence Officer   We won't be needing your assistance.

Voice   It's no biggie, we're already on the –

Intelligence Officer   You can move the Predator away.

Voice   It'll take like ten minutes to check these guys out. I gotta tell ya, this is like the first thing I've picked up in three fucking weeks and I'd kinda like to see if they're a legitimate –

Intelligence Officer   You can move the Predator away. We have a Heron in the area. We'll investigate further ourselves.

Pause.

Voice   A fucking Heron? Instead of a Pred?
Fuck it. It's your country.

A burst of static as he hangs up.

The **Intelligence Officer** *starts to direct the Heron, a less sophisticated drone, towards the scene.*

Intelligence Officer   It is indeed, brother. It is indeed.

Blackout.

Five

Semira *with her husband* **Hüsnü**. *He's packing to leave.*

Semira   It's not you I'm worried about.

Hüsnü   Thanks.

Semira   It's the boy.

Hüsnü   The boy can handle it. Strong for his age. Be good for him.

Semira   He's not your responsibility.

Hüsnü   A lot of the lads are sending their kids. It's the derby.

Beat.

Semira   Ferhat. Can you divorce a brother?

Hüsnü   You know why he can't go, Semira. If you'd been there, seen what he saw, you wouldn't –

Semira   You were there. You can still go.

Hüsnü   Some men have straw inside. Some men have rock.
The way we're born.

Semira   Is the dog going?

Hüsnü   Of course the bloody dog's not going.

Semira   Then I don't know how Ferhat's gonna get Savaş to
go. (*Beat.*) It is you I'm worried about.

Hüsnü   I know.
I've done it before.

Semira   I know.

Hüsnü   So many times. Hundreds of times. What's so
special about this one?

Semira   I don't know.

Hüsnü   We've told the border guards we're coming, there's
no reason to −

Semira   But now.
Why does it have to be now?

He touches her stomach.

Hüsnü   A couple more trips, some money in the bank for
when he arrives, and I'll stop. I promise you.

Look at me.
I'll be fine.

She looks up. They kiss.

Semira   I'm afraid and I don't know why.

Hüsnü   I'll bring you something back.

Semira   You're carrying diesel.

Hüsnü   Something *nice*. Jewellery maybe. A necklace off one
of the Iraqi lads.

She gives him a little package wrapped in gold paper.

Hüsnü   What's this?

He starts to open it. She stops him.

Semira   My mum has this superstition. If you give someone a gift, nothing bad can happen to them till they open it.

Hüsnü (*smiling*)   I've not heard that one.
Alright then, I'll keep it.
I'll open it when we get back to the head of the valley. To a place as beautiful as you are.

Semira (*smiling*)   If I want cheese, I'll milk the goats.

They kiss. She stops.

I feel sick.

Blackout.

Six

The spotlit microphone.

Cast Member   Erkan Encü was thirteen years old. His best mate was Davut Encü. They sat next to each other in school. They studied the Quran together and dreamed of being footballers. Erkan was the only boy from a poor family. One day he told Davut he was going smuggling. Davut told him he was too young. Erkan said he needed the money to pay for school.

On the first trip, Erkan fell and injured his arm. On the second trip . . .

Davut says, 'I miss my friend so much. I hope God forgives him, and I hope He punishes the people who did this to him.'

Erkan Encü. Thirteen.

Blackout.

Seven

A plush awards ceremony in the capital. A costly logo. A caption: 'Political Columnist of the Year'. Thunderous applause.

A celebrity columnist in an expensive dress steps forward, smiling rapturously. She milks the applause. It eventually fades. Beat. She begins to read.

Columnist   The harsh truth is they want their children to die. They take them on their demonstrations, their smuggling missions, let them play near their caches of rockets and bombs. If you care for your children you keep them safe, as we do ours. But they do not. They take them up into the mountains, into harm's way. And when tragedies occur in the course of national security, they mercilessly exhibit them dead. They exploit their mangled bodies because they know their children are more telegenic, more beneficial to their 'cause', dead than alive.

If they will do this to their own, what will they do to us?

This is not our conflict. It is theirs. We are the ordinary citizens of a legitimate state, merely going about our daily business. They are the armed and fanatical terror machine that yearns to destroy that state. We know from our history how dangerous such movements are, how implacably resistant to compromise. They refuse to integrate. They push again and again for *their* language, *their* schools, *their* culture. For their *independence*, which inevitably means the dissolution of our beautiful and storied country. So when they claim only to assert their right to exist, what they mean is they want to destroy ours.

We cannot allow that to happen. We must, against the odds and in the face of Western prejudice, stand up for ourselves. Stand up for all that is good and admirable about our nation.

This is not our conflict, but we will, with sorrow and reluctance, win it.

Thunderous applause. She basks in it. Pause.

Blackout.

Eight

Military barracks in the mountains. A tough veteran soldier sits cleaning his boots. He stares up at pictures of soldiers on the wall. Pause. He resumes cleaning.

A rookie just arrived for national service enters, carrying an army-issue backpack. He puts down the pack, salutes awkwardly and stands expectantly in front of the veteran, growing increasingly uncomfortable as he is ignored. Pause.

Bully Soldier   Here for the disco?

Raw Soldier   Pardon?

Bully Soldier   Doesn't start till ten.

Raw Soldier   No, I . . . I'm not here for the disco.

Bully Soldier   Course you're not. This is an army barracks, there's no disco here.

Raw Soldier   No, I –

Bully Soldier   Why would there be a fucking disco in an army barracks?

Raw Soldier   I didn't –

Bully Soldier   I don't know why you brought it up.

Beat.

Raw Soldier   They told me to report to you.

Beat.

Bully Soldier   Where are you from?

Raw Soldier   From the capital.

Bully Soldier   From the capital. Course you're from the capital.

The lads had a vote last month: if we were in charge of the nukes and we could choose one place we'd bomb into oblivion, where would it be? And everyone voted for the capital. Every single man.

Not saying I agree.
Just pointing it out.

Beat.

Down the corridor, first on the left, lower bunk.

He turns back to polishing his boots. The **Raw Soldier**'s *attention has been caught by the pictures on the wall.*

Raw Soldier   Is that them?

Bully Soldier   Is that who?

Raw Soldier   The twenty-four.

The **Bully Soldier** *rises slowly, with genuine hostility. Beat.*

Bully Soldier   Who the fuck do you think you are?

Raw Soldier   No, I –

Bully Soldier   You don't mention the twenty-four. You don't get to put their names in your *mouth*.

Raw Soldier   I didn't mean any –

Bully Soldier   You have to *earn* the twenty-four, you useless little cunt. You don't get to rock up here and steal their sacrifice.

Raw Soldier   I only – I was told about them and I –

Bully Soldier   You gonna call all your mates now? 'Yeah, I'm in the mountains where the PKK killed all those soldiers, I'm one of them, I'm part of it, I'm a real person instead of some weak lazy ignorant little urban *parasite*.'

Raw Soldier   Respect. I only meant respect.

Bully Soldier   How the fuck can you, *you*, respect those men?

Raw Soldier   I don't know.

Bully Soldier   What the fuck can you do that they did? Can you march twelve hours through a blizzard?

Can you track a man in a ravine of scree?
Can you take a bullet for the man next to you?

Pause.

Raw Soldier   No.

Bully Soldier   SIR.

Raw Soldier   Sir.

Bully Soldier   GET DOWN!

*The **Raw Soldier** dives to the floor.*

Bully Soldier   GET UP!

*The **Raw Soldier** leaps to his feet.*

Bully Soldier   GET DOWN! ROLL OVER!

*The **Raw Soldier** dives to the floor and rolls over.*

Bully Soldier   GET UP!

*The **Raw Soldier** leaps to his feet. Beat.*

Bully Soldier   Then what possible use are you to me?

Raw Soldier   I can learn.

Bully Soldier   You can *learn*?

Raw Soldier   Yes, sir.
I can learn.
Sir.

Pause.

Bully Soldier   Down the corridor, first on the left, lower bunk.

Raw Soldier (*saluting*)   Yes, sir. (*Beat.*) I won't let you –

*The **Bully Soldier** raises a hand to silence him, then points down the corridor.*

Bully Soldier   Go.

The phone rings. The **Bully Soldier** *answers it.*

(*To* **Raw Soldier**.) Stay.
Hello?
Yes.
Yes, sir.
Understood, sir.
As you wish.

He hangs up.

Get your gun.

Raw Soldier   Are you sure –

Bully Soldier   Get your fucking gun.

Blackout.

Nine

The spotlit microphone.

Cast Member   All the weddings are off. The huge Kurdish weddings, a hundred people dancing a *govend* in a green field between the mountains, are over. Nobody feels like celebrating, and nobody can say when they will resume.

The women still wear black.

Rojin Encü lost her thirteen-year-old brother Bedran. She no longer goes to school. When asked about her future, she says, 'I will never get married, never. The boys are dead.'

Rojin Encü is eighteen.

Blackout.

Ten

Hüsnü *and his nephew* **Savaş** *in the mountains with donkeys and barrels of diesel.*

Hüsnü 'My name is Savaş Encü. This is my uncle Hüsnü. We are diesel smugglers. We have no weapons. We've been this way a hundred times before.'

Beat.

'My name is Savaş Encü. This is my uncle Hüsnü. We are diesel smugglers. We have no weapons. We've been this way a hundred times before.'

Come on, Savaş. Learn it. Whatever they ask you, stick to that and we'll be fine.

Savaş I miss my dog.

Hüsnü I know you do.
Are you scared? Don't be scared. The first time is intimidating but we have a deal with them, it's fine.

Savaş Why do you hate my dad?

Hüsnü What? I don't hate your –

Savaş You never talk to him. You never invite him over.

Hüsnü We don't have people round very –

Savaş You had me over last week.

Beat.

Hüsnü You talk to Ferhat about it?

Savaş He doesn't talk. Except to the TV.

Hüsnü I don't hate your dad.

Savaş Why not? Everybody else does.
Is it because of your brother?

Hüsnü This is a long conversation for another –

Savaş   Because he got your brother killed?

Hüsnü   He tell you that?

Savaş *shrugs non-committally.*

Savaş   He doesn't talk. And when he talks he talks really carefully about nothing, like he's tiptoeing round a massive stack of plates and if he tips one over they're all gonna smash into a million pieces.
But I listen.
I know how to listen to him.

Beat.

Hüsnü   The checkpoint's coming up. We need –

Savaş   My name is Savaş Encü. This is my uncle Hüsnü. We are diesel smugglers. We have no weapons. We've been this way a hundred times before.

Beat.

Hüsnü   Good lad.
Head up. Chest out.

Savaş   He's not what people say he is, you know.

Blackout.

Eleven

A TV news **Reporter** *at the scene of a bombing. She's shaken by what she's seen, but tries to maintain her professional composure. Beat. The disembodied voice of her producer comes to her through her earpiece.*

Producer   Coming to you soon, OK?

Reporter   What's taking so long?

Producer   Finishing up with the commander.

Reporter   Still?

Producer   He asked for extra time.

Reporter   What's his line?

Producer   They're terrorists.

Reporter   That's it? That's what he needed all this extra time for?

Producer   It is, yes.

Reporter   Well, it's not true. They're civilians.

Producer   That's not what the army says.

Reporter   Well, they would, wouldn't they?

Producer   Sorry?

Reporter   I'm here. I've seen the bodies. I've talked to them.

Producer   Who?

Reporter   The survivors.

Producer   There are survivors?

Reporter   There are. Yes. You sound surprised.

Producer   And you're taking their word over the army's?

Reporter   There are four of them. And thirty-four dead.

Producer   What difference does that make?

Reporter   To their families quite a bit, I'd imagine.

Producer   Is that the line you're going to take? That they're civilians?

Reporter   Yes it is.

Producer   You don't think that's a bit simplistic?

Reporter   No more than calling them terrorists.

Producer   Why would a civilian convoy be crossing the border, at night, in a terrorist area?

Reporter   Because they *live* in a 'terrorist area'?

Producer   Why would a civilian convoy –

Reporter   They were smuggling diesel.

Producer   Right. So illegal activities, across borders, in a known terrorist area –

Reporter   There's no other work.

Producer   By people known to have terrorist affiliations –

Reporter   They try to keep sheep, the army mine their fields. They try to grow crops, the army mine their fields.

Producer   People known for terrorist affiliations, in an area known for terrorist activities, and you're telling me there's absolutely no chance they're terrorists?

Reporter   I've met them.
These are, in my professional judgement, civilians.

Producer   And that's what you're going to report?

Reporter   Yes. I am.

Beat.

Producer   Look, it's a complex situation.

Reporter   Not really.

Producer   What evidence is there that terrorists were not involved?

Reporter   Pardon?

Producer   Where's the evidence that this convoy did not contain terrorists?

Reporter   Where's the evidence it did? That's how evidence *works*.

Producer   Listen. You're new here.

Reporter   So?

Producer   So we need to be even-handed. *Balanced*. Any accusations of bias –

Reporter   So why are you giving the army three times as long as me?

Producer   When you grow up, you will realise that without army co-operation we have no *access*, and without access we can only tell one side of the story. All I'm asking you to do is tell both sides of the story.

Reporter   What if there's only one side? What if a group of powerful people killed a group of powerless people and that's all that happened?

Producer   Have you been in journalism long?

Reporter   What if the whole idea of 'balance' is a professional delusion?

Producer   Would you like to stay in it?

Reporter   What if 'balance' is actually the problem here?

Producer   Coming to you in five. Get it right.

Reporter   What if the real question is why there are drones here in the first place?

Blackout.

Twelve

An arms factory. Two employees, **Steve** *and* **James***, one on a laptop, the other assembling a complex device. Beat.*

Steve   Check this out.

James *moves to look at* **Steve***'s laptop. They observe.*

Steve   Beautiful, isn't it?

James   Bloody hell. It really is.

Steve   Something so sinuous about it. Seductive even.
The brushed gleam of steel. The grace of movement.

James   The way it hangs so effortlessly in the air. Like a bird
of prey.
The curve of that wing. Phwoar.

Steve   Incredible.

James   Which one is that?

Steve   That, my friend, is the new Predator.
If all goes to plan, *we* will be getting the contract for the
arming unit.

James   Bloody hell. I'd love to work on that.

Steve   Fingers crossed, eh?

James   Fingers crossed.

Steve   You're never alone with a drone.

James *moves back to his laptop. Beat.*

Steve   Plans for tonight?

James   Take it easy, I think. Family dinner maybe. I fancy
an Indian.

Steve   Lovely little Indian round the corner from me.

James   Yeah?

Steve   Very authentic. I mean, as far as I can tell.

James   Sounds good.

Steve   I'll give you the address.

James   Only thing is, I don't want to go too far. Still got a
lot of unpacking to do.

Steve   Course you do. How's the new place working out?

James   Fine, yeah. Kids whingeing about leaving their
friends behind, she can't find the plug sockets, nothing major.

Steve   Where were you before again?

James   British Aerospace.

Steve   Course. Lovely Farnborough. I've always had a soft spot for the A331.

James   Frimley Green. You can't go wrong with a bit of Frimley Green.

Steve   Now there speaks a wise man.
What's it like? Coming from BAE to here?

James   Great. Lower profile. Less stress. I still get to do my sighting devices, my electrical connectors.

Steve   Fair play.

James   That's always been my thing, electronics. Really satisfying, like solving a puzzle.

Steve   I get that.

James   Just, like, the real world falls away and it's just you and this brain-teaser.

Steve   You know we do guiding devices too?

James   Really? Nobody told me.

Steve   Shed 3. You should take a look.

James   I will. Deffo. I've always fancied a pop at guiding devices.

Steve   Gotta keep challenging yourself. That's the key for me.

James   Absolutely. Evolve or die.

Steve   Right, we'd better get a wiggle on. This consignment needs to be with Shed 6 before end of play today. Customer's put in an urgent order.

James   Oh yeah? Where's it going to?

Steve   No idea.

Blackout.

Thirteen

The spotlit microphone.

Cast Member   Mahsun Encü was a tech geek. All he wanted was a laptop. He lived far from his school, ten kilometres down a horrible muddy rocky road to nowhere on which he used to twist his ankle all the time, and as he laboured along it he would dream of his laptop, his magical machine that would bring the vibrant life and richness and colour of the whole world into his narrow little room.

He went smuggling many times. With the money, he bought his dream laptop on instalments. By the time he died, he had paid for half of it.

His mother says they cannot afford to pay for the remaining half.

Mahsun Encü. Seventeen.

Blackout.

Fourteen

The army barracks. **Hüsnü** *and* **Savaş** *tied to chairs. The* **Raw Soldier** *nervously points his gun at them. The* **Bully Soldier** *stands. Beat.*

Hüsnü   My name is Hüsnü Encü. This is my nephew Savaş. We are diesel smugglers. We have no weapons. We've been this way a hundred times before.

Beat.

My name is Hüsnü Encü. This is my nephew Savaş. We are diesel smugglers. We have no weapons. We've been this way a —

The **Bully Soldier** *punches him in the face. Beat.*

Bully Soldier   You smell of shit.

The **Raw Soldier** *gets close to* **Savaş** *and speaks low and urgent.*

Raw Soldier   Just tell us where they are.

Savaş   Where what are?

Raw Soldier   Don't make me do this.

Savaş   I'm not making you do anything.

Raw Soldier   Give us the guns.

Savaş   We don't have any guns. You know we don't have any guns.

Raw Soldier (*sotto voce*)   Please.

Savaş   Why are you doing this to us?

The sound of rain. The **Bully Soldier** *looks idly out of the window.*

Bully Soldier   Snow's turning to rain. Shouldn't rain here. Some places suit rain.
Norway.
I haven't been to Norway but I've seen their boring detective shows on DVD.
The bird in the jumper and the shit plot-twists and the implausible number of suspects and the constant fucking rain.
It's atmospheric. Suits them. Their gloomy personalities.

Doesn't suit here.
Here everything drips and seeps and sags and falls apart.
The garbage rots and turns to mush. The grey landscape turns even more grey. Your boots moulder on your feet. You've a long way to go in mouldy boots.

It baffles me why you cunts choose to live here.

Beat.

Hüsnü   Where's Kerim?

Bully Soldier   Who's Kerim?

Hüsnü   The guy I speak to. The guy we give the Camels to and he lets us –

Bully Soldier   What are you trying to say, fucker?

Hüsnü   Just let me speak to Kerim.

Bully Soldier   There's no Kerim here.

Beat.

Savaş   Denmark.

Bully Soldier   You what?

Savaş   Those detective shows are from Denmark. Not Norway.

Pause.

Bully Soldier (*to* **Raw Soldier**)   Go to the latrines.

Raw Soldier (*to* **Savaş**)   Last chance.

Bully Soldier   Fill up a bucket.

Savaş   You should be ashamed of yourself.

Beat.

Raw Soldier   I don't have a choice.

He leaves.

Bully Soldier   If you scumbags are going to smell of shit, I want it to be our shit.
Our shit. Not your shit. Do you understand?
Our land. Not your land.
Our government. Not your government.
Everything is ours.

The **Raw Soldier** *returns with a bucket of shit.*

Savaş   Hüsnü! Hüsnü!

Hüsnü   Savaş! It's OK, be strong, it's OK.

Bully Soldier   Last chance to tell me where the guns are.

Hüsnü   Please, leave him alone, he doesn't know anything.

The **Bully Soldier** *nods at the* **Raw Soldier**. *The* **Raw Soldier** *rubs shit on* **Savaş**'s *face as he yells and gags.* **Hüsnü** *tries desperately to comfort him.*
The phone goes. The **Bully Soldier** *answers it.*

Bully Soldier   Yes sir.
That's right.
I have them here now, sir. As requested.

They seem like smugglers, sir, if I'm honest.
But it's up to you.
Who do you want them to be?

Blackout.

Fifteen

A corporate presentation. Title on screen: WHEN EXCELLENCE
MEETS INNOVATION. *An* **Executive** *in black-framed glasses.*

Executive   Recent events in the Middle East.
Troubling, traumatic, the cause of anger, concern and
passionate debate all across the globe.
A human tragedy.
And perverse as it may seem, of enormous importance to this
company and to the economic environment within which we
operate.

Clicks a slide.

By its nature, 'battle-tested" is the best endorsement the
defence industry can devise. Combat is the only true seal of
approval for our products in the eyes of international markets.
And it's essential to realise that with the advent of social
media, the nature of combat has fundamentally changed.

Clicks a slide.

Now, anyone with a mobile phone and access to YouTube can
instantly upload the impacts of missiles, bombs and tank shells
within a given conflict, giving a global audience direct
experience of a war zone almost in real time.

Clicks a slide.

Essentially, modern warfare is now a feature-length, hi-tech ad campaign for the defence industry, giving us market penetration and exposure we could only dream of through conventional advertising. During the course of the recent tragic events in the Middle East, billions of people turned on the news or went online and saw our products in action. That is pressure, but it is also, undeniably, opportunity. In Turkey and in Israel, to name only two conflict zones in which our products are operational, not only did our conventional weaponry perform impeccably, some of our more experimental products absolutely shone.

Clicks a slide.

Super-smart MPR-500 multi-purpose rigid bomb, penetrates reinforced concrete structures and other difficult targets.

Clicks a slide.

Flechette tank shell, releases thousands of sharpened darts over an area approximately 300 metres by 90 metres, maximising ground clearance.

Clicks a slide.

Thermal-imaging night-vision equipment, not affected by the glare of bombs or of urban lighting, rendering target identification and elimination easier.

All these products are now the subject of intense interest from foreign and domestic military operatives.

Clicks a slide.

I know some investors are concerned that worldwide austerity measures might mean a reduction in military expenditure. I'm happy to report that our findings are quite the opposite. Military expenditure as a proportion of public budgets is rising across the board, particularly in the Middle East, but in Western countries also. These are strange times, difficult times, times which are seeing the rise of religious extremism, terrorism, threats to national and personal security.

Governments are deciding, and in my view wisely, that their obligations to their citizens require an increase in defence spending. To keep us all safe.

Clicks a slide.

I know it's hard to see images of what's happening in Gaza, or in Syria, and not wonder, 'Are we really on the side of the angels?' I think that's a natural human response. We would be irresponsible *not* to reflect on such things. But just take a look at one of those ISIS videos and ask yourself, 'Where would we be, where would civilisation be, without our work?'

In my view, we are essential to eventual peace.

Now, without further ado, we move on to what you've really come for: the results for our most recent financial year.

Clicks a slide.

Blackout.

Sixteen

The deafening sound of helicopters. **Semira** *shields her eyes from the dust.* **Ferhat** *appears. His face is haunted. He carries a cheap plastic bag with lumps of flesh inside. Blood oozes from the bag. He stumbles towards her, puts down the bag as if in a dream. The helicopters fade. Pause.*

Ferhat   This is my son.

Beat.

Semira   Where's my husband?

Ferhat   Hands claw at my legs but I tread on them. Voices scream for help but I stick my fingers in my ears.
All I want is to find my son.

Semira   Where is he?

Ferhat (*shouts up at the sky*)   These fucking helicopters!
Here now, aren't you? To make sure we don't riot. But where
were you then?

Semira   Please, Ferhat.

Ferhat   I recognise him by his shoes.
Stuck out from under a dead donkey.
All the air rushes out of me. I drop to my knees to pull him out
and save him.
Save my son.
I grab his feet and pull, and . . .
They came away in my hands.
There was nothing there except his feet.

(*At the bag.*) I put what I could find in there.

Semira   Please.
I'm begging you.

Ferhat   Last summer he helped me plant apple trees.
He asked me when there would be apples. I told him he would
still be eating them long after I'm gone.

Semira   Where is my husband?

*He pulls out the present, gold wrapping torn and stained with blood. She
gasps.*

Ferhat   I'm so sorry.
I'm so, so sorry.

Pause.

Semira   It should have been you.

Ferhat   I know.

Semira   Instead of both of them. It should have been you.

Ferhat   God forgive me, I know.

Blackout.

Seventeen

The two soldiers playing backgammon. The **Bully Soldier** *smokes a pack of Camels. Pause.*

Bully Soldier   Clean under your nails?

Raw Soldier   I did, yeah.

Bully Soldier   Cos they're mad about hygiene, you know.
Upstairs.
Obsessed with it.
If you come down with something nasty, we'll have to fill out no fucking end of paperwork.

Raw Soldier   Cleaned right under. With one of those little nail brushes they issue us.

Bully Soldier   Good.
Good, those little nail brushes, aren't they?

Raw Soldier   Very effective, yeah.

Beat.

Bully Soldier   Not a bad first day, was it?

Raw Soldier   Yeah, no.

Bully Soldier   Get your feet under the table, see what's what.

Raw Soldier   Get my hands dirty.

Bully Soldier   That's a good one, Disco. I like that. 'Get my hands dirty.'

The **Raw Soldier** *wins. The* **Bully Soldier** *looks at him in surprise.*

Bully Soldier   Well played, lad.

Raw Soldier   Getting the hang of it now.

They start another game. Beat.

Bully Soldier   Won't be that much action every day, of course.

Raw Soldier   Nah, course not.

Bully Soldier   Lot of standing around, mainly. My first week I didn't see anyone. Just wind and snow and rocks. You get used to it, though.
You'll get used to it.

Raw Soldier   Yeah, no, it feels . . . feels good.
Knock the paint off.
I needed that.

Blackout.

Eighteen

The spotlit microphone.

Cast Member   There were two football teams in the village. Team Young and Team Old. They used to play the neighbouring village, Alancik. One time Alancik smashed Team Old, absolutely destroyed them. Team Old trudged back home, tails between their legs, and told Team Young they had no chance. But for the honour of the village, Team Young went to Alancik to take them on.

Half-time, three–nil down.
Heads are hanging.
But Cevat Encü tells the boys, 'We got this.'
Cemal Encü played striker, Serhat Encü was in defence, Faruk Encü in the middle of the park.

They won eight–four!
Eight–four!
A famous victory, never to be forgotten.

They stayed up till one in the morning, laughing and texting their girlfriends and telling war stories. Cemal bought everyone Coca-Cola to celebrate.
They even got an apology from Team Old!

Six of the eight members of Team Young were killed.

Şervan Encü, nineteen.
Selman Encü, eighteen.
Selahattin Encü, sixteen.
Cemal Encü, seventeen.
Serhat Encü, sixteen.
Cevat Encü, seventeen.

Faruk, one of the two who are left, says, 'We were going to get our own strip. Whenever I see a football strip in a sports shop now, I cry.'

No one in the village has played football since.

Blackout.

Nineteen

The **Reporter** *with her* **Producer**.

Reporter   Why?

Producer   Because it's pretty clear.

Reporter   Is it? I don't think so.

Producer   It was a tragic blunder.

Reporter   A 'tragic blunder'?! You're even speaking like a headline now?

Producer   The army got the convoy confused with terrorists and they made a mistake. A horrible, terrible mistake.
I don't see the story.
Time to move on.

Reporter   The Americans are briefing that it wasn't their call. Any time the Americans don't want to take credit for killing Muslims –

Producer   Easy.

Reporter   Sorry, for 'intervening in the global war on terror', there's a story.

Producer   They're outsourcing their whole foreign policy to drones. They don't want this incident to get dirt on that policy. It's perfectly logical.

Reporter   Let me tell you what isn't perfectly logical. It isn't perfectly logical to turn down help to confirm the identities of thirty-four people before you kill them. It isn't perfectly logical to fail to get accurate confirmation from troops on the ground. It isn't perfectly logical to bomb a group of teenage diesel smugglers four separate times in an hour and a half without being absolutely sure they're the PKK.

Producer   There's an inquiry. All this stuff will get sorted out in due time –

Reporter   Unless, in fact, it *is* perfectly logical.

Pause.

Producer   Let me tell you something.

Reporter   That's what the Kurds think anyway.

Producer   Journalism is all about timing.

Reporter   They think it was deliberate.
To intimidate them.
To stop them talking separatism with their cousins across the border.

Producer   And the timing for this is not right.

Reporter   To *start* them talking separatism with their cousins across the border.

Producer   There are four thousand members of the BDP, a *legal* political party, in jail.

Reporter   To stir up the ancient spectre of the 'enemy within'.

Producer   A hundred and fifty writers and academics in jail.

Reporter   To give these brutal assholes the enemy they cannot do without.

Producer   Forty-two of Öcalan's own lawyers in jail.

Reporter   Because they hate the Kurds so deeply, *still*, that they're willing to cut deals with anyone that will hurt them. Even the nightmare boys.
ISIS.
The ones who always kill their own paymasters in time.

Producer   Seventy-one *journalists* are in jail.
The timing is not right.

Reporter   I'd say that's exactly why the timing *is* right.

Producer   I've had a call.

Beat.

Reporter   A call?

Producer   A call.
Yes.
On a telephone.

Reporter   About me?

Producer   About you.
Yes.

Pause.

Reporter   Right.
What did they say?

Blackout.

Twenty

Hüsnü *and* **Savaş** *sit amidst their gear.* **Hüsnü** *chews.* **Savaş** *stares at the floor.* **Hüsnü** *throws him a piece of bread, which he ignores.*

Hüsnü   Should eat something.

Beat.

Savaş   Not hungry.

Hüsnü   You need to eat something.

Savaş   You did fuck all.
You sat there and took it.

Hüsnü   It's called being a man.

Savaş   Letting someone punch you in the face is being a man?

Hüsnü   In the circumstances we're in, yes.

Savaş   Didn't you want to hurt them back?

Hüsnü   I could hear their face bones cracking under my fists. I could *feel* them.

Savaş   Then why didn't you *do* it?

Hüsnü   Because I kept my dignity.

Savaş   I don't want fucking dignity. I want revenge.

Hüsnü   Listen. You're not standing there as you. You're standing there as *us*. You hit back, you know who gets hurt? Your mum, your aunt, your uncle, your dog.

Savaş   My mum's dead.

Hüsnü   They judge every one of us on how *you* behave. They judge themselves as individuals but us as a group. It's not fair, but that is how it is. So you have to swallow your ego, swallow your pride, and keep your dignity.

Savaş   What about the ones that do fight back?
Take me to them.

Hüsnü   Don't start that shit.

Savaş   Take me to the PKK.

Hüsnü   I'm not taking you to the PKK.

Savaş   Why not?

Hüsnü   Thirty years is a very long time to fight the Turkish army, kid. A long time to keep up the spirit of moral purity. Lot easier to come to some – what would you call it? A mutually agreeable arrangement.

Savaş   What are you talking about?

Hüsnü   Let's just say some of the consignments I've brought through here over the years haven't ended up where I thought they would. Quite the opposite.

Savaş   The PKK fight the enemy.

Hüsnü   Do they now? Or do both sides just prefer you to think that?

Savaş   You're a pussy. You're too chickenshit to fight and so you make up –

Hüsnü *grabs* **Savaş**'*s shirt.*

Hüsnü   Don't talk to me about . . . !

Beat. He lets his shirt go. Beat.

I had five brothers and now I have none.
Three dead, one's a vegetable, and one nobody's heard from in seven years.
They all joined and they're all gone.
I'm the only one left.

Savaş   The pussy.

Hüsnü   That's right. Got it in one.
The pussy.

Savaş   There's worse things than death.

Hüsnü   Who for?
That's the only question. Who for?
It can't be about you.

What would your dad say?
What would your aunt say?
Who'd look after Messi?

You have to live for the people you love and who love you.
That's the only answer I've been able to find.
It's not perfect but it's true.

Beat.

Come on. Eat something. Still a fair way to go.

Beat. **Savaş** *slowly eats the bread.*

Blackout.

Twenty-One

The arms factory. Steve and James on laptops. Beat.

James I'm thinking about a greenhouse.

Steve Yeah?

James To grow tomatoes.

Steve Mmm. I love the smell of fresh tomatoes.

James Problem is the soil in this area is quite chalky.
Tomatoes prefer a slightly acid soil.

Steve I did not know that.

James Well, now you do.
With a greenhouse I could pot 'em up, control the temperature,
get round the problem of the chalky soil.
When we first got here I didn't think we could afford one, but
with the bonus . . .

Steve Makes sense.

James I sort of think I should put it to real use, you know?

Steve Buy something tangible with it. Instead of it just
dribbling away on bills.

James Exactly. Not like we're gonna get a bonus regularly,
is it?

Steve   Not normally, no.
Only in very good years.

Blackout.

Twenty-Two

A dog howls long and mournfully in the distance.

Ferhat *emerges from his house. He holds a plate of food.*

Ferhat   Come here, Messi.

Here, Messi.

Come here, Messi! Now! Get over here!
I'm ordering you.
Fucking get over here!

The dog howls and howls. **Ferhat** *holds out the plate of food.*

His favourite.
I know you like it.
He always gave you the best bits.
Eat. It's been days.

Beat. He places the food on the floor.

Come here, Messi.
There's plenty. For you and me to share.

Please.

Come and eat with me.

Please.

The dog howls inconsolably.

Ferhat *puts his face in his hands and starts to sob.*

Twenty-Three

*The **Bully Soldier** with a **Superior Officer**.*

Superior Officer   Captain.
Good.
At ease.

I'm sure you're aware of the consequences.
Of the unfortunate incident in the mountains.
Some time ago.

Inquiries.
Discord.
Threats to the security of our nation.

Bully Soldier   I am, sir.
I just want you to know that I'm willing to do whatever it takes
to restore order in the region. Quell these protests.
Whatever it takes. *Whoever* it takes.
Nothing is beyond me, sir.

Superior Officer   I'm very glad to hear that, Captain.
Very glad to see just how much the well-being of your country
means to you.

Bully Soldier   Everything, sir.
'My existence shall be dedicated to the Turkish existence', sir.

Superior Officer   Absolutely.
Country above all.

Bully Soldier   And I also wanted to say, sir, that I know
certain people have received promotions as a result of the
operation, and I wanted to tell you that I don't wish to be
considered for one, sir.
I was only doing my job. There's no need to celebrate that in
my eyes.

Pause.

Superior Officer   You're a remarkable man, Captain.
Rest assured that your devotion and your valour, while they

will never be publicly acknowledged, are noted and
understood here.

He touches a closed fist to his chest above his heart.

Are noted *here*.

Bully Soldier   Thank you, sir.
It really means a lot to me.

Beat.

Superior Officer   Very well then.
These are your orders.

Beat.

Hand in your gun, your security clearance, and your conduct
and service medals immediately.
Clear out your locker by 0700.
Delete all your access passwords and codes.
Do not attempt to make contact with any members of your
regiment, members of central command or any other military
operatives, or you will face prosecution.

You are hereby summarily and dishonourably discharged
from the army on grounds of gross misconduct during the
Roboski incident.
Do I make myself clear?

Pause.

Bully Soldier   I . . .
I don't . . .

Beat.

Superior Officer   Somebody always has to pay the price,
Captain.
This time, that somebody is you.

Country above all.

Blackout.

Twenty-Four

Another plush awards ceremony. Another costly logo. Another slogan:
PROVOCATEUR OF THE YEAR. *The columnist in a different dress.*
More thunderous applause.

Columnist   The most moral and humane army in the world
has outdone itself again. While the Americans and the British
carpet bomb the Middle East without breaking sweat, we are
not so blasé. We hold ourselves accountable. The firing of the
captain who so plainly failed in his duties not only quiets the
manipulative troublemakers who tried to politicise this
unfortunate incident, it shows that we as a nation hold
ourselves to a higher moral standard than those around us.

And yet there is more.

Not content with safeguarding us from the threat of terrorism,
the army now compensates terrorists! It visits the houses of
people whose relatives were eliminated while attempting our
destruction – and it rewards them not with punishment but
with money!

The kind part, the forgiving part of my woman's heart,
naturally swells with pride at this astonishing display of
generosity. But another part, the part which proudly beats
with our nation's bright red blood, harbours a different
impulse.

I want them all wiped out.

Behind every terrorist stand others without whom he could not
engage in terrorism.
I am thinking particularly of the women.
The wives and mothers.
The women who cook their meals and service their needs and
whisper encouragement into their ears, who tell them their
sacrifices will not be in vain and they will be loved and
remembered for ever more.
These women should not be compensated.
They should be *targeted*.

They must go, and their homes too must go.
The nests in which they raised the snakes.
For if they are not eliminated, more little snakes will be raised there.

She nods to the adoring crowd like a triumphant gladiator.

Blackout.

Twenty-Five

The spotlit microphone.

Cast Member   Cemal Encü went smuggling to pay his debt to the school canteen. It was fifty Turkish lira. Fourteen pounds. Eighteen euros. Twenty-two dollars.

His mother kissed a thousand times what was left of her son.

Cemal Encü was thirteen.

Blackout.

Twenty-Six

Semira *and the* **Raw Soldier**. *She reads a document. He holds out a pen. Beat.*

Semira   Eight thousand.

Raw Soldier   Under the circumstances, we believe it's a rather generous –

Semira   Under the circumstances.

Raw Soldier   Yes.

Semira   What circumstances?

Raw Soldier   We're dealing with a large number of cases –

Semira   The more people you kill, the less you have to pay their families?

Raw Soldier   No, that's not –

Semira   Budget restrictions.

Raw Soldier   There's no legal obligation on the army to make these payments. No judgement has been found against us. We have admitted no liability –

Semira   So because you won't apologise, you get to pay us less? I see.
Why eight thousand?

Raw Soldier   It's a non-negotiable figure.

Semira   Who's negotiating? I'm just asking.
Why not seven? Or nine?

Raw Soldier   I really can't go into detail.

Semira   Eight thousand. Do you know what I can get for eight thousand?

Raw Soldier   What you spend the compensation on is entirely your affair.

Semira   A year's supply of rice. A new septic tank.

Raw Soldier   Now if you could sign the –

Semira   A secondhand Fiat Punto. Are you comparing the value of my husband's life to a second-hand Fiat Punto?

Raw Soldier   I'm not making any –

Semira   If I killed your fiancée, your dad, your brother, what would you ask from me? More than a second-hand Fiat fucking Punto. (*Beat.*) How do you have the balls? Is it because we're poor? You look around at our shabby floors and cracked walls and you think, 'These people are desperate, I can kill their men and leave them a bag of money, and they'll hug my feet with gratitude, and I can stop feeling bad?' Is it because you think I'm that desperate for money?

Look at me.
Look at me, you little flunkey.

I'll show you how desperate I am for money.

She pulls out a banknote, holds it up to his face, and rips it slowly and methodically into pieces. She throws the pieces in his face. Then she rips up the document. Beat.

Here's what I want from you.
I want an apology.
I want an admission of guilt.
I want the men who killed my husband prosecuted and sent to jail.
Strictly speaking, I want them hung from lamp posts so crows can peck out their eyes while they scream.
But I doubt that's in the law book.
So I'll settle for prosecution.

Money?
You can stick yer fucking money up yer arse.

Pause.

Raw Soldier   I don't feel bad.

Semira   I know you don't.

Raw Soldier   I'm glad.
I'm really glad we killed him.
Glad we –

She vomits suddenly and copiously on to his face and shirt.
He's too stunned to hit her.
She wipes her mouth.

Semira   They told me I could never have kids.

Raw Soldier   You whore.

Semira   He cried about that. Cried more than I did.

Raw Soldier   You disgusting whore.

Semira   Eight years we tried. And now he'll never see his son.

Raw Soldier   I won't forget this.
I'll be waiting for you in the mountains.

Semira   I'm having his baby.
And I hope it grows up to kill you.

Blackout.

Twenty-Seven

Hüsnü *and* **Savaş**.

Savaş   You never told me that!

Hüsnü   Didn't want to jinx it, you know. Kept it quiet till
after the danger point.
Whaddya reckon?

Savaş *gives* **Hüsnü** *a huge hug.*

Savaş   I've always wanted a cousin, brother, anything. It's
lonely at home.
I thought you didn't want to?

Hüsnü   No. Couldn't.
Thought we couldn't anyway. Except we can!

It was the timing more than anything.
The doctors told her there was a problem just after my brother
was killed. They were close. The combination knocked her
hard.
She cried for months. Years, really. I couldn't . . .
But now everything is good. So good.

Beat.

Savaş   What happened to your brother?

Beat.

Hüsnü   Shrapnel.
The most horrible, drawn-out, helpless way to go.
When my time comes, I hope I'm vaporised, eradicated,

eliminated from the earth without ever knowing a thing about it.

Savaş   Cheery thought.

Hüsnü   Better than going out like my brother.
Big white eyes rolling in terror like a cow that knows it's gonna be killed.
Bright thick blood gushing between his helpless fingers.
Knowing that they could save you, but they won't. They're watching you up there, their eye in the sky, laughing at you, enjoying watching you die slowly.

He didn't speak for three days. Your dad.
Wouldn't speak. Wouldn't eat. Wouldn't wash my brother's blood off.
Flies crawling all over his face and arms.
Disgusting.

Savaş   He was there.

Hüsnü   It was his very first trip.
He was afraid, and made my brother go with us.
His best mate. Growing up, they did everything together.
Inseparable.
He made him come down out of the mountains to go with him.

I hated your dad for years.
Hated him.
Wouldn't have him in the house.

Savaş   He wants to make it up.
It hurts him so much.

Pause.

Hüsnü   Does he talk about it?

Savaş   Never.

Hüsnü   Then how do you know?

Savaş   I told you. I know how to listen. To more than words.

Pause.

Hüsnü   I'll talk to him when we get back.
Invite him over for dinner.

Savaş   He'd like that.
A lot.

Hüsnü   About time, I suppose. (*Beat.*) There's a treat before
we get home.

Blackout.

Twenty-Eight

*The reporter squints into the camera. We see her live broadcast on a
nearby TV.*

Reporter   This is my final broadcast.

As such, I wanted to share a couple of observations with you.
Things I've learned in the course of my work here.

A noise in her earpiece.

There is no such thing as a happy colonised people.
Never has been and never will be.
That is our basic delusion.

A squawking in her earpiece but she cuts it off.

Whether or not *you* think they are colonised, that is what *they*
think.
And you can't stop them thinking that by hurting them.
It only proves to them that they're right.
And so we go round in circles.

Louder, angrier squawking. She presses on.

Trying to 'talk' to them, to 'bring them round'. Failing.
Bafflement becoming frustration and then anger.

Short furious squawk. The TV picture starts to wobble.

Anger turning to hatred.
Hatred to contempt and rage and violence.

The live broadcast abruptly cuts out and is replaced by an advert for washing powder. She doesn't know. She presses on.

Turning the story around so *we* are the victims, we are the ones who try for peace, and *they* are the ones who kill. Even though we have the army and the government and the weapons and the land.

Reaching the point we are now: where in our minds they are so intractable, so full of hate, so impossible to deal with, there is only one answer for them.

Roboski.
The answer no one will acknowledge but everyone believes in.

There is no such thing as a happy colonised people.
You either cease to colonise them, or you kill every last one.

Blackout.

Twenty-Nine

Hüsnü *and* **Savaş** *at the head of the valley. They drink in the view.*

Savaş   I've never come this far up before.

Hüsnü   High point of the whole journey for me, this.

Savaş   Is that the village?

Hüsnü   It is.

Savaş   Looks tiny.
This is what God must feel like. Looking down.

Hüsnü   Downhill all the way now. The home stretch. The donkeys feel it too. You'll have trouble keeping up with them the rest of the way.

They take a last look.

Hüsnü   Right, let's see what she has for me.

He reaches into his pocket and pulls out the gold-wrapped present.

Been saving it for here. For good luck.

They're instantly vaporised by a missile strike.

Thirty

The spotlit microphone.

Cast Member   Hüsnü Encü, thirty.
Savaş Encü, fourteen.

Blackout.

Thirty-One

*The **Intelligence Officer** at his monitoring desk, speaking into his headset.*
Armed men wave the black flag of the Islamic State.

Intelligence Officer   I have it in my sights, sir.
Convoy is crossing the border now.
Bit different from the Kurds, aren't they? Professional outfit.
Trucks and tanks and armoured vehicles. No fucking mules here.
You sure people will believe it's just 'food and clothing', sir?

If you say so.

Hold on.

They're not over-familiar with the word 'discretion', are they sir?

They're waving the flag.
The Islamic State flag.
The border guards might just connect them to ISIS doing that, sir.

Can someone have a word?

Beat. Blackout on the men with the flag.

Thank you.
Yeah, should be fine now.

Pause.

Convoy is over the border now and into Syria, sir.
As you ordered.

No problem. Just doing my job.
Securing the safety of our glorious nation.

He shakes his head where nobody can see him.

Blackout.

Thirty-Two

Semira *and* **Ferhat**. *He stands in her doorway holding a bowl of tomatoes. Pause.*

Semira   You know you can't come in here.

Ferhat   I brought you something.
They're from the garden.

Semira   He wouldn't have you in here.

Ferhat   Tomatoes.
Good for a woman in your condition.

Beat.

Semira   Who told you?

Ferhat   Word gets around.

Beat.

I only came to say how happy I am for you.
What an incredible, wonderful, beautiful thing.
I cried when I heard.

I'm so glad.
And if there's anything you need, anything at all . . .

Pause.

Anyway.
Congratulations. I'll be thinking of you.
Do you mind if I . . .
Just to drop them off.

She nods. He enters the room. Looks about briefly. Puts the tomatoes down on the table. Looks at her. Pause.

You can keep the bowl.

He turns to go.

Semira   Don't.
Stay.

He turns back to her.
Lights gradually down.

Thirty-Three

The spotlit microphone.

Cast Member   Ferhat Encü, who lost eleven relatives, says
that every young person in the village is growing up with a
sense of revenge, but not in a violent way.

They either want to be lawyers, or judges.

Some want to be journalists, to uncover the secret details of
the massacre.

Blackout.

Thirty-Four

The village graveyard. A communal mourning celebration, which the villagers have quite often. One person reads out each of the names of the thirty-four dead, and after each they all cry out, 'He is here!' So the men and boys are not lost for ever.

Villager   Özcan Uysal.

Village   He is here!

Villager   Seyithan Enç.

Village   He is here!

Villager   Cemal Encü.

Village   He is here!

Villager   Vedat Encü.

Village   He is here!

Villager   Selim Encü.

Village   He is here!

Villager   Selahattin Encü.

Village   He is here!

Villager   Nadir Alma.

Village   He is here!

Villager   Celal Encü.

Village   He is here!

Villager   Bilal Encü.

Village   He is here!

Villager   Şirvan Encü.

Village   He is here!

Villager   Nevzat Encü.

Village   He is here!

Villager   Salih Encü.

Village   He is here!

Villager   Osman Kaplan.

Village   He is here!

Villager   Mahsun Encü.

Village   He is here!

Villager   Muhammet Encü.

Village   He is here!

Villager   Hüsnü Encü.

Village   He is here!

Villager   Savaş Encü.

Village   He is here!

Villager   Erkan Encü.

Village   He is here!

Villager   Cihan Encü.

Village   He is here!

Villager   Fadil Encü.

Village   He is here!

Villager   Şerafettin Encü.

Village   He is here!

Villager   Hamza Encü.

Village   He is here!

Villager   Aslan Encü.

Village   He is here!

Villager   Mehmet Ali Tosun.

Village   He is here!

Villager   Orhan Encü.

Village   He is here!

Villager   Salih Ürek.

Village   He is here!

Villager   Yüksel Ürek

Village   He is here!

Villager   Adem Ant.

Village   He is here!

Villager   Hüseyin Encü.

Village   He is here!

Villager   Bedran Encü.

Village   He is here!

Villager   Serhat Encü.

Village   He is here!

Villager   Şivan Encü.

Village   He is here!

Villager   Selam Encü.

Village   He is here!

Villager   Zeydan Encü.

Beat.

Village   We are here!

Blackout.

End of play.

Kingmakers

Kingmakers was first presented as part of 'The Magna Carta Plays' at Salisbury Playhouse on 22 October 2015 with the following cast and creative team:

Earl Grabber	Tim Frances
Duke Venal	Trevor Michael Georges
Lady Plunder	Juliet Howland
Sprocket	Mark Meadows
Lord Lamprey	Michael Mears
King Henry III	Ben Stott

Director   Gareth Machin
Designer   Ellan Parry
Lighting Designer   Johanna Town
Sound Designer and Composer   Helen Skiera

Characters

Lord Lamprey
Duke Venal
Lady Plunder
Earl Grabber
Sprocket
King Henry III

1225. England. A luxurious dining hall in a baron's palace. Feasting at the table are the assembled peers of England, clad in silks, furs and jewelled finery. Among them: **Lord Lamprey**, **Duke Venal**, **Lady Plunder**, **Earl Grabber**, *and sundry divers others. Standing discreetly in the shadows, watching them with some distaste, is* **Sprocket**, *a man of poor birth risen to be advisor to* **Lamprey**. *He is sombrely dressed and holds a copy of the Magna Carta. He steps forward and addresses us.*

Sprocket
My name is Sprocket, and my function's same:
I wheel the deals of bigger cogs than I.
Though small in size, my turning gear will make
Wheels crunch, their axles spin, and burdens shift.
Though scarcely known among the men I serve,
Many of whom can't quite recall my name,
Machines don't work without me. Parts don't start.
And noble ranks, of pomp and circumstance,
Throw up their arms and look for someone poor
To blame. Or fix it. Either way. No odds.
Gold pays for words their wits refuse to shape
And crafts delights their hands could never make.
But there we are. Of me, in brief, let's say:
I am a man who turns the world my way.
And like all cogs, two things give me most peace:
Sharp teeth, and generous supply of grease.

Let's take advantage of this antique style
To bring you up to date with where we are.
It is the year of twelve and twenty-five.
Ten years ago, these barons I do serve
Did cut a deal with John, their loathsome king,
To divvy up the ruling class's loot.
It's fair to say that in the press release
That's not how they described their little coup.
They lauded it the triumph of liberty!
The ripping down of monarchy's dead shroud!
A move from dark and tyrannous night to bright
And shining freedom's day, where rights and powers

Did wax and grow like glorious summer flowers
Released from brutal winter's frigid grip.
That last bit's mine. It's how I earn my keep.
I sell my wit for dear, and honour cheap.

Not long thereafter, John mysteriously died
(Before you ask, we all have alibis)
And left his young son Henry in the care
Of William Marshal, Regent, hard but fair.
Who, thank the Lord, has gone to meet his Lord
Which lets them now put Henry to the sword.
That's why this boisterous roistering's happening here:
To mark a royal dispatch drawing near.
For when the young pretender's out the way
This vulpine lot will have untrammelled sway.

An argument breaks out at the table.

Venal

Which of you scum has purchased Hertfordshire?

Grabber

Don't look at me.

Lamprey

          Nor I.

Venal

                Then who?

Plunder

                      'Tis mine!

Venal

Fuck you!

Plunder

          Tough cheese, old bean. Hard lines. Is that
How English people talk? I think 'tis so.
A Norman noble finds it hard to master
England's incomprehensible vernacular.

Venal
> I've had my eye upon that spot for time.
> But had to squeeze the cash out of my peasants.

Lamprey
> Don't call them that. We did discuss. Not smart.

Venal
> Who cares? In closèd chamber we need not
> Stop our mouths. But how –

Plunder
> With foreign finance swift sought out, I bought
> That bounteous county's fields and streams and roads,
> To bar the way to ravening hordes of poor
> Which now upon its bounties feast for free.
> In future years, should peasants want to drink,
> Or farm, or walk, they'll have to pay.

Lamprey
> Subjects!

Plunder
>   Whatever.

Venal
>   You bitch. That deal was mine.

A brawl breaks out, with lots of shouting and shoving.

Sprocket
> They're not a charming bunch, I have to say.
> Lamprey, my master, like that sucking fish
> Which lately brought demise upon King John,
> Doth drain the life and vital force from men.
> His cohorts, Venal, Grabber, Plunder, all
> Like licentious philanderers masked at ball,
> They swing from grasp to grasp, from haunt to haunt,
> Looking to see who'll give them what they want.
> Charming as leprosy, gracious as the grave,
> This is the class which owns this country now.
> Their banquet has that nasty edge which comes

From being one-up on someone else. The foolish
Would-be king believes this noble feast
Is held to mark ascension to his throne.
This lot believe he'll play the Banquo role.
But I in turn must make this story whole.

He steps from the shadows and addresses the brawling throng.

My lords! Gentlemen! My nobles! AHEM!

They turn and vengefully take his presence in.

Venal
Who's this now? That dares disrupt our sport?

Lamprey
My retainer. Springet is his name.

Sprocket

Sprocket, sir.

Lamprey
Though short –

Sprocket

I'm average height.

Lamprey

He's smart with cash.

Venal
How nice.

Sprocket

My lord, your kindness makes a splash.

Grabber
Hush your mouth, you sarky little twat,
And still your tongue, else see it loll and flop
Salted and chilled upon a plate for lunch. Mmm.

Sprocket (*aside*)
Looking at him, I would not guess
Another meal to be his greatest need.

Grabber
What?

Sprocket
Good sir, please know, my sole intent
Is saving you from harsh predicament.

Grabber
What does he mean? Predicament there's none!

Sprocket
It's called democracy, monsieur.

Grabber
                                    Eh?

Sprocket
                                              And tax.

Plunder
Fuck me, is English hard!
I've sat for hours, hunched o'er my books piled tall,
But neither word rings any bells at all!

Grabber
Tax is the thing the little people pay
To fund the noble privilege of our stay.
The other thing's all Greek to me.

Lamprey
Good friends, we must confront a brutal truth.
We are not popular. In fact, we're hated.
Our towering castles, built at great expense,
Loom high above the hovels of the poor.
Our copious feasting lodges in their craw.
Our sumptuous robes, our carriages of gold,
Consumption that bespeaks a life of ease.
For poor, consumption's merely a disease.

Plunder
Our function's simple: we inspire! Perchance

The common man looks up at us and thinks
'One day I'll be like them!'

Sprocket (*aside*)

> He's got no chance.

Plunder
And back he turns to worthy toil and graft.
And thus we decent men create from knaves.

Sprocket (*aside*)
Whose sole reward is sleep in early graves.

Lamprey
You miss the point.
It's not the wealth that hacks them off. It's not
The sprawling piles or endless holidays.
It's broken promises. We said, when we
Took power from king, we'd open up these new
Found rights to all mankind to be enjoyed.

Plunder
 And so we did!

Lamprey

> Er, not so much.

He takes the Magna Carta from **Sprocket** *and quotes from it.*

Lamprey
'No man to be arrested or imprisoned,
Outlawed, exiled, in any way destroyed,
Save by the lawful judgement of his peers.'

Plunder
Ah. Ooops. Missed that bit.

Lamprey
'To no one will we sell, to none delay,
Rights or justice.'

Grabber (*looking*)
There are no footnotes there?
Exceptions?

Lamprey

       There aren't.

Grabber

                     Not e'en for those
We can accuse betray our state abroad?
Who go unto the Middle East to fight
Religious wars, crusades, conflicts of faith?
We may not lock them up? For public health?

Lamprey

This text says no.

Venal

             Then let it burn to ash.
As now it has. Our late and unlamented former king
Did have it quashed by papal intercede
Mere months beyond the deal at Runnymede.
Its work is done. In years come after
Who'll remember Magna Carta?

Lamprey

                 The point is this:
Those crimes of which we did accuse the king
And held above his head to cast a light
Disfavourable and tyrannous 'pon his face,
We now do ourselves! John raised his levies,
Grievous and oppressive as they were,
To fund an army, fight in France,
Restore the heady scent of empire to our land.
(He lost, but hey, at least he tried. And why
We need an empire to have pride
Is for another time.)
We take men's tithes to buy luxurious clothes
And shining jewels, like worthless sybarites.
We nothing give to nation, merely take.
Or so it is alleged by Common Man.

Venal

And so? Have we not weapons, guards and flame?

The military might of conquering power?
What care we that these peasant scum resent
Our sumptuous sovereignty and reign?
What can they do? Who now grips England's balls?
The dukes and lords, with money and with swords.
Us. We are the state now. Money is power.
You don't agree? Detained within the hour.

Lamprey

That's one approach. For which we have the means.
But Sprocket proffers gentler, more melodic themes.
(*To* **Sprocket**.) Speak.

Sprocket

The knotty matter's this: you all are frauds.

Rage among the nobles.

Grabber

Now do I feel that threatened snack enforced:
Ill-mannered tongue beslabbered with special sauce.

Sprocket

Mistake me not. I speak not my own mind
But that of all your subjects, whose hot rage
And fiery anger turns upon the schism
'Tween those who should have rights and those who get 'em.
Full half the men of England see no boon
From what this vaunted treaty claims to give.
The villeins of this state, the men and women
Who do base work and labour in your fields,
Receive no rights at all. If it's your whim
To turn them off or someway dispossess
Them of their homes and livelihoods, they have
No recompense nor choice but to submit.

Plunder

Let me the simple logic of this give:
It's called an economic incentive.
The average worker's lazy, thick, and steals.
Why should we pay for unentitled meals?

Grabber

> We must be lean and mean and so compete
> Or suffer economic cruel defeat.
> Our aptest tool to best our foes, you see,
> Is labour-market flexibility.

Sprocket

> I heartily concur, and would not stop
> The rise of business to the very top.
> The problem's this: resentment of my lords
> Stirs up enraged antagonistic ire.
> There are three ways to overcome this flaw.
> Repression's one. The second is to grant
> Rights full and true to all who populate
> This land, the women too.

Venal *draws his sword.*

Sprocket

>   I'll take that as
> A 'no'. That leaves us number three, which is
> A subtler answer, twisty as a snake.
> Take all this strident rage and turn to joy
> Where people flood the streets to clap not burn.
> In place of scowling faces conjure smiles
> And ballèd fist unclench to waving hand.

Plunder

> Sounds great.

Grabber

>   But how?

Sprocket

>   Bring back the king.

Consternation and hubbub among the nobles. **Venal** *waves his sword at* **Sprocket**.

Venal

> Have you full lost the plot? For one, he is
> A *child* of bare eighteen, hapless and weak.

What man would cheer for him? For two, have you
A clue how hard we've scrapped for ten long years
To get these royal fuckers off our backs?
His dipshit dad was tough enough to shift,
His Regent pain in the behind, and now
Just as he reaches his majority
And we can slip some hemlock in his food
(Eighteen's the proper age to poison kings
Go younger and the history books are harsh)
You want to put him back above our heads
And undo all the graft we have put in?

Sprocket

When were you last beloved? When there was king.

That stops them in their tracks. Pause as they think about it.

For every farm you took, King John stole two.
What monies you did swallow, he took double.
However deep into the trough you dipped,
He shoved his snorting snout yet further in.
Your own delinquencies were overlooked
In light of kingly gross indulgent greed.
And as an ugly man when sat with leper
Doth manage by the contrast to look fair,
So did your lordships in the public eye
Wax bountiful and generous as our Lord.

Grabber

I see where he doth lead. 'Tis like in form
To when a group commits a robbery.
One fellow's often set in front to fool
The armoured men whose job is staunch defence,
With japes or noise distract them from their task,
While others ransack treasury at will.

Plunder

Is that how's done?

Grabber

                    I would not know.

Plunder

                                  Nor I.
I'm merely asking for a friend.

Venal

                          Set up
This royal stripling as new king? Make of
His dim and pretty face a mask to hide
Our own true ugly nature, and distract
Attention from our wanton shameful acts?
Then make him sign a Magna Carta making
Us the Magna? Interesting.

Beat. He puts his sword away.

                         I may
Not kill you after all. Go on. How would
We tell this new un-sceptred isle they've been
Re-sceptred?

Sprocket

                The English are a doleful race,
Uncertain who they are. They spit their bile
At immigrants new landed 'pon their shores
Who rob them (so they say) of old traditions.
And yet the king they claim they have been called
'Politically incorrect' to cheer
Is immigrant himself! They *yearn* to turn
The clock back on their own society.
Bend knee, tug forelock, humbled and debased
Before a golden throne, and so relieve
Their frightened spirits of the awful load
That actual freedom places on the spine.
They're spineless. You'll have no problem there.

Plunder

What of the Scots and Welsh?

Sprocket

You'll have to kill them. They have balls.

Lamprey

It may take time. And swords. We have
Them both. My lords, list close. There's more.

Sprocket

When formerly you signed that treaty bold,
Your adversary was a slippery eel,
A cunning fox, a haughty eagle high.
Now John is dead, and in his place there stands
A new-fledged chick, his feathers damp with egg.
He nothing knows of politics, that dark
And stormy long night of the soul, whereby
Control's achieved, accounts are fixed. Let's speak
Of gold: he'll need a ton, to fund his own
Strange misadventures here and o'er in France,
Where sultry empire croons her loony tune
Like fatal Circe's song. Who's got gold? You.
You strike a deal, he'll cede authority
Greater than any which now to you befalls.
He'll wear the crown. You'll be the king. That's all.

Plunder

How do we know this puppet king plays ball?

Sprocket

Ask him yourselves. He's waiting in the hall.

An approving hubbub. The nobles intrigue among themselves. Pause.

Venal

Send him in.

Sprocket *bows and withdraws to the antechamber beyond the hall. The
nobles huddle into a welcoming committee, plastering on sickening rictus
smiles.* **Sprocket** *returns with a swaggering teenager,* **Henry III**.
The nobles bow sycophantically.

Lamprey

Your Royal Highness, welcome. On behalf
Of England's noblest gentry gathered here,
On your exalted visage may we wish

The glow of noble Apollo's fiery steed,
The sun herself, may shine, and bring –

Henry III

    Whatever, fam. Your chat is long. I have
    Got untold tings I need to do. To make
    Me wait's a liberty! You get me, blood?

Plunder (*sotto voce to nobles*)

    What language does he speak? It is not French,
    Nor English from the books I have perused.

Henry *looks admiringly round at the sumptuous dining hall.*

Henry III

    Your yard is off the chain though, bruv! Whose crib?

Sprocket (*to nobles*)

    He compliments your chamber, and inquires
    To whom it may belong.

Lamprey

                    It is mine own.

Henry *holds out a fist for* **Lamprey** *to bump.* **Lamprey** *looks baffled.*

Henry III

    My don! Your shit is tight! But why you keep
    These sidemen here on lock? Where are the yats?

Lamprey

    The who?

Henry III

          The yats, hot chicks, the fit to hit
    It, yeah? It is a partay up in here!

Sprocket

    He wonders –

Venal

          Yes, I know. I have a son
    Not far in age who speaks in similar tone.

From what I can discern, it is the speech
Of streets, not he upon the threshold of the throne.

Henry III

I speak the tongue of bredrins at the club.
That's where my true skills lie: as a DJ.
Next week I drop the mandolin remix
Of 'Auld Lang Syne'. You *know* that shit will bang.

He does a hiphop dance.

Lamprey

My Lord, perhaps a drink? To quench your thirst?

Henry III

An epic fail. *You* drink.

Grabber (*sotto voce to nobles*)
                              'Tis shame he's not
Exact as dim as language makes him sound.

Lamprey *picks up a flagon from the banquet tables and drinks deeply
from it. He hands the flagon to* **Henry***, who drinks with enthusiasm.*

Lamprey

Drink up, Your Highness. Please don't stint. There's more.

Henry *drinks again.*

Henry III

Hear what, when you give me my crown, I'll wear
It in a different style. Like, back to front?
I saw it in a woodcut sent from France.
The shit is sick.

Lamprey

                    I doubt it not, though do
Not know the meaning to be good or bad.
Yet look now, Highness, to that very theme:
Ascension to the gilded throne of state.

Henry III

  My birthright and my role when come of age.

  As I am now. Today. You feel me, fam?

Lamprey

  Well, yes and no.

  I'm sure your honoured Regent did make clear

  Before his much lamented death –

Henry III

                        It's odd

  You say it made you sad: I don't recall

  One of your faces at his funeral.

Plunder

  We did send flowers.

Henry III

              Big whoop.

Venal (*to nobles*)

                   This cocky twat

  Does not perceive the way the balance shifts.

  It's time for nasty, less of nice. (*To* **Henry**.) My lord.

  You will not get the crown. We fought too long,

  Against the depredations and excess

  Of your benighted pa, to hand the keys

  To noble kingdom to his half-formed sprog.

Henry III

  I'm not my dad. You can't blame me for his

  Mistakes.

Venal

         Why not? It's only being his son

  That puts you in the frame to wear the crown!

  What other skills do you possess? Fuck all!

  I see your future: gap year off, then join

  The army, long way off. The dumping ground

  For thick and privileged since dawn of time.

Henry III

I don't feel well. This drink's too strong. I'm used
To Breezers. Five per cent. I must sit down.

He sits heavily in a chair. His façade has gone.

Grabber

You fancy that? A stint abroad? Amidst
The dust and blood of misbegotten wars?

Plunder

Or do the things the normals do to eat:
To have to get a *job*? Or e'en the fate
Accompanying the useless fallen nags
Who lose the kingly race? To be put down?

The nobles draw their fingers across their throats. **Henry** *retches.*

Henry III

I think I'll puke.

Lamprey

    Not there!

Grabber

       Too late.

Henry *pukes copiously on to the carpet.*

Sprocket (*aside*)

The least right fact I ever learned at school?
It's *class* that lets the ruling classes rule.

Lamprey (*angrily, to* **Sprocket**)

That Turkey carpet is brand new. If puke
Does not come out or scheme does fail, you'll pay.

Sprocket

Fear not, my lord. The hook is in. 'Tis now
The time to reel the fish on to the shore.

He sits **Henry** *up and passes him some water.*

Sprocket
My lord, sit up. A drink. Of water. Clear
The head. You know, it doesn't have to be
That bad. You can still rule.

Henry III (*pointing at* **Venal**)
But that man there –

Sprocket
A rash impetuous blunt ignoble noble
Is the duke. Oft times he knows not where
His mouth doth lead. Pay him no heed, I swear.

Henry III
How can I rule without consent of peers?

Sprocket
A thing called Magna Carta ring a bell?

Henry III
The charter Dad knocked on the head? I did
Not think it was that big a deal.

Sprocket
                              'Tis not.
A bagatelle. Yet that by which you will
Gain friendship of these barons gathered here.
You'll make these knights of honour bend the knee.
Great England's serried ranks of high-born men
Doff cap, defer, acknowledge you in place.
As he whose glow enlightens all our stars,
Our blazing sun, true monarch of our hearts,
Our king!

Henry III
            I am!

Sprocket *whips out a new version of the Magna Carta and holds it aloft.*

Sprocket
            Then SIGN!

The new Magna Carta is a lot longer than the old one. It trails to the floor. **Henry** *looks doubtfully at it. Pause.*

Henry III

It is. Quite long.

Sprocket *hands it to* **Henry***, pointing out a part.*

Sprocket

Quick skim should do. The germane chapter for
Your eyes is this: that gives you lots of cash.

Henry *reads. Contentment among the nobles. Pause.*

Henry III

I must confess I do prefer to have
My reading stuff engravèd with hot chicks
And know not well the grand affairs of state.
Yet seems all powers and ingots go to you.

Sprocket

Uh. Oh.

Henry III

And none to poor. Not that I care. But seems
You take the rights my father used to have
And aggregate them to yourselves, without
Fulfilling promises you've made to men
Of ordinary rank. Or am I wrong?

Sprocket *(to nobles)*

It seems we've underestimated him.
Now does this gormless poshboy fool
Begin to show a smarter, wiser side.
He seeks to cut a better deal for self
And frame it like he's doing us a turn.

Venal *(to* **Henry***)*

Shut trap, get pen, sign name. It's growing late.
Unless you're keen on grim mysterious fate.

Henry III

But seems to me, my duke, that if you wished

Me swim with fish, I'd already be paddling.
What could you want of me, a lad not twenty?
Ah!
There is but one of king: of nobles, plenty.

Major muttering and concern among the nobles.

Venal (*to* **Sprocket**)
　　You've screwed the pooch. He sees the scheme. And I'll
　　Screw you if you don't sort this matter out.

Sprocket
　　Good duke, but stay your ire, I'll bet you'll see
　　You have good cause to thank not threaten me.

Henry III
　　Don't get me wrong. I have no love for those
　　With whom I've passed the time in bars and clubs.
　　We lounged like lads, had proper bantz, but all
　　It was was mere distraction. Now's the time,
　　Like Henries yet to come, to shrug off plebs
　　And peasants, take my place in pantheon
　　Of glittering absolutist kings beloved.
　　The tsar's the star in England, so they say.
　　My fear is how to do it, given Dad.
　　His darker deeds; the promises you made.
　　The English people do not trust your type
　　Nor mine. We must do something. Make concession.

Sprocket (*aside*)
　　Now it is clear John gives him ancestry.
　　The apple does not fall far from the tree.

Plunder
　　You cannot mean we must fulfil what's in
　　The Magna Carta for the mass? I'm ill
　　At very thought!

Henry III
　　Fear not: though like all kings I am derived
　　From shallow gene pool, yet I have not dived

Into its deep end and concussed my head.
You may allay your well-entitled dread.
Such policy would nakedly be dense
The cost in power and cash beyond immense.
The trick is this: *distract* the people from
The promises you've made to them. Allay
Their new-found hopeful expectations of
A better, happier, less cruel world to come.

                                                    But how?

Pause. He smiles.

There is one thing in England trumps all else:
A royal wedding.

The nobles break into huge smiles and mutual congratulations.

Venal
The kid is good.

Lamprey
                              I told you so.

Venal
                                        You did.

Sprocket
In fact 'twas me.

Venal (*pushes* **Sprocket** *away*)
Shut up and let me hear.

Henry III
In slack moments inside strip joints, I did
Read up upon the history of kings.
(I hid the book inside some porn. It does
Not do to look too smart.) Time after time,
There was a panacea for discontent.
It stopped rebellion in its tracks, assuaged
The sharpest hurts of grim austerity,
Made men forget they could not feed their kids.

It was, of course, the wedding of a prince
To beauteous blushing bride, oft-times princess,
Or even commoner (though *really* posh)
To give the average Joe a sense of hope.
It's quite remarkable the strong effect
A royal wedding has upon the minds
Of men and women (God's grace, the women! Obsessed
With dress and nails and hair and all that shit)
Who think themselves of independent mind.
They all melt down to dribbling pools of goo
Who burble 'Majesty' at every turn,
As if somehow their family's hopes and fears
Were sublimated into ours. I guess
They are, if only in the sense we spunk
Their taxes on our fripperies, and so
Take food directly from their kids' own mouths.
The more we get, the less they have: of hope
And power, education, food, the lot.
And yet they love it. Stand and cheer. Seems wrong.
It mystifies me why they go along.

Venal

They do. That's all. The ones that don't, we'll call
Unpatriotic and a threat to state.
We'll lock them up and say they're driven by
Irrational and misbegotten hate.
Agreed?

Henry III

        Agreed. How like you then my plan?

Venal, **Lamprey** *and the rest of the nobles kneel.* **Sprocket** *doesn't.*

Lamprey

Most Royal Highness, please forgive our ways
Untimely, crude and foolish as they are.
We thought you'd be a puppet on a string.
Now do we see the strings you pluck are ours.
Let us from now on be your mandolin
And let us make sweet music all together!

The nobles cheer as one.

Plunder

    Enthusiastically we do accept
    Your proposition of a royal wedding.
    And let me swift propose a perfect match:
    My own beloved girl shall be your bride!

Grabber

    When she doth say she'll eat a horse, she means
    It literally. She weighs a ton. Now *my* –

Plunder *punches* **Grabber**.

Plunder

    You nasty man!

The nobles cluster round **Henry***, waving woodcuts of their daughters
in his face.*

Venal

            My daughter is for miles
    Around renowned for beauty unsurpassed.

Lamprey

    She also could not spell a word like 'cat'
    If gifted with the c and with the t.
    My own fair child –

Henry III

            Enough! There is no lack
    Of time to find the lucky lady who'll
    Be fortunate enough to bear my heirs.
    Cos that's the thing, good barons, don't forget.
    The marriage is the porn flick, but the key,
    The money shot? The *kids*. The final nail
    In independent England's rotten coffin.
    You think a wedding makes 'em bow and cringe?
    Just wait until we show our first-born son.

The nobles cheer.

With that in mind, come, let's away and send
For shots of hotties all round Europe, then
As with a medieval Tinder, swipe
To left until we find the one that's right.

They all begin to move off. **Henry** *raises the new Magna Carta.*

One issue left. This thing will have to change.
Returning power and fiscal wealth
My way. An equal partnership requires
An equal share.

The nobles look at each other for a moment, then acquiesce.

But worry not. We'll dump
The worst effects on bad old Dad and make
The history books record it as his shame.
We'll share the cash; he and the people, blame.

They all move off triumphantly, **King Henry III** *at their head.*
Sprocket *manages to catch* **Lamprey**'s *arm just before he exits.*

Sprocket
Sir, what of me?

Lamprey
What of you?

Sprocket
All I did
To bring this reconciliation on,
And solve your pressing woes, does not deserve
A little something?

Beat. **Lamprey** *grudgingly pulls out a bag of gold.* **Sprocket**'s *eyes light up.* **Lamprey** *reaches inside and pulls out a single gold piece. He hands it over.*

Lamprey
A little something. As you asked.

He laughs contemptuously and exits after the rest. Beat. **Sprocket** *sits mid-stage, single coin in hand, contemplating it like Hamlet with Yorick. Pause.*

Sprocket

    Why do we do it? When we know full well
    The rich are turds? What full and deep contempt
    They hold us in? They laugh at us from yachts.
    It's not their thievery, their cruelty, e'en
    Their clear intent to turn the real-life clocks
    Back to this era we do play. It's what
    They make us do to us. A smarter man
    Than me once said, just as no two objects
    Can in one time take up one single space,
    So must one mode of life squeeze out the rest,
    Must choke at source the vital oxygen
    From other ways of life that seek to breathe.
    So does our love of rich asphyxiate
    Our thoughts of better, fairer, happier worlds.
    There are right now, you may have seen, a rash
    (I use the word advisedly) of plays
    And books and films about the royals, which make
    These hapless plastic twats into great figures
    Of weight and moral dignity and power,
    Shakespearian in scope. A joke. At time
    When elites want our cash and power, it seems
    They also want our *sympathy*. The rub:
    Where are such tender ministrations for
    The ones they rob? The normal men? The poor?
    It's propaganda for austerity.
    If you can't see that, rather you than me.

Beat. He stands.

    And yet I am no better man, of course.
    I've made my bundle from the same discourse.
    If bundle it be called.

He throws the coin to an audience member.

                  Here, take, and spend.
    Or maybe save. By time that lot in there
    Are done, you'll need it for some healthcare for

Your mum. What can we do, eh? Something *better*.
Shrug off this worthless lot, and selves unfetter.

He bows to the audience and strides off in the opposite direction to the one the nobles exited.

End of play.

The Insurgents

'Those that live by the sword shall die by the sword.'

'And those that don't? How will they die, Uncle?'

George Tabori, The Cannibals

The Insurgents was first produced at the Finborough Theatre, London, on 9 September 2007 with the following cast and creative team:

Wassermann   Andrew McDonald
Abdullah   Robert Carragher
Metin   Adam Dahrouge
Yilmaz   George Antoni

Director   Alexander Summers
Designer   Rachana Jadhef
Lighting Designer   Tom White
Sound Designer   Matt Downing
Producer   Serenah Cole

Characters

Abdullah
Wassermann
Metin
Mr Yilmaz

Early morning, late winter. Lights up on a dingy low-ceilinged office-cum-bedroom above a corner shop in a Kurdish enclave of North London. Boxes of products and bottles are stacked precariously along both side walls and on top of an unmade bed, spilling into the centre of the room. A table to one side is piled high with receipts and paperwork and a first-aid kit in a plastic box. A huge flag in the Kurdish colours of red, green and yellow occupies most of the upstage wall, alongside pictures of the Kurdish leader Abdullah Öcalan and an unattractive London University campus. Upstage right is the entrance to a small and untidy kitchen. Upstage left a door which leads downstairs to the shop.

In the centre of the room, a fifty-something man, **Wassermann***, is standing on a rickety chair with a noose around his neck. His polished wingtips and tailored suit seem ill-matched to the grime of his surroundings. His hands are tied behind his back and a gag is tied around his mouth; the noose, stretched taut, leads up to a joist in the roof. He would be a good-looking man if not for his expression of faintly haunted cruelty. Right now he betrays nothing. He stares out in front.*

Long pause. Enter **Abdullah***, early twenties, wiry and feisty, born in the Kurdish part of Turkey but largely raised in this very house. He carries in his hand a sheaf of notes. He slams the door behind him and moves in front of* **Wassermann***, staring him in the face. His pent-up energy means he can't stay in one place.* **Abdullah** *picks up an open pack of Pringles from one of the boxes and chews loudly in* **Wassermann***'s face for a moment.* **Wassermann** *stares imperiously in front of him, refusing to meet* **Abdullah***'s gaze.*

Abdullah *goes into the kitchen, emerging a few moments later with a long sharp machete. He goes up to the man on the chair, holds the machete to his face for a moment, then in a sudden motion cuts away the gag and steps back.*

Abdullah (*holding the pack out*)   Pringle? (*Beat.*) Lost yer appetite? (*Beat. He puts the pack down.*) So. This is it. Our humble abode. Nice, yeah? Well, we like it. (*Beat.*) You must have known this was coming, surely? One day? (*Beat.*) Alright then. Since you ask. Let's do it.

He takes a step towards **Wassermann***.*

Abdullah   You are not welcome here. I repeat that: you are not welcome here. Our organisation has taken a grassroots democratic decision. We have made protests over the irreversible damage caused to this community by the OurFolks Corporation. Those protests have been ignored. We are thus obliged to take measures to cut out this burgeoning cancer from our body politic. This is the first of these measures. The OurFolks Corporation is required to cease all operations in the United Kingdom within twenty-four hours. It will also liquidate its holdings in all other UK industries. If these demands are not met, our organisation will undertake some corporate downsizing of our own. We will demonstrate, physically, that we are not willing to live under your thumb, Mr Wassermann.

Pause. **Abdullah** *may be a little disconcerted that* **Wassermann** *isn't more disconcerted.*

Abdullah   In this strategy, we follow the sage wisdom of B. Reed Wassermann, vice-president of the OurFolks Corporation, as expounded in the *Daily Telegraph* of – (*Checks the article.*) 13 November 2006. 'The Saviour of Crockney'. The Saviour of Crockney! This is supposed to be a *newspaper*! I quote. 'Too many executives want the rewards of success without the suffering. A real leader gets out in the trenches and faces the bullets. If you gotta spill blood to do the right thing, then that is what you do.' (*Beat.*) I thought the point of trenches was that you don't have to face the bullets?

Beat. Still no reaction from **Wassermann.** **Abdullah,** *a little fazed, stuffs a couple of Pringles in his mouth and looks at his notes.*

Wassermann   We own them.

Abdullah   Huh?

Wassermann   We own Pringles.

Abdullah   No, you don't.

Wassermann   Sure we do.

Abdullah *consults his notes.*

Abdullah   Pringles are owned by . . . Rayfield Nutritional
Group.

Wassermann   A majority stake in Rayfield Nutritional
Group is now held by Mannheim Lawlor Enterprises, a wholly
owned subsidiary of the OurFolks –

Abdullah   The OurFolks Corporation. (*Beat.*) I'm hungry.

Wassermann   Be my guest.

Abdullah *tosses the Pringles away and roots around in the supplies
again. He comes up with a packet of biscuits. He slowly opens the
packet, takes one out, tentatively raises it to his mouth, hesitates a moment
and finally puts it in.* **Wassermann** *is impassive right up until the
moment when* **Abdullah** *bites into the biscuit, then gives him an
affirmative nod as if to confirm that his company owns the biscuit
makers too.* **Abdullah** *spits out the biscuit in vexation.*

Abdullah   For fuck's sakes! When did you buy them?

Wassermann   I believe 13 March.

Abdullah   I don't have that down here. (*Indicates notes.*)

Wassermann   Then I guess you're out of date.

Abdullah   I can't keep up with you lot. You turn your back
for two minutes and you have to throw out half your stock.
How do we stay ethical with scum like you around?

Wassermann   This you call ethical? (*Pause.*) What do you
want here?

Abdullah   I was gonna ask you the same thing.

Wassermann   I don't have to explain anything to you. You
have thirty seconds to let me –

Abdullah *steps up to the chair and wiggles it slightly, causing*
Wassermann *to rock from side to side somewhat. The first flash of
fear and panic appears on* **Wassermann**'s *face.* **Abdullah** *sees it
and stills the chair. He steps back, satisfied. Pause.*

Abdullah   You are not in charge here, Mr Wassermann. I know that's a foreign language to you, so I'll say it again slowly: you are not in charge here. Say that to me.

Wassermann   You are not in charge.

Abdullah   Are you twelve?

He shakes the chair harder. **Wassermann** *wobbles.*

Wassermann   Hey. HEY!

Pause.

Abdullah   What are you doing here?

Wassermann   I'm acquiring this store.

Abdullah   We call it a shop over here.

Wassermann *takes a deep breath.*

Wassermann   Then I'm acquiring this shop.

Abdullah   No, you're not.

Wassermann   Are you enjoying this as much as I am? Can we make it a regular date?

Abdullah   You're not 'acquiring' this shop because this shop is not for sale.

Wassermann   This shop is not only for sale –

Abdullah   Not to us.

Wassermann   It has already been sold.

Abdullah   Not to us. And we live here.

Wassermann   The shop has been sold as a part of a far wider commercial transaction –

Abdullah   We *live* here.

Wassermann   – involving the fundamental regeneration –

Abdullah   We live in this house.

Wassermann   – by a partnership of government initiatives, commercial actors –

Abdullah   WE LIVE HERE!

A phone chirps. An incongruous ringtone. **Abdullah** *looks at* **Wassermann** *askance, then fishes it out of* **Wassermann**'s *jacket and places it on the table. Beat.*

Abdullah   Always ring when you're tied up, don't they?

It continues to ring.

Wassermann   People are expecting me.

It stops.

Abdullah   My father has lived in this house for sixteen years. It is the only place in England he has ever lived. During that time, he has never once been on holiday. Can you even begin to imagine what that is like, Mr Wassermann? I don't know if he's even been out of London more than twice. When he leaves Crockney, he starts to sweat, which is ironic cos most people have that reaction coming *in* to Crockney.

Wassermann   Listen, kid, can we just cut to / the chase?

Abdullah   During those sixteen years, my father has attempted to purchase the freehold on this property from Crockney Council no fewer than nine times. On each and every occasion he was rebuffed with a new and more original excuse. You can imagine our surprise last year, then, when although my father held first option on this property, we were informed that it had been sold to an unnamed bidder.

Wassermann   We're an aggressive organisation, I make no apology for it.

Abdullah   At the same time, we began to receive a steady and unexpected stream of visitors. Health and Safety. Inland Revenue. They didn't buy much, those people. Asked a lot of questions, though.

Wassermann   You should be grateful your public officials show such a commendable work ethic.

Abdullah   My father, with beautiful naivety, thought gentrification might be good for us. More customers, he said. But there's not much call for Spam among the upwardly mobile, is there, Mr Wassermann?

The phone rings again.

Wassermann   I need to answer that. I am expected.

Abdullah *rejects the call.*

Abdullah   I know you are. At the – (*Reads from sheet.*) 'Regeneration Community Gala: Celebrating a New Dawn for Crockney'. You're the keynote speaker, I believe.

Wassermann   What do you think you're gonna achieve here?

Abdullah (*reading*)   'The Regeneration Community Gala is an invitation-only event.'

Wassermann   You are fortunate enough to live in a democracy.

Abdullah   You really don't know much about this country, do ya?

Wassermann   Why don't you take your problems to your elected officials, as one does in a democracy?

Abdullah   How is Number Ten, Mr Wassermann?

Beat.

Wassermann   Surprisingly spacious inside.

Abdullah   I'll bet it is. I will fucking bet it is. Not quite enough room for ordinary people though. When we went to deliver this petition (*Waves document about.*) no one was available to speak to the representatives of more than a thousand citizens of this country, requesting that the Crockney 'urban reclamation' project be blocked. I can't get near the home of my elected government. Yet you've been there four times in the last fourteen months.

Take my problems to my elected officials? We did a Freedom of Information request after the council knocked us back: lo and behold, who should be 'donating' three quarters of a million pounds to the council war chest in April 2004 but the OurFolks Corporation? Then we went to our local MP, who turns out to be a non-executive director of the UK arm of a large American conglomerate with which both of us are intimately familiar.

Beat.

Wassermann   We are undertaking a regeneration process, at considerable exposure to ourselves, that has incorporated an exhaustive range of stakeholders –

The phone starts to ring again.

Abdullah   For fuck's sakes . . .

Wassermann   We provide a community investment programme to benefit local hospitals and schools, a –

Abdullah (*reading from newspaper article*)   'The single most essential attribute for business success – '

Wassermann   We bring opportunity, employment, wealth –

Abdullah   'The single most essential attribute for business success – '

Wassermann   – a massive upgrade in available facilities and consumer choice –

Abdullah *chops the phone in two with the machete. A stunned silence.*

Abdullah   'Saviour of Crockney', paragraph 4. 'The single most essential attribute for business success is the ability to listen.'

Beat. **Wassermann** *inclines his head a fraction.*

Abdullah   Thank you. (*Beat.*) Why here?

Wassermann   There is a market demand.

Abdullah   Why here? You've got Hoxton, you've got Shoreditch, you've even got fucking Peckham. This is the last place people like us have left.

Wassermann   This is an authentic, up-and-coming neighbourhood. People wanna move in.

Abdullah   Authentic is middle-class for 'shithole with gastropub'. If you would like to live to lunchtime, Mr Wassermann, please do not use the words 'authentic' or 'up-and-coming' to describe my neighbourhood.

Wassermann   Your father agree with what you're doing?

Abdullah   While we're on the subject of authenticity, let me read you something from your brochure. 'This development is embedded in a vibrant, exciting, rapidly regenerating community' . . . 'Gated access and twenty-four-hour security protection.' You don't see any contradiction between those two sentences? (*Reading from brochure.*) 'Luxurious living spaces featuring state-of-the-art contemporary design. Massage salon. Private gymnasium. On-site juice bar.'

Wassermann   You'd like those things, everybody would.

Abdullah   It doesn't matter what people like us want, Mr Wassermann. We never get it.

Wassermann   If we don't do this, somebody else will. There is a demand.

Abdullah   Not from us, not from the actual people that make this place 'authentic'. You 'regenerate' away the very thing you're selling, Mr Wassermann, do you not see that?

Wassermann   I understand if this is upsetting for you, but you gotta know this isn't personal.

Abdullah: You're taking my home. How is that not personal?

Wassermann   This is a business transaction. You have to detach yourself emotionally from –

Abdullah (*reading from notes*)   *The Economist*, 12 June. 'Corporate Cowboy Rides Herd on Rivals' . . . '"You know what I love most about what I do? The thrill of the hunt," says the ebullient Wassermann. "I don't do this for the money. I do it for the same reasons the old-time cowboys did it: the thrill, the buzz in your guts when you lasso the beast you've been pitting wits with and bring it down in a welter of sweat and panic."' Rather poetic, that. You're wasted doing this. (*Beat.*) That's us, is it? 'The beast'?

Wassermann   All I'm saying to you is that this is business.

Abdullah   Why do you call yourself a cowboy when you were born in New Jersey?

Wassermann   We work with your government to make this place better than it was. Bottom line.

Abdullah   You're buying our homes and kicking us out. Bottom line.

Wassermann   People are selling us their houses?

Abdullah   They aren't. The council are.

Wassermann   Homeowners whose property is compromised by the new facility are compensated at rates well above market value.

Abdullah   What about the people who don't own their homes, the shops that are already here?

Wassermann   There is a necessary corollary to competition.

Abdullah   Look out the window.

He gestures at the window in the downstage wall. **Wassermann** *refuses to look.*

Wassermann   Thanks, I already took a stroll around the neighbourhood. I like to get a feel for the communities in which we're investing.

Abdullah   So look out the window.

Beat. No movement. **Abdullah** *wobbles the chair again.*
Wassermann *looks, simmering*

Wassermann   I know people like you.

Abdullah   Really? Who are they, your cleaners?

Wassermann   People whom history has passed by. Who can't accept the truth.

Abdullah   Which is?

Wassermann   That folks want what we sell. Tell me when we build these spaces that folks won't buy them.

Abdullah   But you're not going to build these 'spaces', Mr Wassermann. What do you see?

Wassermann   Won't they? They will sell. People will buy them of their own free and sovereign will, because we can offer them a form of modern happiness.

Abdullah   What d'ya see?

Wassermann   What do I see? (*Squints, reads a shop sign.*) 'Fat Benny's Takeaway Takeover: Curry, Chinese, Fish and Chips. All meat halal.'

Abdullah   Fat Benny is a versatile geezer.

Wassermann   There's a guy eating something out of a box, but I can't tell if it's curry, Chinese or fish and chips.

Abdullah   What else?

Wassermann   Not a whole hell of a lot. Houses.

Abdullah   Houses. Yes. Where people live. Now look over to the left. What do you see? (*Beat.*) The building with the white lettering over the entrance, what does it say?

Beat.

Wassermann   Public Library.

Abdullah   Public Library. Isn't that a nice building? Tell me it's a nice building.

Wassermann   It's a nice building.

Abdullah   It's more than a nice building, Mr. Wassermann, it's a public building. Look at the detail in the carving work. Know when that was built?

Wassermann   Suck my dick.

Abdullah   No, 1874. 1874, and it still looks like that. Ordinary people, real people, have used that building for a hundred and thirty-three years to think, to learn and thus to become a little more human. Soppy, but true. Under your proposals, it will become – (*Checks brochure.*) 'An exclusive harmonisation of cutting-edge paradigmatic modernity with the cream of historic period features.' I will not permit this.

Wassermann   Really.

Another mobile on **Wassermann***'s person goes off.* **Abdullah** *raises an eyebrow. A third one chirps into action.* **Abdullah** *reaches into* **Wassermann***'s jacket and withdraws them both.*

Wassermann   People know I've come here. They will be looking for me.

Abdullah   You're going to cancel this project, Mr Wassermann.

Suddenly **Abdullah***'s younger brother* **Metin***, teens, bangs in through the door, shivering with cold. He has a pair of tights over his head.*

Abdullah   What the fuck are you doing?

Metin   Need a cup a tea, rudebwoy. Cold to rhas outside, get me? Can't feel my nads, dread!

Abdullah   I mean with the tights.

Metin   Disguise, innit.

Abdullah   You've been standing outside with that on your head?

Metin   Thass how's it's done, bruv. You never see *Crimewatch*?

Abdullah   I told you not to draw attention to yourself.

He pulls the tights off **Metin**'s *head.*

Metin (*seeing they have ripped*)   Never sell 'em now. Dad's gonna be well vexed.

Abdullah   This is important . . .

Metin *moves towards the kitchen. To* **Wassermann**, *as he passes him.*

Metin   Alright, boss? Metin. I smacked you in the bonce with a extra-size tin of Spam. Always said that shit's bad for you. Cup a' tea?

Wassermann   Thanks, no.

Metin *disappears into the kitchen.*

Wassermann   Friend of yours?

Beat.

Abdullah   My brother.

Metin *re-emerges from the kitchen. He picks up* **Abdullah**'s *discarded pack of Pringles and eats one.*

Metin   No bloodclart milk. Affe get some from downstairs.

Abdullah   Metin!

Metin   What?

Abdullah   Now is not the time for a cup of tea. And don't eat the Pringles.

Metin   Come on, bruv, not Pringles now . . .

Abdullah   He owns them.

Metin   Not the sour cream and chives one an' all?

Abdullah   Yes, even the sour cream and chives one.

Metin   Allow it! Thass my favourite, like . . . Bloodclaart! Tellin ya, man, this terrorism shit's a lot more tricky than it look onna TV, y'know.

Abdullah   This is not terrorism, we discussed this. Go away.

Metin   Rah! Tryna help, innit.

Abdullah   Get out!

Metin *leaves. He slams the door behind him. A loud shout of 'Wanker!' as he trudges downstairs. Beat.* **Wassermann** *laughs hard.*

Wassermann   Is that all of you? Please tell me that isn't all of you. Your 'organisation'?

Beat.

Abdullah   It doesn't matter how many we are.

Wassermann   Two fucking guys?! Jesus H. Christ! I'll bet Al-Qaeda doesn't have this problem.

Abdullah   We represent the thousands of / people

Wassermann   I'll bet Al-Qaeda doesn't run out of milk.

Abdullah   We represent the thousand people on this petition –

Wassermann   You 'represent'? You wanna know who I represent? One point five million individual shareholders, kid: that's like the entire population of Botswana chooses to put their fiscal faith in me each morning. And as you're no doubt aware, the principal obligations of the corporation, legally, financially and morally, are to those shareholders. They include your father.

Abdullah   Bollocks.

Wassermann   He's a businessman. Maybe he –

Abdullah   Bollocks, you lying –

Wassermann   Maybe he did what good businessmen do, and hedged his risks.

Abdullah   My dad doesn't have money to piss away on shares.

Wassermann   Maybe you just don't know him as well as you think?

Metin *crashes back in through the door, can of drink in one hand, in a sulk.*

Metin   No milk downstairs neither! And no Coke! Terrorism is rubbish!

Abdullah   Go. Away.

Metin   I can't even get a proper drink an iss your fuckin fault.

Abdullah   How is it my fault?

Metin (*to* **Wassermann**)   You know what this idyat did? He only made the old man stop buyin Coke cos of 'ethical reasons'.

Abdullah   Coca-Cola is draining the groundwater out of Kerala right this second.

Metin   So?

Abdullah   So what are the local people supposed to drink?

Metin   Lemme think: it's brown, it's sticky –

Abdullah   Don't be a wanker.

Metin   People like Coke, Apo. That is why they buy it. They don't like 'Fairtrade Hibiscus and Linseed Infusion'. That is cos it tastes like donkey piss.

Abdullah   If people want Coke, they can go somewhere else.

Metin   They are goin' somewhere else, Apo, thass why we don't have no customers no more.

Wassermann   Apo?

Metin (*to* **Wassermann**)   'Slike a special thing for Abdullah, innit.

Abdullah   Metin –

Metin   The old man called him after his fucking hero, Mr. Őcalan, leader of 'the revolution'.

Abdullah   Can we stop discussing family affairs in front of the hostage, please?

Wassermann   Hey, don't mind me.

Abdullah   What do you want? You want a Coke? Here. (*Digs in his pocket, pulls out some change.*) Go get a Coke.

Metin *spots the phone and picks it up.*

Metin   Two beats, yeah. Got some fit ting on lock, dread!

Abdullah   Where's your phone?

Metin   Pay as you go, innit? I di'nt pay, it fucking went. Wha 'appen, darling?!

He moves into the kitchen with the phone.

Wassermann   Abdullah? It's nice to put a name to the face, by the way.

Abdullah   Fuck off.

Metin *(off)*   Girl, you so sweet, you gimme diabetes!

Wassermann   I do owe you an apology for one thing.

Abdullah   Oh yeah?

Wassermann   When I said you were two guys?

Metin *(off)*   Dem call me Mista Boombastic . . .

Wassermann   I overestimated by 50 per cent. I have places I need to be now. (*Beat.*) Whaddya got to be so angry about? Everybody's life is full of changes. Things change and people move on. Your pop gets to quit humping boxes at five in the morning. You should be happy for him.

Pause.

Abdullah (*quiet, and thus genuinely unnerving*)   What have I got to be so angry about?

Wassermann   Let's go home now, boys, 'kay?

Metin *emerges from the kitchen during* **Abdullah***'s speech.*

Abdullah   When I was born, my dad didn't call me Abdullah, not at first. He called me something else. He called me Newroz, it's Kurdish for New Year. It means hope and rebirth. N-E-W-R-O-Z; the third letter there is quite important.

My first day at school, the teachers wouldn't let me register. They said my name didn't exist. They said that in Turkey there's no such language as Kurdish and in Turkish there's no such letter as W, so obviously there's no such word as Newroz. So I didn't exist.

But I must have existed for somebody, because later the paramilitaries came. They asked for my father, but he was in the fields. So they took away my mother, and when they found her body three days later by the roadside her tongue and eyes had been cut out.

My father left his sons somewhere safe and went into the mountains and lived through things the merest ghost of which would cause your soul or mine to shrivel up like burning paper. And when he came out, he took his sons far, far away. Somewhere they could live to be every letter of themselves. And he succeeded.

This is the man whose home you are taking. This is a man who has spent his life running from the powerful. I will not let you make him run again.

Beat.

Wassermann   I'm sorry for those things, kid, but I didn't do any of them. I'm only here to buy this store.

Abdullah   I ask you again: will the OurFolks Corporation stop its acquisition of my father's house?

Wassermann   The deal is already done.

Abdullah   Will the OurFolks Corporation stop its acquisition of my father's house?

Wassermann   Are you having problems hearing me? The contract is signed.

Abdullah   Contracts can be torn up. Will you stop the Crockney 'urban reclamation' project?

Wassermann   There is nothing I can do.

Abdullah   Metin, get me the machete please.

Metin   Apo, c'mon, bruv, you said we wouldn't –

Abdullah   The machete please.

Wassermann   You won't do anything.

Metin *passes him the machete.* **Abdullah** *struggles to hold* **Wassermann'**s *thumb.*

Wassermann   Get the fuck off me! Get the . . .

Abdullah   Metin, hold his hands.

Wassermann   No! Metin, don't!

Metin *moves to help restrain* **Wassermann**'s *arms.* **Abdullah** *prises* **Wassermann**'s *thumb away from his fingers and raises the machete high above his head to cut* **Wassermann**'s *thumb off.*

Abdullah   We are no longer willing to live under your thumb, Mr Wassermann.

Wassermann   No . . . No . . . PLEASE!

The door opens and a man of about fifty with a weatherbeaten face enters: **Mr Yilmaz,** *father of* **Abdullah** *and* **Metin**. *He is not a big man, but he exudes a patriarchal authority of which his sons are somewhat in awe. He stands dumbstruck at the scene before him.*
Abdullah *hides the machete behind his back and both boys jump back from* **Wassermann**. *Pause.*

Abdullah   Alright, Dad? You're back early.

Yilmaz   The cash and carry was closed.

Beat. **Wassermann** *squirms.*

Yilmaz   Go on then.

Wassermann *grunts and writhes as the brothers hold him in place.*

Abdullah   What?

Yilmaz   Do what you will do.

Abdullah *hefts the machete again.* **Wassermann** *looks away.*
Abdullah *looks at his dad and hesitates.* **Yilmaz** *strides towards him.*

Yilmaz   Come on! You want to play, play! Finish your game,
come on!

Beat. **Abdullah** *slowly lowers the machete.* **Yilmaz** *takes it from*
Abdullah's *hand and places it carefully on the table. He crosses the*
room and slaps **Metin** *in the face.*

Yilmaz   Get out.

Metin   It was him!

Yilmaz   Go downstairs.

Metin   Why you always put it on me? It's his fucking idea!

Yilmaz   I know you are in the middle of this somehow. Get
out.

He virtually marches **Metin** *to the door and slings him out of the room.*

Wassermann   Do you fucking maniacs have any idea what
you just did? Do you know how long you are going to prison –

Yilmaz *stuffs the gag back in* **Wassermann**'s *mouth. Pause.*

Yilmaz (*to* **Abdullah**)   You do this.

Beat.

Abdullah   Yes.

Pause.

Yilmaz   You disappoint me, Abdullah. You hurt my heart.

Abdullah   No, Dad –

Yilmaz   Who is this man?

Abdullah   This is him, Dad. The one who can stop it.

Yilmaz   You know so so little of the world, Abdullah, to think this? Let him go, Abdullah.

Abdullah   No, Papa.

Yilmaz   Let him go.

Abdullah   No! I'm in charge now.

Yilmaz   You are in charge? In my house, you say this to me? (*Pause.*) Why you are here?

Abdullah   This is my home.

Yilmaz   No. Your home now is the university. (*Beat.*) You are not in trouble with no English girl? You remember what I say –

Abdullah   Let's have that conversation another time, Dad, please?

Yilmaz (*gesturing to picture on the wall*)   The university –

Abdullah   Forget the university. It's not even a real university, Dad, it's just an ex-poly where everyone wants to be either a management consultant or a suicide bomber.

Yilmaz   I don't understand.

Abdullah   Yes you do. You get what you want in this man's world by taking it. It's the only language they understand!

Yilmaz   This is not your fight.

Abdullah   I'm doing what you did.

Yilmaz   No. Not what I did.

Abdullah   What you did. Pick up the gun, make the Turks run.

Yilmaz   This is your idea of a fight? Why you think I pick up the gun, Abdullah?

Abdullah   Because the Turks killed my mother.

Yilmaz*'s face clouds with angry disgust.*

Yilmaz   Hah! The way you say this.

Abdullah   What?

Yilmaz   Selfish, like Englishman.

Abdullah   Selfish?!

Yilmaz   She was my wife before she was your mother.

Abdullah   If you don't want me to be English, why'd you bring me to England?

Yilmaz   Not for pretend be Kurdish, I know this!

Abdullah   Pretend?! And what if I stopped 'pretending' to be Kurdish? You'd be the first one to give me a bollocking. (*Beat.*) Why are you doing nothing, Papa? Why are you letting yourself get pushed around?

Yilmaz   You don't tell me I am so bad man. You listen your brother now?

Abdullah   No, I listened to you. From when I was that high, you talking about Kurdistan, our people –

Yilmaz   You are so Kurdish, you know so much of our people, why you don't speak me in our language? Speak me. Go on. (*Pause.*) When I pick up the gun, is because there is nothing else I can do. Someone is shooting at me, what else I can do?

Abdullah   Someone is shooting at us now, Dad. The bullets are made of paper but they do just as much damage.

The noise of shouting and chanting from outside. Both men look at the window.

Yilmaz   What is this?

They move to the window and stare out in disbelief at what they see for some moments. The chanting continues. They look at each other.

Abdullah/Yilmaz   Metin . . .

Yilmaz   I go talk to them, make them go.

He hurriedly leaves the room. **Abdullah** *turns and bellows for his brother.*

Abdullah   Metin! METIN!

Metin *enters sheepishly.*

Metin   Alright, bruv?

Abdullah   The entire community centre is holding a rally outside our front door.

Metin   Yeah, yeah, I saw that, yeah . . .

Abdullah   Your mate Mustafa's got a ten-foot banner with 'Go On My Son, Hang the Motherfucker High' written on it. 'Motherfucker' spelled wrong. And 'Son'.

Metin   Maybe people'll think it's like a Kurdish festival or su'in . . .

Abdullah   Tell me, bruv, what part of 'Don't tell anyone' do you not understand?

Metin   I was, like, proud to be doin' it with you, Apo, and when Mustafa belled me when I was outside it just kinda . . . slipped out . . .

Abdullah   You're a fucking joke, do you know that? (*Beat.*) I'm gonna help Dad. Stay here; do nothing, say nothing, give him nothing. You think you can manage that?

Abdullah *pushes past him and leaves.* **Metin** *looks at* **Wassermann** *uncertainly, then meanders over to the phones, turns one of them on and starts fiddling with it. A series of choking noises emanate from* **Wassermann**, *increasing in volume and urgency; it seems like he might really be asphyxiating.* **Metin** *starts to panic and look around for help; eventually, with some trepidation, he leaves the phone on the table, comes over to* **Wassermann** *and pulls the balled-up gag out of* *his mouth, stepping quickly backwards.* **Wassermann** *takes a huge gulp of air.*

Wassermann   Thanks, kid. Thanks a lot. You couldn't fetch me a glass of water, could ya?

Metin   Why?

Wassermann   Because if I don't drink enough water my complexion goes to shit? Jesus Christ!

Metin *goes into the kitchen and emerges with a glass of water which he holds up tentatively to* **Wassermann**, *who merely drinks the water with apparent gratitude.* **Metin** *goes back to the phone, his back to* **Wassermann**.

Wassermann   Thanks, kid. Appreciate it. (*Beat.*) He was pretty tough on you there. (*Beat.*) Your pop. Hit you pretty hard. (*Beat.*) He do that a lot?

Metin (*without looking*)   Am I a thick cunt?

Wassermann   Say again?

Metin   Am I a thick cunt?

Wassermann   Well, no, I mean as far as I –

Metin   Then why you chattin' bare shit like I'm a thick cunt? People underrate me, y'know! You reckon you gonna get me vex with my dad and I'm gonna let you go? Cha! Allow it! Tings dem nah kyan run dat way, seen?

Wassermann   Fine.

Metin *has been dialling a number.*

Metin   Yeah, whass gwaanin, darling, down at the shop, you know, same old same old. How 'bout this Sat'day we go down – What you sayin, baby?! So – (*Beat.*) Yeah, but . . . You need 'space and time'? Who are you, Stephen Hawking or su'in? Hello? (*He snaps the phone shut. Pause. To* **Wassermann**.) Ah well, plenny more fish in the sea, innit. Although thass not what Greenpeace says, you know.

Pause.

Wassermann   Women, huh?

Metin   Yeah.

Wassermann   Trust me, it don't get any easier. (*Beat.*) You liked her?

Metin   She was alright. (*Beat.*) I did, yeah.

Wassermann   Then I'm sorry.

Beat.

Metin   Hear what, I'm sorry about mashin' you in the head, like. Them Fray Bentos people have gotta lot to answer for.

Wassermann   That's OK. I wasn't the only one got hit. (*Beat.*) Does he do that a lot?

Metin   What?

Wassermann   Your father, hit you?

Beat.

Metin   Iss no joke runnin a gaff like this. Seventeen, eighteen-hour days. Man go proper bruk a'ter dat. (*Beat, more savage.*) Straight sucker business if you arks me an I tell 'im dat to his face. You should hear him down there, 'Yes sir, no problem sir, whatever I can get you sir.' No pride, rudeboy. Scrabblin' around on his hands and knees to get a single can a' Red Stripe for some pisshead? Fuck that! An' then he wants to be the big man wid me!

Wassermann   Yeah, I saw that.

Metin   He got me graftin' eight hours in the gaff fe nuttin an' when I arks him for a coupla dollars he mek out like I'm some kinda ponce! Man affe mek him ends so, right or wrong?

Wassermann (*uncomprehending*)   I would imagine so, yeah . . .

Metin   Ennit! Apo goin' uni, the brer gonna get paid good. So I starts a lickle runnins, lickle shottin bisness on road, you know, support meself, be a man like him arks me to, an' he's givin me licks about that as well! (*Beat.*) He thinks I'm just leftovers, my dad. Thass why when Apo arksed me fe do this, I come in. Cos the two a' dem nah believe I can do nuttin good but shot peng an tief.

Wassermann   Like you said, people underrate you.

Metin   Thass what I'm *sayin*, dread!

Wassermann   You love your brother, huh, Metin?

Metin   Nah, drop me out. This ain't no *Trisha* tings.

Wassermann   Course you do, you idolise him. Even when he does something as stupid as this, you idolise him.

Metin   I shouldn't even be speakin' to you, blood.

Wassermann   What did he tell you? It'd be you and him, right? Partners?

Metin *looks flustered and moves away, picking up the phone again.*

Metin   Hush and move, man. Shouldn't even be speakin to ya.

Wassermann   You think he respects you the way you respect him?

Metin   What you talkin about?

Wassermann   He's got you on a string, son! Running around, doing all the dirty work. He's setting you up, Metin.

Metin   Suck ya mum! I ent bein' set up.

Wassermann   Look who took the heat when your dad found out.

Metin   Yeah, but thass Dad, he always / blames me for –

Wassermann   He threw you under the bus, kid! You think he won't do it again when the police get here? Apo doesn't respect you, Metin. What could *you* ever do to make a guy like him respect you?

Beat. **Metin** *looks* **Wassermann** *in the face for a moment, then starts fiddling with the phone again.*

Wassermann   You should hear him and your father when you're not around. Laughing at you. You wanna know who really thinks you're a thick cunt? (*Beat.*) Come over here. Just come over here a second.

Metin *hesitantly moves over to* **Wassermann**, *leaving the phone propped up on the table.*

Wassermann   What do you need, Metin? Tell me what you need.

Metin   So he's wrong, my brother?

Wassermann (*irritated*)   What?

Metin   He don't know what he's talking about?

Wassermann   Not wrong, no. Just naive.

Metin   Where's he gone wrong then?

Wassermann   What do you care? Loosen my wrists, Metin.

Metin   I'm interested, innit. I juss got Apo in my ear all day long, I don't never get to talk to the real big boys dem.

Wassermann   He has no idea of how things work, Metin. I mean, yeah, we pay people where we need to pay people, but you would not believe how little we have to do that. Take the authorities here. Now there were a few instances where we had to help the process along a little with some extra-curricular finance, but most of these people can't do enough for us. You know how much we bought this whole street for, Metin? Nothing. Spare change. It's almost embarrassing to steal assets from a public authority like that. Crockney Council couldn't give it to us fast enough, and you wanna know why?

Metin   Because they're really fucking stupid?

Wassermann   Because they believe in us. Because what else is there to believe in? Who else is *doing* anything, Metin? We are the ones changing the world, not your brother's kind. We are the insurgents. We're the ones you wanna be with. Loosen my wrists. (*Beat.*) Just loosen my wrists, that's all. No one even needs to know it was you.

Yilmaz *opens the door. He regards the tableau with some suspicion.*

Yilmaz   Get out, Metin.

Metin   It's not what you think . . .

Yilmaz   GET OUT! You cannot obey me even one little thing?

Metin   Trust me, Dad, it's –

Yilmaz *starts to force him out.*

Metin   I'm gone, I'm gone.

He half runs out of the door. **Yilmaz** *slams it shut and stares hard at* **Wassermann**.

He moves to the sofa, lights a cigarette, picks up **Abdullah**'s *notes and starts to leaf through them. Long pause.*

Wassermann   You know what 'accessory' means, right?

Yilmaz   I know. I sell this. The girls, they put in their hair. (*Beat.*) This is joke. With the humour I am very good.

He waves the sheaf of notes at **Wassermann**.

Yilmaz   My son's work.

Wassermann   Congratulations. You must be very proud.

Yilmaz (*frighteningly neutral*)   I do not understand the way you talk to me. I think maybe a little more nice is better for you.

This is the first threat that really cuts through **Wassermann**. *He deflates slightly.*

Yilmaz   Very much information. Look. All this knowledge of you and your company. (*He rifles the pages.*) I cannot read it. Any of it. Turkish yes, some, but English no. Only what I need in shop. Crosse and Blackwell Branston Pickle, Bird's Custard Powder: these are my literature. (*Beat.*) What is your name?

Beat.

Wassermann   Reed Wassermann.

Yilmaz   My name is Mehmet Yilmaz. Pleased to meet you.

Wassermann   Delighted, I'm sure.

Yilmaz   It is strange for a man to take your home and you do not know his name. (*Beat.*) You have children, Mr Wassermann?

Wassermann   Why do you ask?

Yilmaz   I ask.

Pause.

Wassermann   Two sons and a daughter.

Yilmaz   You love them?

Wassermann   Of course.

Yilmaz   They love you?

Beat.

Wassermann   I would hope that they do, yes.

Yilmaz   You would do any things for them?

Wassermann   I would rather not talk to you about my children.

Yilmaz   You would do any things for them?

Pause.

Wassermann   Yes, I would.

Yilmaz   Tell me about them. (*Pause. No reply.*) Children. I have one son who wants to be Kurd but behave like Englishman, and one son who wants to be Englishman but behave like Kurd, and I do not understand either of them. But I love them, both of them, very much. (*Beat.*) But I never can say this to them. I don't know why. I can say to strange man in my house, but I never can say this to them. When I try, every time my mouth go dry like a root. (*Pause.*) You don't know your children, do you, Mr Wassermann? When is last time you see them?

Wassermann   That has nothing to do with you.

Yilmaz   If there is one thing you can do for your children, what is it?

Wassermann   I am here on business. Can we please talk business?

Yilmaz   Business.

Wassermann   Yes. Business. (*Pause.*) How much?

Yilmaz   How much what?

Wassermann   You know what. How much? (*Beat.*) How much do you want to let me go?

Yilmaz   You have strange way to do business, Mr Wassermann. I cannot sell what I do not own.

Wassermann   Come on, Yilmaz –

Yilmaz   Mr Yilmaz. (*Beat.*) I prefer. It is polite.

Wassermann   Mr Yilmaz. Come on. You're a businessman. You see an opportunity, you take advantage. It's perfectly natural. I don't even blame you hardly. So why don't we just cut the blushing bride shit and you tell me how much it's gonna take.

Beat.

Yilmaz   What you think of my son Abdullah?

Wassermann   I think he's going to prison.

Yilmaz   Because if my son go to prison anyway . . .

Beat. He blows out smoke and stubs out his cigarette.

When my son is little boy, he have birthday party. We are not long time this country, maybe one, two year. We ask come all little boy and girl from area, and they play together. Is very nice day, the sun shine, people are happy. For his birthday, Abdullah get only one present. Is toy car, big one, what is word in English? Yes, I think 'truck'. He love it, he play with it all the day. He don't want other children to touch it, but I tell him no, is not good to ask other children to come and not to play with them. So my son give truck to them, and they break it. They break his truck. My heart is feel very much pain, I do not think I feel this pain for so small thing. My son, he go upstair, and I think he go his room for cry, and I about to go to him. And then he come out, and he bring old toy. He start to play with it, and other children come, and he give his toy again to other children to play with.

Pause.

Wassermann   Why are you telling me this?

Yilmaz (*quietly*)   My son is so so good in his heart, Mr Wassermann.

Wassermann   Your son tried to cut my thumb off, you'll forgive me if I don't shed a tear at his youthful benevolence.

Yilmaz   I do not understand you.

Wassermann   Benevolence. It means –

Yilmaz (*sharp*)   English I know. It is you I do not understand. I do not understand why you are so angry.

Wassermann   You don't understand why I'm angry with a noose around my neck?

Yilmaz   You are angry long long time before this day. I do not understand why you hate so strong when everything in this world, it is for you.

Wassermann   Everything in this world is not for me.

Yilmaz   Then who it is for?

Wassermann   The world works a certain way, Mr Yilmaz. I can't be held accountable for that.

Yilmaz   Then who can? (*Beat.*) My son make mistake, Mr Wassermann.

Wassermann   Not my fault.

Yilmaz   When you are young man, Mr Wassermann, do you make mistake?

Wassermann   Listen, Mr Yilmaz, with respect, after this I would love to get better acquainted, but –

Yilmaz   When I am young man, I make mistake. I kill five men.

Beat. **Wassermann** *pales despite himself.*

Yilmaz   Four men are from Turkey *jandarma*, the army, I don't want kill them but they want kill me so what I can do? But one man, he is Kurd but he help Turks to fight us, I don't know what is call in English. When we go to mountains, Turkey army give them our village. I go back one time only for see what is happen. It is night. I go my house, I see four, five guards live there. I see my window break, my roof break, my house dirty. My wife, she always keeps house so clean. My heart so so angry. I go in, quiet, quiet, nobody see. I go to bedroom and there is this man, he sleep. He sleep like this – (*Motions lying on his back.*) and his . . . ?

He runs his hand up and down his throat and looks at **Wassermann** *inquiringly.*

Pause. Genuine fear.

Wassermann   Throat.

Yilmaz   Thank you. His throat open to me like when we kill sheeps. I look this man long long time. My heart is so long time – (*He mimes a violent twisting or wringing motion with his hand.*) inside me, you know? But I cut his throat and my heart go flat, like a big lake on a calm day. (*Beat.*) If there is one thing you can do for your children, Mr Wassermann, what is it?

Pause.

Wassermann   I should have let them make their own mistakes.

Yilmaz   Tell me.

Beat.

Wassermann   You ever hear that song 'A Boy Named Sue'?

Yilmaz (*baffled*)   This is the name of boy?

Wassermann   No. That's the . . . The point is the guy knows he's not gonna be around much for his kid, so he tries to leave him with something that's gonna help him out, you know?

Yilmaz   The name of girl?

Wassermann   I tried to leave my kids something that would get them through. When I wasn't around.

Yilmaz   Money.

Wassermann   Yeah. Money.

Yilmaz   And what is happen?

Beat.

Wassermann   It didn't work out.

Yilmaz   When is last time you see your children?

Pause.

Wassermann   Charlie about three years ago, Vanessa maybe five. Leo . . .

Beat.

Yilmaz   You don't know your children.

Pause.

Wassermann   No. I don't know my children.

Yilmaz   I want my son, Mr Wassermann.

Wassermann   I didn't take him from you.

Yilmaz   But you hold him, Mr Wassermann. You hold him in your hand like dust. You wipe your hands and he is gone.

Wassermann   Let me go, Mr Yilmaz.

Abdullah *and* **Metin** *return to find the door locked. They bang from the other side calling for* **Yilmaz**.

Yilmaz (*going to let them in*)   I cannot let you go, Mr Wassermann. I must let him make his own mistake, you see.

Abdullah *and* **Metin** *enter.*

Abdullah   What's going on, Dad?

Yilmaz   We talk.

Abdullah   What about?

Yilmaz   There is a boy with the name of a girl.

Abdullah   What?

Wassermann   Listen, kid –

Abdullah   I'm not talking to you, Mr Wassermann. I'm talking to my father. Metin, put the gag back in please.

Metin *gags the irate* **Wassermann**. **Abdullah** *doesn't want to ask the next question.*

Abdullah   Dad . . . It's not . . . You don't have shares in the OurFolks Corporation, do you?

Beat.

Yilmaz   There is not time for this now, Abdullah.

Abdullah   Yes or no, Dad.

Yilmaz   Yes. Yes, I have.

Abdullah   You have?

Yilmaz   Maybe three thousands of shares I have. Is not so much, three thousands, I think.

Abdullah   Where d'you get the money, Papa?

Yilmaz   Where you think? I save from work here.

Abdullah   What happened, Halliburton was all sold out?

Yilmaz   What is problem?

Abdullah   You gave the profit you made from your business to the very same people who are taking your business away from you?

Yilmaz   I buy their shares because their shares go up high, is very simple. Is how it works.

Abdullah   I know how it 'works'! It 'works' because they keep buying up dipshits like us and putting them out of business!

Yilmaz   I try to make a bit money for my family, Apo, what is wrong with this?

Abdullah   What is wrong with this? Are you or are you not the father who gave me a cartoon version of the Communist Manifesto for my sixth birthday?

Yilmaz   You want I always must work here?

Abdullah   Does everyone give up? Does everyone bottle it in the end?

Yilmaz   You come back one day and I am dead, baked beans are my gravestone? This is what you want?

Abdullah   What happened to you, Dad?

Yilmaz   We are leaving this place, Abdullah. (*Beat.*) I need money so we can leave this place.

Abdullah   We are not leaving!

Yilmaz   Everybody leave this place.

Abdullah   Because of him! Because he's kicking them out!

Yilmaz   It does not matter. Our people all leave this area, we don't have no more customers. I cannot live on shop money no more. You know this. Long time you know this, Abdullah.

Abdullah   This is our home. This is our community.

Yilmaz   There is no 'community' now. All people are gone, my son. (*Unconscious echo of* **Wassermann**'s *earlier line.*) Things change and people move. They make money, they buy nice flat Palmers Green, they leave us. Even those men outside with flags, they have to take bus to get here now.

Abdullah   I'm not going to leave, Papa.

Yilmaz   You are already gone. You don't live here no more, Apo. You go study and you don't see everybody all gone.

Beat.

Abdullah   Why, Papa?

Yilmaz   Apo, I am tired. I am so so tired. I am tired to get up five o'clock in morning, to wash floor, to carry box. I work like horse in field all my life, Abdullah, push and pull and carry. All my life I fight. I want to stop now. I want rest. I want rest and watch my son become big man in England. (*Beat.*) I want holiday. Fifteen years I live in England and not one time I take holiday.

Abdullah   You're giving up for a holiday?

Yilmaz   I think maybe I go Benidorm. The man who bring bread to shop, he say me is very nice. Sunshine.

Abdullah   Benidorm.

Yilmaz   Maybe, how is call, Torremolinos also is good?

Abdullah   Please tell me you're joking. (*Beat.*) How can you be so selfish?

Yilmaz   Selfish you call me? Abdullah, how I can pay your studies without money?

Abdullah *is extremely discomforted at the mention of his studies.*

Abdullah   We're not giving up for me . . .

Yilmaz   For so long time when you are child we have no money. I want to get for you some things, you can study better. Maybe you want also to study for longer time, become doctor, maybe professor, you need money for this –

Abdullah   Can you please stop going on about my studies for one fucking minute?!

Beat.

Yilmaz   Why you say this?

Abdullah   I don't belong there.

Yilmaz   What is happen?

Abdullah   I want to do things the way you did, do something proper, get my hands dirty –

Yilmaz   What is happen, Abdullah?

Beat.

Abdullah   They kicked me out, Papa.

Pause.

Yilmaz   The university?

Abdullah   Yeah. They kicked me out.

Yilmaz   Why they do this?

Abdullah   They said I wasn't keeping up with the work.

Yilmaz   Is not true, they make mistake. You work hard always, I see –

Abdullah   Yeah, I was working hard. But I was working on this.

He grabs the sheaf of notes from his father's hand and waves it at him.

I don't want to go back.

Yilmaz   You say to me I am selfish?

Abdullah   I hate it. I only went for you.

Yilmaz   I work too hard to let you to waste this chance.

Abdullah   I don't want it.

Yilmaz   I don't care what you want! You are so English now you think is only matter what *you* want?

Abdullah   I DON'T WANT IT, PAPA! This is the fight I was given. And I can't even win this one. You were running round the mountains risking your fucking life, and all I can do is . . . I'm ashamed, Papa. People need love more than anything. It ain't right what's he doing. Something should be done.

Yilmaz   What something?

Abdullah   Whatever it takes.

Yilmaz   You don't get what you ask, you kill him?

Beat.

Abdullah   Whatever it takes.

Yilmaz   My son. What do you know of the killing, Apo? When you kill a man, he die inside your body. He stay there, and he rots. You can taste him. In my shop I taste. Many times I think there is something problem with frozen meats, but when I check freezer there is no problem. Only problem in me. (*Beat.*) I only ever do what I do because I have no choice. I never never feel the deep way you do inside. I am not as deep a man as you, Abdullah. You shame me. I am the one who should feel the shame. (*Beat.*) I want you let him go now, Apo.

Abdullah *steps back, turns to* **Wassermann** *and removes his gag.*

Abdullah   If I let you go, Mr Wassermann, what will you do?

Wassermann   I owe you nothing.

Abdullah   No promises?

Wassermann   No promises.

Beat.

Abdullah   Alright, Mr Wassermann, I'll say this. I'm going to put you on your honour.

Wassermann   My honour?

Abdullah   Your honour.

Beat. **Wassermann** *shakes his head and blows air from his nose.*

Wassermann   OK.

Abdullah *unties his hands, then loosens the rope and removes the noose.*

Wassermann   Thanks.

He steps down from the chair, gingerly rubbing his neck. He then strides over to **Abdullah** *and pokes him hard in the chest.*

Wassermann   Give me one good reason why I shouldn't have you people destroyed.

Metin *goes to help* **Abdullah** *but* **Yilmaz** *holds him back.* **Wassermann** *rubs* **Abdullah**'s *head and laughs before going to leave.*

Metin   I can give you one.

Wassermann   Yeah, Einstein? And what is that?

Metin   You've been on videophone for the last half hour, blood.

He holds up **Wassermann**'s *phone and plays the recording. We hear the excerpts from where* **Metin** *set him up before:*

Wassermann (*recorded*)   'Yeah, we pay people where we need to pay people' . . . 'Some extra-curricular finance' . . . 'It's almost embarrassing to steal assets from a public authority.'

Beat.

Metin   This phone is the bollocks, Mr Wassermann. You get proper quality on this. Give us two secs . . . There we go, it's all teed up to go to your whole address book. You wanna do the honours?

He holds the phone up, out of **Wassermann***'s reach. He thinks about making a grab for it, then pulls back.*

Wassermann   So? You think that's enough? Put it on YouTube, I don't give a fuck. You think we don't have lawyers.

He goes to leave but is caught in the doorway as **Metin***, who has been fast-forwarding through the recording, plays another extract:*

Wassermann (*recorded*)   'I don't know my children.'

Pause. **Wassermann** *starts to walk back into the room.*

Wassermann   Gimme that. Give me that phone.

He is blocked from getting to **Metin** *by* **Abdullah** *and* **Yilmaz***.*

Yilmaz   Leave my house now, Mr Wassermann.

Wassermann   Give me my fucking phone! That is my –

Metin   Come out the drum, blood!

Yilmaz   You leave now, Mr Wassermann.

Wassermann *pulls away and straightens his clothes, trying to regain his dignity.*

Wassermann   That is my phone.

Metin   It's ours now, rudeboy – taxed!

Wassermann   What are you gonna do with it? (*Beat.*) What are you going to –

Abdullah   Goodbye, Mr Wassermann.

Beat. **Wassermann** *leaves. Pause.*

Metin   Bloodclaart! Totally forgot.

He runs into the kitchen. **Yilmaz** *ruffles* **Abdullah***'s hair tenderly.*

Abdullah   I'm tired, Papa.

Metin *runs back in holding three cans of Coke in triumph and gives the others one each.*

Metin   Secret stash. Tiefed 'em when you threw the rest out.

Yilmaz   I always like Coca-Cola.

Metin   Yes, dread!

He holds out a closed fist to his father. **Yilmaz** *somewhat tentatively holds his out in reply, and* **Metin** *enthusiastically bangs them together.*

Abdullah   They're corporate scum, Dad.

Yilmaz   I know this. But it taste good. Better than this donkey piss you make me sell.

Abdullah   For fuck's sakes . . .

Metin *and* **Yilmaz** *open their cans and hold them up.*

Yilmaz   To my sons.

Beat. **Abdullah** *reluctantly cracks his can and holds it up to theirs.*

Yilmaz   I have something I need to tell you.

End of play.

Bloomsbury Methuen Drama Contemporary Dramatists

include

John Arden (two volumes)
Arden & D'Arcy
Peter Barnes (three volumes)
Sebastian Barry
Mike Bartlett
Dermot Bolger
Edward Bond (eight volumes)
Howard Brenton (two volumes)
Leo Butler
Richard Cameron
Jim Cartwright
Caryl Churchill (two volumes)
Complicite
Sarah Daniels (two volumes)
Nick Darke
David Edgar (three volumes)
David Eldridge (two volumes)
Ben Elton
Per Olov Enquist
Dario Fo (two volumes)
Michael Frayn (four volumes)
John Godber (four volumes)
Paul Godfrey
James Graham
David Greig
John Guare
Lee Hall (two volumes)
Katori Hall
Peter Handke
Jonathan Harvey (two volumes)
Iain Heggie
Israel Horovitz
Declan Hughes
Terry Johnson (three volumes)
Sarah Kane
Barrie Keeffe
Bernard-Marie Koltès (two volumes)
Franz Xaver Kroetz
Kwame Kwei-Armah
David Lan
Bryony Lavery
Deborah Levy
Doug Lucie

David Mamet (four volumes)
Patrick Marber
Martin McDonagh
Duncan McLean
David Mercer (two volumes)
Anthony Minghella (two volumes)
Tom Murphy (six volumes)
Phyllis Nagy
Anthony Neilson (two volumes)
Peter Nichol (two volumes)
Philip Osment
Gary Owen
Louise Page
Stewart Parker (two volumes)
Joe Penhall (two volumes)
Stephen Poliakoff (three volumes)
David Rabe (two volumes)
Mark Ravenhill (three volumes)
Christina Reid
Philip Ridley (two volumes)
Willy Russell
Eric-Emmanuel Schmitt
Ntozake Shange
Sam Shepard (two volumes)
Martin Sherman (two volumes)
Christopher Shinn
Joshua Sobel
Wole Soyinka (two volumes)
Simon Stephens (three volumes)
Shelagh Stephenson
David Storey (three volumes)
C. P. Taylor
Sue Townsend
Judy Upton
Michel Vinaver (two volumes)
Arnold Wesker (two volumes)
Peter Whelan
Michael Wilcox
Roy Williams (four volumes)
David Williamson
Snoo Wilson (two volumes)
David Wood (two volumes)
Victoria Wood

Bloomsbury Methuen Drama Modern Plays
include work by

Bola Agbaje
Edward Albee
Davey Anderson
Jean Anouilh
John Arden
Peter Barnes
Sebastian Barry
Alistair Beaton
Brendan Behan
Edward Bond
William Boyd
Bertolt Brecht
Howard Brenton
Amelia Bullmore
Anthony Burgess
Leo Butler
Jim Cartwright
Lolita Chakrabarti
Caryl Churchill
Lucinda Coxon
Curious Directive
Nick Darke
Shelagh Delaney
Ishy Din
Claire Dowie
David Edgar
David Eldridge
Dario Fo
Michael Frayn
John Godber
Paul Godfrey
James Graham
David Greig
John Guare
Mark Haddon
Peter Handke
David Harrower
Jonathan Harvey
Iain Heggie

Robert Holman
Caroline Horton
Terry Johnson
Sarah Kane
Barrie Keeffe
Doug Lucie
Anders Lustgarten
David Mamet
Patrick Marber
Martin McDonagh
Arthur Miller
D. C. Moore
Tom Murphy
Phyllis Nagy
Anthony Neilson
Peter Nichols
Joe Orton
Joe Penhall
Luigi Pirandello
Stephen Poliakoff
Lucy Prebble
Peter Quilter
Mark Ravenhill
Philip Ridley
Willy Russell
Jean-Paul Sartre
Sam Shepard
Martin Sherman
Wole Soyinka
Simon Stephens
Peter Straughan
Kate Tempest
Theatre Workshop
Judy Upton
Timberlake Wertenbaker
Roy Williams
Snoo Wilson
Frances Ya-Chu Cowhig
Benjamin Zephaniah

For a complete listing of Bloomsbury
Methuen Drama titles, visit:

www.bloomsbury.com/drama

Follow us on Twitter and keep up to date
with our news and publications

@MethuenDrama